COMPARATIVE POLICING ISSUES

The British and American System in International Perspective

R. I. Mawby

Steven Greer
Bristol
March 1991

London
UNWIN HYMAN
Boston Sydney Wellington

Published by the Academic Division of

Unwin Hyman Ltd
15/17 Broadwick Street, London W1V 1FP, UK

Unwin Hyman Inc.,
8 Winchester Place, Winchester, Mass. 01890, USA

Allen & Unwin (Australia) Ltd,
8 Napier Street, North Sydney, NSW 2060, Australia

Allen & Unwin (New Zealand) Ltd
in association with the Port Nicholson Press Ltd,
Compusales Building, 75 Ghuznee Street, Wellington 1,
New Zealand

First published in 1990

British Library Cataloguing in Publication Data

Mawby, R. I.
Comparative policing issues.
1. Police
I. Title
363.2
ISBN 0-04-445545-3
ISBN 0-04-445544-5 pbk

Library of Congress Cataloging in Publication Data

Mawby, R. I.
Comparative policing issues: The British and American system in international perspective/R. I. Mawby.
p. cm.
Includes bibliographical references and index.
ISBN 0-04-445545-3 (hardbound): $44.95 —
ISBN 0-04-445544-5 (pbk.): $16.95
1. Police—Cross-cultural studies. I. Title.
HV7921.M38 1990 90-12526
363.2—dc20 CIP

Typeset in 10 on 11 point Bembo by Fotographics (Bedford) Ltd
and printed in Great Britain by Billing and Sons Ltd, London and Worcester

Contents

List of Figures and Tables

Figure *page*

Tables

Preface

I first became interested in carrying out some systematic work on comparative policing in 1985. At the time I was already teaching on the Diploma in Public Administration (Police Studies) course at Plymouth Polytechnic, and was involved in the submission to CNAA for a degree in police studies. During the preliminary meetings, I suggested that a specialist degree ought to incorporate a unit on comparative policing in the final year, and wrote out a brief, very general outline of a course structure. I then disappeared on sabbatical and reappeared at the end of the year to discover my outline had been left intact in the final document and I was scheduled to teach the course in two years time!

My response, in the time-honoured tradition of academics, was to forget the matter for eighteen months and panic for the remaining six months. My panic was heightened when, again following academic tradition, I attempted to develop a course by plagiarizing the reading lists of my counterparts in other universities and polytechnics. Unfortunately I was unable to unearth one course on comparative policing, and spent an uncomfortable couple of months writing my own course. Overwhelmed by physical and mental exhaustion I resolved to make my efforts more worthwhile by writing a text which would be of help to my students and, hopefully, students elsewhere.

My course on comparative policing issues ran for the first time in 1987–8 and has subsequently been offered for both police students on the BA (Hons) Social and Organisational Studies (police studies) and conventional students on the BA (Hons) Social Policy and Administration. During the two and a half years that I have taught it, I can safely say that I have learned considerably more about policing worldwide than I have contributed. Additionally, as I have been more aware of the relevant literature, and indeed of the wider areas that have a relevance to comparative policing, so my appreciation of my own ignorance has grown!

As a result, I have written much of this text with my fingers crossed, which has increased the burden on the secretaries for whom even my normal handwriting is a challenge. In addition to them I would like to thank all my students who have taken the comparative policing course for their enthusiastic response, or otherwise for pointing out the more boring or inadequate aspects of the course. I am also grateful to my former colleague Martin Gill for his enthusiasm in chasing up various pieces of information, and for the considerable help I received from the Police College library at Bramshill, and especially Sue King.

The result is, I hope, a text which breaks new ground and raises some interesting questions about police systems from an international perspective.

Rob Mawby
February 1990

1

A Comparative Analysis of Policing

INTRODUCTION

Until well into the 1970s most published, easily accessible studies of the police were concerned with police work in the United States. With the exception of Banton (1964) and Cain (1973), research on the British police was minimal, and indeed when labelling theory drew attention to the role of the police in the definition of deviance and deviants, the major references were to the American literature.

Ironically, perhaps, most of the writings from the United States were parochial and, ultimately, non-comparative, leading Punch (1983b, 14) to suggest that 'Americans are fundamentally ignorant about police systems in other countries'. Police work was described in terms which assumed a universal commonality, and indeed, despite Fosdick's ([1920] 1969a) early text, variations between the multitude of different forces in the United States received very little attention. For example, even Wilson (1968), in identifying three alternative policing styles, paid scant attention to the extent to which these different styles might be located in different types of community, with historical, social and political underpinnings. While this situation has changed in recent years, comparative analysis is still relatively underdeveloped. It is still commonly assumed that policing in modern societies is a constant rather than a variable; that the similarities between countries in their policing patterns outweigh the differences. As Brogden (1987, 4) noted:

> Ethnocentricity, inadequate comparative knowledge of policing, and a historism are the hallmarks of the Anglo-American sociology of the police. Chauvinism still prevails . . . The failure to consider the wider contours of the emergence of the professional policeman has been near-total.

To illustrate the point, one need look no further than the special issue of the *British Journal of Criminology* in which Brogden's article appeared. With this exception, the issue contains little reference to societies other than Britain and North America. Yet there is no commonly accepted definition of the 'police', or what 'police work' actually entails, a prerequisite of any serious attempt at comparative analysis.

The term is actually derived from the Greek *politeia* and then the Latin *polita*. However, in its original context it referred to the general instruments of government, the wider administration of the state, and it is in this context that the term was resurrected in seventeenth-century Europe (Chapman 1970; Radzinowicz 1956b; Williams 1979). In a discussion of the 'well ordered police state', for example, Raeffe's (1975) analysis contains scant reference to any body of agents which a contemporary reader would recognize as police. In fact, Radzinowicz (1956b, 4) accredits Maitland, writing in 1885, with the earliest modern definition of the police as 'such part of social organisation as is concerned immediately with the maintenance of good order, or the prevention or detection of offences'. Thirty years later, in comparing police systems throughout Europe, the American Raymond Fosdick ([1915] 1969b, 4) concurred: 'Today we mean by the police the primary constitutional force for the protection of individuals in their legal rights'.

However, as academic discussion of policing became more common, definitions of the police tended to be avoided. Writing in 1979 Maureen Cain noted that few of the numerous writers she reviewed defined the term. To her: 'Police, then, *must be defined in terms of their key practice*. They are appointed with the task of maintaining the order which those who sustain them define as proper' (Cain 1979, 158). In some respects, this equates with the earlier definition, although not surprisingly it includes a more critical and analytical edge. Rather than the police being seen as self-evidently a public service, it is identified as an arm of government control. The legal authority of the police, and its appeal to the law for a mandate, and the authorization of force to maintain law and order, are emphasized by the Canadian criminologists Shearing and Leon (1976) and by Bayley in his comparative policing text:

> Whenever the word *police* is used in this book, it will refer to people authorised by a group to regulate interpersonal relations within the group through the application of physical force. This definition has three essential parts: physical force, internal usage and collective authorisation. (Bayley 1985, 7).

But does this definition hold across a range and types of society? In their analysis of policing in primitive societies Schwartz and Miller (1964, 161) employ a more restricted definition, describing the police as a 'specialised armed force used partially or wholly for norm enforcement'. We are left then with a number of definitions which share some features in common but contain variations in emphasis, and indeed necessarily leave room for considerable differences in interpretation. Here it is important to focus on the core elements of these definitions and note areas of differences. The latter point will be developed at the end of Chapter 2 when a clear picture of comparative analysis has been presented.

Essentially, though, when we move on to consider policing in different societies we mean by the police an agency which can be distinguished in terms of its *legitimacy*, its *structure*, and its *function*. Legitimacy implies that the police are granted some degree of monopoly within society by those with the power to so authorize, be they an elite within the society, an occupying power, or the community as a whole. Structure implies that the police is an organized force, with some degree of specialization and with a code of practice within which, for example, legitimate use of force is specified. Clearly, however, the extent of organization or specialism, and the types of force considered appropriate, will vary. Finally, function implies that the role of the police is concentrated on the maintenance of law and order and the prevention and detection of offences. Again, there will be considerable differences here in terms not only of different definitions of crime, but also the balance between law and order, or prevention and detection, and the extent to which other duties are assigned to the police, be these service-related, administrative or concerned with political control.

Such variations will be a persistent theme of this text. It is, however, imperative that some baseline is identified before one can proceed into comparative analyses. That established, we can consider the comparative approach in more detail.

COMPARATIVE ANALYSIS IN THE SOCIAL SCIENCES

Comparative analysis is, of course, one of the foundations on which the discipline of sociology was built. While physical scientists or psychologists could control for different variables in the laboratory, sociologists have tended to use regional comparison as an alternative with, ultimately, the world as one huge macro-laboratory which allows consideration of a wider range of alternative situations. In introducing comparative analysis of welfare systems, Joan Higgins (1981) likens it, on a basic level, to a blind person discovering the essential features of an elephant. One touch is misleading, two better, and a multitude of tactile experience from as many varying angles as possible necessary if one is to get any clear impression of the nature of the object! Taking the analogy further, we might add that sight and smell (but perhaps not taste) are also essential if we are to gain an overall impression which has any validity. The wider the approach to the subject and the more elements it incorporates, the more complete the picture we get.

International comparisons also give us the most opportunity for developing theoretical models. In sociology, Durkheim's ([1897] 1951) classic analysis of suicide was based on comparisons of the suicide rates of different population groups across a range of societies, and the analysis of individual decisions in terms of the impact of alternative structures and cultures. Moreover, suicide is but one aspect of Durkheim's concern to account for social order and the varying methods by which group cohesion was secured in societies differing widely in their size and complexity (Durkheim [1893] 1947; [1912] 1948). Equally, Weber's classic analyses of the rise of capitalism, the place of bureaucracy in society, and the nature of authority (Gerth and Wright Mills 1958) were dependent upon international comparisons. A similar theoretical orientation, but necessitating rather different methodologies, is central to anthropology. Starting from a functionalist perspective, academics like Radcliffe-Brown (1952) and Malinowski (1926) were concerned not merely to explain the social structure of specific primitive societies, but to draw parallels across societies and tease out the constants and variables of social interaction.

It is interesting that, anthropology apart, disciplines which emerged around a subject matter, rather than a theoretical orientation such as political analysis or social policy and administration, initially accorded rather less emphasis to international comparisons. In social policy, for example, the first priorities among postwar British academics concerned the description of the key features of welfare administration within British society, an approach devoid of theoretical or comparative emphasis.

That said, the last twenty years have seen a marked growth in texts which have attempted to compare and explain the development and differing patterns of political structure and welfare in different societies (see, for example, Ashford 1978; 1986; Deacon 1983; Heidenheimer, Heclo and Adams 1983; Higgins 1981; Jones 1985; Rose and Shiratori 1986). In contrast, police studies, which is itself of more recent origin, has a less substantial comparative tradition. Consequently, as we focus on policing, it is important to bear in mind the lessons learnt by those from other disciplines who have made international comparative analysis.

However, comparative analysis is clearly not restricted to *international* comparisons. We can draw comparisons historically by considering, say, the police at different times within one society; intranationally by looking at differences between regions within one county; and on an inter-agency level by considering a similar issue as it impinges upon, for example, police and social work. In writings on the police, a host of studies have considered policing, or clients of policing, at different points in time. Robinson (1978), for example, in addressing the political location of the police in the United States, argues that in some periods the police demonstrated radicalism and a willingness to identify with 'their' community rather than their employers, and that one policy priority has been the attempt by authorities to divide police and public. National statistics in many countries provide a basis for making intra-societal comparisons. For example, in the United States, variations between different urban forces were the subject of early texts by Fosdick ([1920] 1969a) and Smith (1940) and national statistics allow one to consider the employment of black or Hispanic officers etc. between forces (Reaves 1989; US Department of Justic 1989). In England and Wales some basic differences between police authority areas are contained in annual reports (Home Office 1989). Similarly, research may focus on policing in different local contexts. One of the first sociological studies of the police in Britain, by Maureen Cain (1973), indeed addressed a comparison of police roles in an urban and a rural force. Finally, some studies make direct comparison between the police and other agencies. For example, the text by Price and Sokoloff (1982) considers the role of women in different law-enforcement agencies including the police, and is thereby able to identify the extent to which issues regarding policewomen are specific to the police or shared by female workers in other professional or non-professional agencies. In Britain, Day and Klein (1987) review accountability in five public services, including police, education and regional water authorities, allowing criticisms of police accountability to be considered in a wider context.

This is not to suggest that studies focus exclusively on one dimension of comparative analysis. Robinson (1978), for example, draws comparisons between England and Wales and the United States *vis-à-vis* the emergence of the modern police, and Mosse's (1975) reader considers police forces across a range of societies in different periods. My own work with Martin Gill on the role of volunteers within the police incorporates a review of how the part played by the community (or sections of it) in law enforcement has varied in Britain from Anglo-Saxon times. It also contains some discussion of variations between different forces, especially emphasizing the greater reliance on volunteers in more rural forces in England and Wales, and the place of the public in policing in other societies (Gill and Mawby 1990a). But a key feature of the research was also our interest in how other agencies within the law-enforcement field, especially probation and victim services, deployed volunteers, and indeed how different agencies might attract and accept different 'publics' as their volunteers (Mawby and Gill 1987; Gill and Mawby 1990b).

That said, the primary focus of this text is on *international* comparisons. The following section contains an overview of the types of study that have been carried out. Then, in the last two sections of this chapter, emphasis is placed upon the advantages to be gained from a comparative approach to police studies, and the attendant difficulties that it entails.

ALTERNATIVE APPROACHES TO INTERNATIONAL COMPARISONS

What alternative approaches, then, have been adopted? Essentially there are three main areas of work which we can label as international comparative analysis: overall comparisons of two or more countries; a focus of policing in one specific county; and a comparison of particular issues related to policing in two or more countries.

If we first consider those texts which have included a comparison of policing systems in various countries, it is appropriate to start with the work of Raymond Fosdick.[1] Fosdick, a former commissioner of accounts in New York City, toured Europe at the beginning of the twentieth century, discussing systems of policing with the senior staff in many of the major cities. His text, first published in 1915 and more recently reissued (Fosdick 1969b), provides both a review of the systems he encountered and an early attempt to classify them according to a number of criteria. Echoing the views of nineteenth-century British politicians and practitioners, he stressed the distinction between policing in Britain and in continental Europe, a point to which we shall return in Chapter 2. While his work is, in retrospect, somewhat uncritical and partly superficial, its importance is perhaps illustrated by the fact that it was unmatched for well over three decades.

Interestingly, another early attempt to provide a comparative analysis was provided by the British practitioner, Sir Charles Jeffries. A former Deputy Under Secretary of State for the Colonies, with considerable colonial experience, his text provided a significant contribution by assessing the emergence of a distinctive police system in British colonies in which law and order was maintained by an occupying power over the majority indigenous population. In comparing countries such as Jamaica and Ceylon, Jeffries (1952) not only provided an insight into policing systems imposed on very differing cultures by the same occupying force (the British), but also the ways in which ideas from one environment were readily translated into another setting.

By way of contrast, *academic* comparisons have been of more recent origins. In one of the first, Banton (1964) compared police work in the United States and Scotland. More recently, McKenzie and Gallagher (1989) provide a more practice-oriented comparison of England and Wales and the US. A number of readers have provided the medium for consideration of policing in a variety of countries (see, for example, Bayley 1977; Bopp 1972; Outrive and Rizkalla 1976; Punch 1983c). A small number of texts, similarly, provide an analysis of policing in a variety of societies, perhaps the most notable being by Shane (1980) and Bayley (1985). Shane focuses on policing in five contrasting societies – England, USA, Netherlands, Israel and India – and then moves on to consider some of the major issues facing the police in different countries. In contrast, Bayley (1985) draws on material from a vast range of countries to address the development of modern police forces, their structure, function and the political context within which they work.

A second source is those texts which focus on policing in one particular society. Of course, this may not be *comparative*, in the strict sense, if policing is seen as a constant and not considered in an international context, but even here it is the raw material of secondary analysis. One difficulty is the problem of language, and thus texts in English are more readily utilized. What makes these accounts *comparative* is where they are either written by foreign commentators, in which case references to 'policing at home' is almost inevitable, or when articles are written by locals for a foreign audience, for example to be published in journals abroad. Again we can also make a distinction between practitioner and academic authors.

Writings in English by locals tend to be less available for countries where English is not the first language, not surprisingly, and common in other countries such as Canada, where one might compare the critical academic analysis of the history of the Royal Canadian Mounted Police by Morrison (1985) with the detailed but less contentious text of policing in Canada by William Kelly, a former deputy commissioner of the Royal Canadian Mounted Police, and his wife (Kelly and Kelly 1976). In the Netherlands, a strong emphasis upon international contacts has resulted in a number of works in English, for example by academics working within the Ministry of Justice, like Wiebrens (1989), senior police officers such as Brink and Bulthuis (1979), as well as 'outsider' academics, the most notable being Punch (1979; 1985; 1989). Gupta's (1979) account of the Indian police can also be compared with that of outside academics such as Bayley (1969) and Arnold (1986).

Outside academics have in fact contributed significantly to our knowledge of foreign police systems. As well as Bayley's (1969; 1976) analyses of Indian and Japanese systems, and Punch's research in the Netherlands, we are dependent on the writings of academics like Brady (1982a; 1982b) on Cuba and China respectively and Stead (1957; 1983) on France. There is also a growing literature on the history of various policing systems: for example Williams (1979) on Paris from 1718 to 1789; Davis (1988) on nineteenth-century Italy; and Arnold (1986) on the Madras police from 1859 to 1947.

Finally, a number of outside practitioners have made contributions to the field. One of the most notable early accounts is that on the Indian police by Sir Percival Griffiths (1971), who retired from the Indian civil service having been a district magistrate in Bengal in the 1930s and then chief whip in the Legislative Assembly. Rather differently, more recent accounts from practitioners have tended to stem from study visits abroad by police like Finch (1984) to China, and Hayes (1986) to Spain.

The third source of comparative analysis refers to those works which focus on specific aspects of policing in two or more societies. Again, some of the more significant contributions are historical analyses of the emergence of the modern police, for example Emsley's (1983) comparison of France and England and Wales, 1750–1870; and Miller's (1977) discussion of the overlap and divergence of police structures in New York and London in the nineteenth century.

Other aspects of comparison, however, vary in the comprehensiveness of the analysis. Certain subject areas, like the role of the police in public-order situations, have attracted considerable attention (Bowden 1978; Brewer *et al.* 1988; Roach and Thomaneck 1985), and the importance of forging international links in order to force internal policy changes is evidenced in some areas, such as *vis-à-vis* policewomen where international comparisons are well established (Mulschlegel and Stolwerk 1989; Sherman 1977) and indeed historically based on the strategies of early reformers (Owings [1925] 1969; Tancred 1931).

However, in other areas analysis tends to be parochial. For example, while Punch (1985) discusses police corruption in Britain, the United States and the Netherlands, and Meyer (1985) analyses police strikes in a number of countries, these are exceptions rather than typical. Despite recent concern over the treatment of crime victims, for instance, discussions of the police role towards victims is at best superficially comparative, and this applies equally to research on domestic violence and rape. Yet one might expect – or one is led from discussions to expect – variations in the treatment of such victims according to the dominance and content of a police culture, the deployment of policewomen and the extent to which police work is crime-focused, to take but three variables. Before moving on, it is perhaps instructive to consider briefly the way in which such comparisons can be made. As illustration two articles on police accountability by Regan (1984) and Bayley (1983) will be described.

Regan (1984) compares police status and accountability in Britain, France and West Germany. To do so, he begins by distinguishing accountability from control and then focuses on three areas which he sees as underpinning the issue: the extent of centralization; the scope of the police role; and the degree of political control. Whether or not these do indeed adequately express different levels of accountability is debatable, but Regan continues by considering each issue in turn for the three countries. Finally he draws the material together, arguing that France is distinctive in prescribing a wider role for policing, Britain for having less political control of the police.

Bayley's (1983) approach is in marked contrast. He also starts with a definition, this time of an accountable police force, and then moves on to consider the mechanisms by which accountability might be achieved, in terms of a fourfold typology based on whether the mechanism is internal or external to the police organization, and whether or not it is specialist. Then concentrating on external, specialized mechanisms, he compares a number of countries in terms of whether they are located within or outside government and whether they are the responsibility of politicians, bureaucrats or both. He also refers to new developments in the creation of locally based community consultative committees. On the basis of examples from a variety of countries, Bayley then argues that the mechanisms of accountability are not related to political regime or police structure. For example, decentralized forces are not necessarily more accountable than centralized ones. This leads Bayley into a discussion where he stresses the importance of internal mechanisms of accountability, but recognizes the necessity for external mechanisms both as a failsafe device and as a means of reassuring the public.

Although both Regan and Bayley use very different approaches, and indeed define accountability in starkly different ways, they share a recognition that in order to draw international comparisons it is crucial to start with a clear definition of one's terms. Any ambiguity about what we mean by 'accountability', for example, will dilute the lessons that might be learnt from the exercise. With that in mind, we can continue by discussing the advantage and difficulties associated with comparative analysis.

THE NEED FOR A COMPARATIVE PERSPECTIVE

We can, perhaps, approach this discussion from two perspectives: that of the practitioner, with a pragmatic view of the lessons to be learnt from other societies; and that of the theorist, attempting to explain practices and predict policy outcomes.

Practitioners have been inexorably drawn into comparative exercises where they have taken on one or other of four roles: as emigrants, conquerors, joiners or borrowers. As emigrants, those moving to a new, 'unpoliced' society have, in many cases, taken with them the traditions of the countries left behind. Settlers in the United States, for example, adopted community-based policing practices from Britain, the Netherlands, France and other European countries, including a nightwatch, the posse and (possibly) the office of public prosecutor (Gittler 1984). As conquerors the Romans bequeathed a legal system and the concept of centralized bureaucratic control on much of continental Europe (Chapman 1970) and later the French (Jammes 1982) imposed policing systems on their new territories. As examples of joiners, we might consider the implications for policing of the transference of Hong Kong back to China in 1997 or advances in co-operation within the EC due to culminate in 1992. Finally, borrowing occurs when police systems adopt practices from other countries. A recent example is the translation of neighbourhood watch from the United States to England and Wales (Bennett 1987; Kinsey, Lea and Young 1986).

In each of these countries, the common assumption of practitioners is that experience in one setting is a guide to success elsewhere: we learn from other successful polices. However, in so far as solutions are sometimes more apparent than real, in many cases such approaches are both ahistorical and atheoretical. A good example from the conqueror tradition is the unfortunate experience of the United States' attempts to impose a devolved policing system on postwar

Japan (Ames 1981; McKenzie 1984) and the equally disastrous attempts by France, Britain and the United States to create a postwar German police system in their own image (Bayley 1985, 65). Essential to good comparative work is the realization that elements of one system cannot necessarily be transferred; that police practices in one society do not automatically translate into another. Similar criticisms have been drawn by the introduction of neighbourhood watch in Britain. Additionally Kinsey, Lea and Young (1986) argue that core features of the American system which explain its success, namely some element of community power, have been omitted from the British model, while Bennett (1987) suggests that assumptions of success in the United States have been accepted uncritically.

A theoretical approach to comparative analysis is not, therefore, necessarily of less practical relevance; rather it is a more thorough assessment of practices in different countries and the extent to which they are dependent upon the wider social, cultural and political structure of the host country. As Higgins (1981) notes in the context of comparative social policy, its advantages are to be found on a number of levels. First, we may draw comparisons in order to see how far different features of a policing system are constant, or in contrast vary between societies: in other words, challenge the assumption that things are always done in a particular way. Second, we may attempt to explain differences: that is, by looking at the wider structural features of different societies over a time period, ask why systems have developed differently in different societies. Third, based on a number of alternative systems, we may suggest middle-range theories, for example, regarding how different police systems might develop in contrasting types of society. Fourth, we may predict outcomes by assessing the extent to which the practices of one society may or may not be applicable in other societies. Finally, such procedures may be used to inform practice, allowing us to attempt policy changes where a comprehensive analysis of the available evidence gives us some good reason to predict success.

The above is, of course, an idealized process. Research within one culture is essentially a vague and messy business and the difficulties are compounded when we widen our horizons. What then are the major problems associated with comparative analysis?

DIFFICULTIES IN COMPARATIVE ANALYSIS

There are at least two levels of difficulty associated with comparative analysis: that which reflects the inadequacy of much of the data on which we depend; and that which is endemic to international comparison.

On the first level, one problem stems from the variable quality of much of the work on policing in various societies. Some accounts are superficial, others simplistic, others frighteningly uncritical. This is to some extent indicative of a new subject area. However, many of these problems over quality, particularly when written by 'outsiders', stem from the inevitable difficulties faced by visiting academics or practitioners. In Japan, for example, the work of Bayley (1976) and more recently Parker (1984) can be contrasted with Ames' (1981) approach. The latter while not a criminologist, is an anthropologist who speaks Japanese and spent considerably longer in Japan than the others, allowing him to 'get beneath' the public face of policing to a greater extent. Almost inevitably, outsiders are more reliant on the formal structure of policing, expressed in official reports, discussions with senior staff etc., than long-term scrutiny of policing in action. Consequently, the standards of validity which we might set in viewing our own policing systems are often laid on one side when we venture abroad.

One recent example of this, in the context of crime and the criminal justice system in Switzerland, surrounds the earlier study by Clinard (1978). He argued that crime levels in Switzerland were relatively low compared with other Western industrialized societies, and sought to explain this. Another visiting academic, Flemming Balvig (1988) from Copenhagen, subsequently spent a month in Switzerland and on the basis of his findings produced a very different image of crime in Switzerland, in the process criticizing Clinard's methodology. Essentially, Balvig argues that crime is not less common than in other European countries but that the ways in which the Swiss process it means that the 'dark figure' represents a larger proportion of crime than in comparable countries. Reviewing Balvig's book a Swiss criminologist, Martin Killias (1989), argues that while Clinard was possibly guilty of relying too much on the views of local experts, Balvig, without a knowledge of the language and with little contact with Swiss academics or practitioners, has produced a serious distortion of the evidence. For example, while Balvig relies on a small local victim survey Killias quotes evidence from the much larger national crime survey. In summary:

> Comparative research in criminology is difficult and time consuming, this is not a field designed for quick and easy studies. The most difficult task may be to overcome language barriers, either by learning foreign languages or by relying on hired staff and/or the views of experts . . . Balvig was thus not eager to listen to whatever Swiss experts might have been able to tell him, but unfortunately he did not care about learning Switzerland's languages either. The result is a series of misrepresentations . . . Since it is impossible to point to all the inaccuracies in a review, the reader may be warned that the sections on statistics, on self-report studies, on immigration policy and the status of foreigners, on white-collar crime, and on the role played by the media are seriously flawed. (Killias 1989, 301).

The inadequacy of the data available is reflected in other ways. Take for example simple issues such as the extent of police personnel in a society (Carr-Hill 1989). Even within Europe it is difficult to collate valid figures over any period of time, but what such figures mean when we have them is open to question. Thus if national definitions of the role of the police vary, for example over administrative responsibilities, then we might expect differences in policing levels. But the issue has wider implications than this. Take the Indian police officer whose traffic-related work is minimal (Shane 1980); or the single officer in Claremont, North Carolina who read the water meters, checked the town pumps and authorized street repairs but drew the line at grass cutting or garbage removal (Hageman 1985, 23)! Such significant differences in police responsibilities will affect motivations for joining the police, job satisfaction, work patterns etc. Further, in societies where traffic wardens or meter maids are employed as a specialist unit within the police, rather than a separate organization, this will dramatically alter not only the recorded numbers of police personnel but also, assuming that such employees are disproportionally female, the apparent gender balance!

However, perhaps the most pervasive difficulty concerns the measurement of crime itself. Of course, the problems of using official statistics as valid indicators of the extent of crime in a specific society, and changes over time, are well recognized. That is not to say that official statistics have no relevance. Clearly, as a measure of the volume and nature of work facing the police they have a reality of their own, although even here police may reshape figures to justify claims for extra resources or to demonstrate efficiency. Additionally some statistics, on, say, homicide or vehicle thefts, may be more valid than others where non-reporting is more of an issue, although even here inducements to report may vary by country for specific crimes.[2] Thus, while international comparisons of recorded statistics, such as that by Kalish (1988), will be referred to throughout this text, it is important to supplement this where possible from other sources.

One such source is the impression given by academics and practitioners who have had the opportunity to express concern over crime 'at street level' in different countries. While not a very scientific approach, my own personal experience of Japan, for example, leads me to accept that when writers express feelings of safety on the streets at night in some countries rather than others we should not lightly dismiss their views. Perhaps more substantial is victim-survey data, now available for a number of Western industrialized countries. Here again, international comparisons are hazardous. As Block (1983) notes, the questions asked vary markedly, and even the recent European victim survey[3] does not overcome all such difficulties, since cultural variations may mean that acceptable responses to the same question may vary across societies.

The difficulties discussed so far nevertheless share the characteristic that they are, at least in theory, surmountable. We can work to ensure that the data we use is adequate, and take care not to draw unwarranted conclusions from it. More serious limitations are those which are endemic to comparative analysis itself. One is the difficulty of understanding a foreign country, still more a number of countries, sufficiently to do justice to the sophisticated analysis required (Blazicek and Janeksela 1978). There is a limit to the extent of our sustained personal experiences. Moreover, the range of variables that need to be taken into account are considerable, and potentially unpredictable (Meyer 1972). For example, it seems fairly obvious that policing cannot be understood without reference to the criminal justice system in total, or the wider legal tradition. But it may also be shaped by the political system of a country, or public administrative structures such as the balance between central and local government or the role of a professional civil service, the military or a political party in administrative affairs. It is at least as important to consider less tangible features of a society like its social structure and cultural expectations. For example, the role of women in policing – or rather the lack of a role for women in policing – in Latin American societies may have less to do with the police system or the political regime and more to do with expectations of women's restricted role in society.

This leads us to a further difficulty, namely the need for categorizations. If we are to attempt to explain developments in policing in different societies and policing systems, we need ultimately to classify both the societies and the policing systems. In terms of societal classification, we may wish to distinguish according to legal traditions, for example as do Cole, Frankowski and Gertz (1988) in their comparative criminal justice text. On the other hand, some measure of social and political structure may be preferable, where we can compare capitalist democracies, rightwing dictatorships, and communist/socialist societies on the one hand and nations according to their lack of development on the other. However, just as there is no classification which is correct, so different typologies may lead us to stress certain similarities or differences and ignore others. Similarly with classifications of police systems: while many authors make distinctions between the police systems of continental Europe, those with an Anglo-Saxon tradition, and (British) colonial alternatives, we could equally distinguish systems according to the balance between public and private police, levels of specialism or professionalism, centralization, militarization, or a host of other alternatives.

The point is that there are no easy solutions. International comparisons are of considerable value, but as the scale of analysis is increased, so the difficulties are multiplied. It is crucial to bear this in mind as we move on to more detailed empirical analysis.

2

The Emergence of Modern Policing Systems

POLICING IN PRIMITIVE SOCIETIES

In the first chapter, some basic definition of the police was suggested, based on notions of legitimacy, structure and function, but accepting that there might be considerable variation between different societies. In these circumstances, can we assume that all societies have some form of policing? Perhaps surprisingly, the answer is no. In a review of work written on fifty-one primitive societies, Schwartz and Miller (1964) concluded that no less than twenty-nine had no form of policing.

Many of these societies had minimal levels of organization, with no form of money, little property and no specialization. One such society, the Eskimo, is described in more detail by Hoebel (1961, 67–9) in a chapter significantly subtitled 'Rudimentary law in a primitive anarchy'. Living in small, transient communities, the Eskimos' level of social structure was indeed minimal, although there were accepted norms, confirmed in taboos. However, where taboos were breached there was little organized, accepted form of response on behalf of the group. For example, despite their extremely permissive sex codes, most homicides were the result of conflict over women. But where homicide occurred, it was viewed as a private matter; consequently, private response – the killing of the killer by the victim's kin – was condoned. Indeed, homicide only became a group responsibility where the offender was guilty of repeated killings and was thus seen as a threat to the group. In such situations the group might agree on united action, either exile or lynching. There was, however, no individual or group specifically designated with any responsibility for controlling even these extreme examples of deviance.

Many other primitive societies have some degree of administrative structure, but still have no police. Schwartz and Miller (1964) found that of the twenty-nine with no police, eighteen had some form of mediation. In many of these societies, property is more significant than in others and some mechanisms are required for dealing with disputes over ownership, inheritance etc. A number of such societies are described by Hoebel. The Ifugao of the Philippines, for example, was a gardening society in which government was minimal but property law substantial. Conflicts, normally over land rights between kinship groups, were handled through official mediators, the *Monkalum*, high-status individuals who were responsible for determining damages. However there was no evidence of any police system (Hoebel 1961, 100–26).

In a number of other primitive societies, however, some form of police could be identified. Schwartz and Miller (1964) argue that, with few exceptions, these fell into two groups: eleven of their sample with some system of mediation and police; and seven with mediation, police and specialized counsel. The exceptions, the Crow and Thonga, had police but no other legal institutions.

What form then do such early forms of policing take? At least three alternatives come to mind: those based on a warrior class, a state agency, or the local community. One example of the former is that of the samurai in Japan prior to the nineteenth century (Ames 1981). Others are some of the Plains Indians described by Hoebel (1961 127–76). Hoebel recounts how the introduction of the horse to Indian society precipitated the need to specify some basic laws of property. Conflicts, over property and sexual relations, formed the main threats to internal cohesion, and the responsibility for policing disputes came to be accepted by the military societies. The Cheyenne had chiefs who acted as peacemakers and a counsel with executive and judicial power. For example, a chief might act as mediator in settlement of an adultery case, while the counsel could impose the sentence of banishment on a murderer. The third branch of Cheyenne government, the six Soldiers' Societies, was responsible for maintaining order especially during the communal hunt and at ceremonial rituals but also at other times. For example Hoebel (1961, 151) details how the Shield Soldiers punished hunters who attacked the buffalo without permission. In this case the offending was obvious, but in other circumstances the Soldiers' Societies had the right to search the property of those suspected of illegal hunting, to look for evidence of fresh meat (Hoebel 1961, 153).

What is particularly significant about the Cheyenne is that when societal conflict reached an unacceptable level at which the need for some regulatory force was recognized, the Soldiers' Societies were deployed rather than some new, specialist organization being created:

> The interesting and utterly reasonable thing about it all is that the need did not result in the creation of new social agencies to wield the stick of power but that already existing agencies were drafted into the job. The primary interests of the military associations had been social. They were nothing more than men's clubs . . . They were military in that all their members were soldiers. Only rarely did they go to war as units. They were not tactical bodies of standing armies nor even militia companies as we understand them. But they were *organised*. And when a job requiring the exercise of force by an organised unit representing not kinship interests, but the tribal whole came up, what was more natural than that the tribes should acquiesce in their taking on of *secondary* functions: the administration of policing and of summary justice where summary action was necessary? Thus an entirely non-governmental type of organisation became a legitimised branch of the government of the tribes. (Hoebel 1961, 154–5).

In some respects, policing by the military was more evident in the Roman Empire, especially in the maintenance of law and order in the provinces (Davies 1968; Stead 1984). However, from a rule of C. Octavius in 27 BC the police emerged as a distinct and separate arm of government, albeit with wider administrative tasks (Bayley 1985; Kelly 1987). Prior to that time law enforcement had involved an unpaid magistracy combined with private law enforcement, with plaintiffs responsible for bringing offenders before the court, and being rewarded for so doing. However C. Octavius (better known as Augustus) organized the Praetorium Guard as a political police and the Urban Cohorts as a uniformed police service for Rome itself. Later in AD 6 he established the *vigiles*, a unit of some 3,500 men, specializing in crime and firefighting duties. About a century later the Emperor Trajan formed a central investigation bureau, the *Frumentarii*, which worked throughout the provinces (Kelly 1987). By the third century Rome had a well-established police force with *vigiles*, based in police stations, regularly patrolling the streets (Bayley 1985, 38).

In marked contrast, the Anglo-Saxon tradition was dependent upon the local small group for law enforcement. Prior to the Norman invasion of England, order was maintained on behalf of the local lord by the *tythingman*. He was held responsible for the good conduct of ten families bound together in a *tything*, reporting 'upwards' to a *hundredman* who himself was responsible to the *shire reeve* (or sheriff) who could, in an emergency, call on the ancient system of 'hue and cry' and summon a posse (Critchley 1978). After the Norman

Conquest the system was centralized to a greater extent, particularly following the Assize of Clarendon in 1166 and the Statute of Winchester in 1285, when the practice of a nightwatch of local citizens, on a rota basis, was introduced in the towns. Magistrates were created in 1361 through the Justices of the Peace Act as the representatives of central government responsible for co-ordinating local services. Up until well into the eighteenth century, then, law enforcement in England was dependent, at local level, on high-status unpaid magistrates supervising lower status constables, appointed within the parish and – at least initially – enjoying considerable local prestige.

Clearly, just as policing is not a universal phenomenon, so alternative police systems can be identified in primitive and later pre-industrial societies. Schwartz and Miller (1964) argue that these early forms of policing emerged as social structures became more complex in terms of the invention of writing, some form of money, property divisions, and other specialist roles, particularly where full-time government officials were established based on non-kinship criteria. Equally clearly, though, these police systems themselves changed as societies became more complex. How then can we identify and explain modern policing systems?

THE MODERN POLICE

In a thoughtful discussion of the comparative literature, Bayley (1985) argues that modern policing incorporates three crucial characteristics: it is public, specialized and professional. In the case of the latter two characteristics, we can consider dichotomies – unspecialized/specialized and non-professional/professional – where there has been a steady move from one extreme to the other. In the case of the third dichotomy, private/public, the situation is more complex since currently private policing is regaining some of its earlier significance.

We may consider Bayley's model in the context of the three key features of policing that were distinguished in Chapter 1, namely legitimacy, structure and function. In terms of a modern police, legitimacy is accorded to a public police force which has a national rather than a local mandate; private, voluntary or informal policing may exist, but it is either subordinate to the public police or has a restricted legitimacy. For example, police volunteers are normally under the control of the public police and have more restricted powers (Gill and Mawby 1990a); private police have less powers than public police and have a responsibility to their employers rather than the public at large (South 1988). In previous periods, in contrast, the role of non-state police (whether community-based, voluntary, private or a combination of all three) was more common.

The second key feature, structure, can be considered with reference to Bayley's non-professional/professional dimension. To a certain extent, the term 'professional' is misleading (as Bayley himself acknowledges) at least in terms of sociological definitions of the term. It is perhaps better to consider modern policing as characterized by being located in an organization whose mandate is clearly prescribed, and which is bound by rules, prescribing training and regarding both acceptable behaviour of employees' or employers' expectations *vis-à-vis* conditions of employment. In contrast, more primitive police structures might be less formal and prescribed. Finally the concept 'function' taps the unspecialized/specialized dimension. While earlier policing systems might be characterized by a lack of specialization, where policing is only one aspect of an individual's occupational responsibilities, modern policing is characterized by both external and internal specialization. That is, police officers are expected to work in law enforcement to the virtual exclusion of other jobs, and internally we find less emphasis on non-crime administrative responsibilities and more specialization on specific aspects of crime.

Clearly the distinction between modern and earlier forms of policing is not as clear-cut as this model implies. Early police systems did incorporate some of the features we have identified with modern forces, and vice versa. For example, the police system of ancient Rome was clearly a public agency. On the other hand, American police are commonly associated with the practice of 'moonlighting', limiting their level of specialism; and no police force could claim to be truly 'professional' in the strict sense of the term. Nevertheless, the distinction is a useful one, and it allows Bayley (1985, 23–52) to attempt to explain the shift towards a modern police not as an unidimensional phenomenon but in terms of the three continua separately. He thus asks how and why police systems have become public agencies, then turns to assess changes in specialization, and finally considers the development of professionalization.

We can perhaps best illustrate the changes briefly with reference to the changing nature of policing in England and Wales and the United States in the nineteenth century. In England and Wales, police systems prior to the nineteenth century can, very broadly, be defined as private, non-professional and unspecialized (Critchley 1978; Radzinowicz 1956a; 1956b). Although there were some police forces financed by local government, the system is best characterized as a mixed economy of policing, in which community, voluntary, private and public services co-existed, with some degree of confusion and little evidence of efficiency (Gill and Mawby 1990a). Although nineteenth-century critics have perhaps overstressed the inefficiency of these various officers of the law, it is equally clear that the public and community sectors failed to attract capable personnel, while the private sector, concentrating on the retrieval of stolen goods rather than the administration of justice, was both inefficient and partial in operation. Finally, while some police agents were specialists, others were designated with police tasks on a part-time or temporary basis. As a review of the role of the Special Constabulary reveals, the deployment of inadequately trained members of the public to maintain order at times of political unrest was at best ineffective, at worst disastrous (Gill and Mawby 1990a).

The police systems which replaced this in the mid-nineteenth century signalled a break from the past in degree rather than kind. Although the London Metropolitan force was established in 1829, and similar forces in other urban and rural areas between 1835 and 1888, there was considerable local variation. Police volunteers and private police continued to exist, the former indeed becoming better established. Many forces were small and scarcely professional (Wall 1987), and central government, through the Home Office, only gradually imposed national standards (Critchley 1978). Moreover, the only public police force was scarcely specialist. Officers earned extra money by acting as 'knockers-ups' and, as Steedman (1984) noted, provincial government, eager to get value for money, deployed its new police in a medley of administrative tasks. Furthermore, while the last century has seen the public police becoming more professional and more specialized, there has also recently been an expansion of the private sector (South 1988) and a resurgence of interest in community participation in policing (Gill and Mawby 1990a).

Early police systems in the United States tended to be based on those familiar to emigrants from Britain and Continental Europe. In the townships law enforcement was provided by a variety of community representatives including nightwatchmen, serving in rotation, and constables paid for by local rates (Lane 1967). There were, however, considerable variations from the British tradition. For example, vigilantism thrived, either in place of a public system of justice or as an alternative to it (Brown 1969a; 1969b). One dimension to the vigilante movement was racist, with organizations like the Ku Klux Klan imposing racial domination. Other community-policing groups also operated so as to control black slaves. Reichel (1988), for example, describes the Southern slave patrols of the late seventeenth and eighteenth centuries as militia-type units specializing in the rounding up of black slaves and in suppressing revolt. Paralleling these, and closely involved in maintaining class domination, the private police have, according to Bowden (1978, 236–60), a more established role in the United States than in Britain.

As in Britain, modern police systems emerged in the United States in the nineteenth century. However, unlike Britain, and reflecting the dominance of local government in the United States, central direction of police developments was minimal. As Emsley (1983, 103) has noted, 'The history of American police during the nineteenth century is the history of separate forces in separate cities.'

In New Orleans, for example, early moves towards a paid police force owed much to French influence (Emsley 1983, 107). In Boston, daytime constables worked alongside a nightwatch from 1823 and separate day and night police units were established in 1837 (Lane 1967). However, New York is accredited with the first truly modern force, formed in 1845 and modelled on the London police (Miller 1977). Notably, though, the United States version was markedly different from the London blueprint in a number of respects. For example, it explicitly recruited personnel from the communities being policed, and was more closely embroiled in local politics (Miller 1977; Monkkonen 1981). Moreover it appears that while the public were more willing to contemplate an armed police, they were reluctant to accept a uniformed force!

The reasons for the emergence of a new police in Britain and the United States are the subject of considerable discussion (Brogden, Jefferson and Walklate 1988, 49–69), not least because no one set of conditions is common to even a majority of the situations within which the modern police became established (Monkkonen 1981, 41–64). Essentially we can briefly summarize the debate by considering three interrelated questions: namely, what problems were the new police designed to confront; why were earlier police systems inadequate; and what determined the characteristics of the new police?

In terms of the problems which gave rise to the emergence of the modern police, it is clear that arguments, advocated at the time, that crime was out of control or that public disorder had reached new heights were grossly exaggerated. At best we might accept that circumstances were considered unacceptable by the emerging urban elites. In some instances, rising crime, or specifically street violence, was identified as the problem; in others, street protests by political activists such as Chartists in England and Scotland have been specified; rather more indirectly, the growth of cities has been associated with the threat posed by a more heterogeneous population, with more immigrants or 'aliens'.

In these circumstances, established forms of policing came to be seen as inadequate. Explicitly, this was often defined in terms of inefficiency; for example the dependence of the watch system on the old or simpleminded who were unable to find better employment. Implicit to such criticism was perhaps a concern that within capitalism the community could no longer be relied on to police itself on behalf of the bourgeoisie. Moreover, at a time of geographical mobility, the expansion of the cities, and industrialization, with associated problems of crime and labour unrest, community-based law enforcement, within small areas, was less appropriate. It was further undermined by the changing structure of society which meant that primary, community-based systems of control were also breaking down. Overall, then, in the Rookeries of London, for example, it made little sense to the middle class to depend on the local community to police itself (Beames 1970; Oben 1974; Stedman-Jones 1971), any more than it did to expect the mill towns to provide sufficient (politically reliable) locals to police the Chartist protests (Mather 1959).

The new police system was shaped as an alternative mechanism that could, through more efficient prevention and detection of crime, maintain order as defined by the establishment. The essential feature of this new system was that it was public, which in turn required that it should be professionally organized and (at least to some extent) specialist. In explaining the centrality accredited to those three criteria, it is important to recognize that they were reflected in a host of other developments in the nineteenth century. In England, for example, Edwin Chadwick, a (partly successful) advocate of a national, rationalized, preventive policing system (Radzinowicz 1956b), was also to the fore of reforms in other areas of public and social policy, most notably with regard to the Poor Law and public health innovations. More generally, nineteenth-century Britain saw governments accepting greater responsibility for the provision of services and the control of standards (Dicey [1885] 1950), and was characterized by early sociologists as heralding an increased division of labour within society (Durkheim [1893] 1947; Spencer 1874).

Such moves were by no means unchallenged. As Radzinowicz (1956b) demonstrates, initiatives for a public police in England met considerable opposition, and counter-proposals advocated a re-emphasis of community responsibilities. Nevertheless, there was gradual acceptance that responsibility for the police lay with government, be it local or central, and that such forces should be professionally organized, with roles and responsibilities clearly defined. Specialization, however, came somewhat later. As already noted, for the English provincial forces Steedman (1984) demonstrates the wide range of responsibilities levied at the police, for example *vis-à-vis* the regulations of the Poor Law, and in the United States the early public police spent considerable time in welfare-related tasks, for example concerning orphans and the older flotsam of the cities (Monkkonen 1981).

As is equally clear, once the Metropolitan force had been formed, innovations took on a momentum of their own. This is neatly expressed by Monkkonen (1981, 55), who argues that cities used early models from London or New York to create police organizations which were compatible with other, newly emerging, arms of local government:

> The causal sequence ran thus: American urban administrations in the last half of the nineteenth century began to provide a growing range of rationalised services – police, fire, health and sewerage – which previously had been provided on an entrepreneurial basis by various organisations. For the largest cities, the conspicuously successful Metropolitan Police of London served as a policing model to be adopted when any one of the several precipitants occurred. Once adopted by larger cities, the new model of policing spread from larger to smaller cities, spurred not by precipitating events any longer, but by the newly developing service orientations of city governments.

Nevertheless, even within England and Wales, and especially the United States (Reppetto 1978), there were marked variations between these separate local forces, differences which in the former more than the later have tended to be eradicated with more central-government influence. There are, moreover, as Brogden (1987) has argued forcefully, considerably more variations on this 'modern police' theme, as examples from Europe and the British colonies well illustrate.

THE CONTINENTAL MODEL

The centralized, monarchical system of government which characterized much of Europe in the late sixteenth and seventeenth centuries provided the framework within which a somewhat different system of policing was constructed. Essentially, government was based on benevolent paternalism: it was the duty of the monarch to act in the best interests of his subjects, accepting that they would often not 'appreciate' what their best interests were (Chapman 1970; Raeff 1975). It followed from this that the ruler was obliged to initiate the regulations and areas of administration necessary to ensure harmony and justice. To do so, available units of government were accredited with a new mandate. In the German states, for example,

> the police activities of the latter half of the seventeenth century are noteworthy for the extent to which they rely on existing estate and corporative institutions and mechanisms to implement controls and regulations. Only a few new offices were created or officials appointed to enforce these controls and regulations. Essentially the task was delegated to existing functionaries, and, whenever possible, it was carried out with the help of corporations and other supervision exercised over the activities of these officials and institutions by the Prince's councils and central offices. The officials becoming increasingly more executors of the instructions and orders emanating from the centre, which provided rational and comprehensive direction. (Raeff 1975, 1227).

This is seen by Chapman (1970, 16) as the basis for the first police state: 'the first Polizeistaat was, therefore, dedicated to three purposes: the protection of the population; the welfare of the state and its citizens; and the improvement of society'.

The Prussian example of the seventeenth century, incompletely translated to French in the eighteenth, became the model for Fouche's reforms in the post-revolutionary republic. Thus, rather than 'police' (in the modern sense) emerging with a specific law and order mandate, the continental pattern was for crime to be added to the main responsibilities of central government, which were initially control, administration and welfare. Consequently, the police systems which subsequently characterized much of the continent were very different from the Anglo-Saxon model, a point emphasized time and time again by Fosdick ([1915] 1969b).

How then can we distinguish the continental model according to the three criteria already identified, namely legitimacy, structure and function? In terms of legitimacy, clearly the model provides for a much wider set of legal powers than in the Anglo-Saxon model. For example, registration of the population was a common requirement. The object of these legal powers was, moreover, to ensure order on behalf of central government, the state, and ultimately the ruler, be he monarch or emperor. The police force was thus the servant of the Crown, not the people, as in the United Kingdom:

> in sharp contrast is the Continental theory, which evolved from the necessity of autocratic government, and makes of the police hence the strong arm of the ruling classes. The continental policeman is the servant of the Crown or the higher authorities; the people have no share in his duties, nor, indeed, any connection with them. He possesses powers greatly exceeding those of the citizen. (Fosdick [1915] 1969b, 16).

This point is re-emphasized later:

> The autocratic spirit of the German government is reflected in the imperviousness of the police to public opinion. The police department is a specialised institution in the details of which the people are held to have no proper interest. (Fosdick [1915] 1969b, 77).

The centralization of the police, its legal powers, and its responsibility to the ruler have considerable implications on a structural level. In particular, the structure which more readily accommodates this model was a militaristic one. Thus most European police systems operated a two-tier entrance system, recruiting to each from the armed forces: the rank structure was also modelled on the military. Weapons were also routinely carried. Additionally, control and supervision of the police was often in accord with the armed services. For example, in Berlin: 'Members of the police force are under military discipline and must mold their conduct while on duty in accordance with military forms' (Fosdick [1915] 1969b, 228).

Finally, in terms of function, it is clear that the continental police had a considerably wider range of responsibilities. At one extreme the role of the political police, including the secret police, was more pronounced than in England and Wales and the USA. At the other, the responsibilities of the police for a range of administrative and welfare tasks were considerable, with consequent implications for the structure of the police organization:

> Thus in Berlin, the fire department, the health department, the prison department, the building department (including the condemnation of land for public purposes) and certain functions of the charity department were all branches of the huge police organisation. The police supervise the markets and the sale of provisions; they pass on the quality of food-stuffs; they exercise an oversight of public assemblies and meetings; they abate nuisances; they inspect lodging houses, cafes and places of amusement; they supervise druggists, veterinaries and the details of various professions; they prepare construction plans

> for street and river-front improvements; they keep a strict watch on certain classes of banking institutions; they frame regulations for the public conduct of citizens and mete out punishment for violations. (Fosdick [1915] 1969b, 21–2).

In Berlin, not surprisingly, responsibility for this range of functions was divided between twelve separate departments, only one of which would have been easily recognized as police by a British policeman of the time. Equally in Paris: 'Matters relating to public health and hygiene, to street railroads, to dangerous substances, to the prevention of fire, to pure food, and to hundred other subjects are all part of the police function'. (Fosdick [1915] 1969b, 127).

In terms of legitimacy, structure and function, then, the continental police model was clearly distinguished from its English counterpart:

> The foregoing account exhibits two main types of police organisation, readily distinguishable from one another – the English and the Continental. The English type is characterised by its simplicity, for it encompasses merely a uniformed force and a detection dimension. The Continental type is complex and intricate, adapted to the variety of functions which the Continental states have committed to their police departments. The English organisation is built up around the work of men in uniform; in the Continental organisation the uniformed force is but one of a number of branches each bearing an equal relationship to the head. (Fosdick [1915] 1969b, 140).

THE COLONIAL MODEL

The very different socio-political structures of Western European states produced distinctive police systems. Equally, as Britain expanded its empire, a police system deemed ideal for colonial rule came to be identified. The model was not, however, the Metropolitan Police Force but the Royal Irish Constabulary.

Protestant-dominated baronial police forces were established in Ireland by the early eighteenth century. In Dublin, this local system was replaced in 1786 when the Dublin Police Act established a new police force. Ironically, the Act was broadly the same as the London Westminster Police Bill of 1785 which had been decisively rejected (Radzinowicz 1956b, 108–23). The problem faced by the English in trying to establish order in a society which rejected rule from Westminster, however, led to the establishment of a centralized police force, the Irish Constabulary, through the Act for the Better

Execution of the Laws in Ireland in 1814 and the Constabulary (Ireland) Acts of 1822 and 1836.

The Irish Constabulary quite clearly sought legitimacy at Westminster rather than among the indigenous population. It was an alternative to an army of occupation with no community mandate whatsoever. This is clearly illustrated if we consider its structure and functions.

On a structural level it was highly centralized, with a recognized chain of command from the individual constable, through chief constable to inspector general and lord lieutenant. The 1822 Act, for example, established the principle that the constable was answerable to the chief constable, rather than the law, the chief constable himself being responsible to central government:

> Thus, subject only to the constraints of the end distance and the familiar problems of control of a large organisation, the Royal Irish Constabulary was responsive to the wishes of the Inspector General, the vast machine being at his orders to carry out the tasks laid upon him . . . The Inspector General was responsible to and bound to obey the orders of the Lord Lieutenant, as conveyed through the Chief Secretary. The Royal Irish Constabulary was part of the Irish Administration, which . . . was a well oiled and effective mechanism, responsible to the commands of its political chiefs. (Tobias 1977, 247–8).

The force, comprising Irish protestant and English recruits, many with an army background, was armed and organized on a military basis. Its location, in barracks, illustrated its source of legitimacy, structure and function as an organ of social control:

> it was not only the single men who lived in barracks; married constables and sub-constables were usually accommodated in the barracks with their wives and children; partly for their protection, partly to make it more difficult for them to form the 'local connection' which their senior officers greatly feared. (Tobias 1977, 246).

In colonies where the indigenous population was in a minority and policing settlers was the priority, such as the United States and Australia, alternative policing systems emerged. In Canada, the English model was appropriated in the growing cities but an Irish-type force, the Mounted Police, was created to impose order in the southern plains and later the north (Macleod 1976; Morrison 1985). In other countries, where British rule was imposed by a small occupying force, combining an administrative division, the military and the police, the police system which emerged tended to follow the Irish pattern:

> In sum, there is evidence of an immediate link between British policing and colonial practices. British institutions, from medicine to law-enforcement, were transplanted to the Empire: to delegitimise indigenous customs; to impose centralised social control; and to incorporate local society as a branch of imperial society. (Brogden 1987, 10).

In India, Sir Charles Napier created an Irish-type police in the province of Sind in the 1840s, and a similar system was later adopted in the other provinces. When W. I. Macartney of the Royal Irish Constabulary and later G. W. R. Campbell of the Indian Police Service were transferred to Ceylon, the structure was duplicated there (Jeffries 1952; Tobias 1977). Indeed, in a review of colonial forces, Jeffries (1952) identified links between the Irish and Indian forces and a range of other police forces in the Caribbean, Far East and Africa. He argued that policing in the colonies could be distinguished in three stages: the first where local, pre-colonial mechanisms of control are preserved; the second, colonial style; and the third, post-colonial phase when policing by consent is prioritized. It is, however, the middle stage which is important for our purposes, when not only ideas, but also personnel, were transferred through the colonies and the Irish blueprint was reproduced as the ideal mechanism for solving a specific set of law-and-order problems:

> It is clear enough that from the point of view of the Colonies there was much attraction in an arrangement which provided what we should now call a 'para-military' organisation or gendarmerie, armed and trained to operate as an agent of the central government in a country where the population was predominantly rural, communications were poor, social conditions were largely primitive, and the recourse to violence by members of the public who were 'agin the government' was not infrequent. It was natural that such a force, rather than one organised on the lines of the purely civilian and localised forces of Great Britain, should have been taken as a suitable model for adaptation to Colonial conditions. (Jeffries 1952, 31).

VARIATIONS ON A THEME?

These are, however, broad generalizations. Writers who have focused on European police or colonial examples have, while

Table 2.1 ***Models of early modern police systems***

	England and Wales	United States	Continental	Colonial
Legitimacy	Local government; based on law	Local government; based on law	Central government, ultimately the ruler	Colonial authority
Structure	Decentralized, unarmed civilian force	Decentralized, armed, civilian force	Centralized, armed, military force	Partly centralized: military force, using armed, alien personnel
Function	Crime and some welfare and administrative responsibilities	Crime and some welfare and administrative responsibilities	Crime only one function: emphasis on political and administrative functions	Crime subsumed within wider concern for political/ administrative functions

accepting that there are variations between countries, tended to stress the distinctions of the model compared with, say, the police systems of England and the United States. In contrast, whereas Brogden (1987) has perhaps overemphasized the similarities between British and colonial policing, in many respects the differences are variations on a theme rather than a reflection of separate species. In Table 2.1 the key features of the English, US, continental and colonial police systems of the nineteenth century have been outlined, using the three criteria of legitimacy, structure and function. As is clear, in many respects the English and US systems share many similarities and are distinct from the continental and colonial systems. In terms of legitimacy, the former are founded on the law and on local-government accountability. In contrast, the will of the ruler, through central government and above the law, is featured in the continental system, while the colonial model is legitimized by an alien authority using its law to suit its purpose. In Madras, for example:

> the role of the police was never restricted to that laid down by law-makers. Police power was often used to circumvent or supplement the legal powers because the latter was too dilatory or too scrupulous to satisfy the colonial need for prompt retribution and collective punishment. In the colonial system the police not infrequently usurped the role of judge, jailor and

> executor. The 'order' imposed by the police did not automatically square with the 'law' with which it was habitually coupled. (Arnold 1986, 3).

Whether the English or US police were always accredited with legitimacy by the public subject to policing is, of course, as questionable as the extent to which the letter of the law was ever strictly applied, but it is clear that on a *formal* level, at least, there are marked distinctions between the different systems.

To a certain extent, the same can be said of the structure. The continental system, for example, is epitomized by a centralized force, based on a military structure, with personnel (but not necessarily senior officers) drawn from the armed forces; police often lived in barracks and were armed. The colonial system also features a military structure, with personnel drawn from the armed forces or other colonial police systems, usually (and certainly in the case of senior officers) aliens, armed, and living in separate quarters. There was, however, some degree of decentralization in many of the colonial forces, including India and Malaya (Jeffries 1952). In contrast the police of England and US were decentralized, civilian, and *not* organized in a military fashion, although in England senior officers tended to be recruited from the military. On the other hand, the US police were commonly armed, and the English police and especially the Metropolitan police tended to be recruited from outside sources, and were not community representatives in the same way as, for example, was the case in New York (Miller 1977).

Different structures are also distinctive in terms of their functions. While the English and US police accepted responsibility for a range of non-crime tasks, their responsibilities for general administration were nowhere as important as in the colonial and especially the continental models. Moreover, their role in maintaining order and protecting the state from political protest, while scarcely ignored, never attained the priority it had on the continent or in the colonies. Indeed, as Arnold (1968, 3) argues, within the colonial system:

> the distinction between political and crime control functions is largely a false one. To the colonial regime crime and politics were almost inseparable: serious crime was an implicit defiance of state authority and a possible prelude to rebellion; political resistance was either a 'crime' or the likely occasion for it. The resources and skills developed in combating the one were freely employed in defeating the other.

While it does, therefore, make sense to distinguish between these alternative models, as with any form of classification we should not overemphasize the differences, and we should be further aware of differences within categories. Moreover, equally clearly, there is no presumption that the classification is universal for modern police. Socialist societies, for example, are ignored, and indeed with the exception of the review by Cole, Frankowski and Gertz (1987) in the context of the legal system as a whole, discussions of policing have tended to avoid socialist examples. Moreover, given the different paths followed by China and the other underdeveloped socialist societies it has influenced, compared with the East European bloc (Dean 1983; White and Nelson 1986), we might anticipate considerable variations between socialist societies. Unfortunately, while there is some material available from the USSR (Karpets 1977; Terrill 1989), discussions of policing in Eastern Europe are minimal,[1] and further discussion will be postponed until after more detailed analysis. A similar problem arises when we seek to incorporate other underdeveloped or developing countries into a model. How, for example, does one categorize rightwing totalitarian regimes, or oil-rich Arab states? Here speculation is perhaps easier to come by than hard evidence!

OUTLINE

The remainder of this book is structured to develop many of the themes and issues discussed so far. The following eight chapters focus on policing systems in a number of societies. The choice of societies has been made on the basis of the available information, with an attempt to include a variety of societies. Chapters 3 and 4 deal with France, perhaps the classic example of the European model, and the Netherlands, with a rather different system. Canada is then considered as an example where English, colonial and US influences can be discerned. Hong Kong is included as an example of the colonial policing system, and Japan is discussed as the first, and perhaps only, Eastern capitalist democracy. Finally, three socialist societies are discussed; the USSR as the model for East European societies; and China and Cuba to demonstrate very different approaches to policing in socialist societies.

It is important that in concentrating on specific countries we do not lose sight of the comparative dimension. In Chapter 11, the emphasis is placed on *issues* rather than specific countries. Again the choice of subjects is to some extent determined by the data available and my own particular interests. However in following community involvement, I hope to cover a range of topics relevant to the legitimacy, structure and function of the police in modern societies. In so doing, material from a range of countries, especially but not exclusively those in Chapters 3–10 are used to illustrate and explain similarities and differences, as they occur. In the concluding chapter an attempt is made to draw together material from the different examples covered in Chapters 3–10.

In order to facilitate comparison, the specific countries included are handled in a similar way. Each chapter therefore begins with a brief review of the country and work on policing within it. This is followed by a discussion of the socio-political structure of the country, and specifically the key features of the criminal justice system. Policing is then discussed: first from a historical perspective, then in terms of the current structure and functions of the police, and finally in terms of the relationship between police and public, which has implications for the legitimacy of the police. In this way I hope to provide a broad introduction which will be of use to those taking up a comparative approach, whether with regard to a specific policy or in order to become better informed about other police systems.

3

France: the Continental System par Excellence

INTRODUCTION

It is appropriate to begin this more detailed focus on specific countries with a review of the French police for a number of reasons. For example, the word 'police', derived from the Greek *politeia*, attained its modern usage in France between the sixteenth and eighteenth centuries and, allied to this, the French police system was arguably the first 'modern' system to be developed. According to Bowden (1978, 140), 'France possesses the largest *continuous* system of policing and the most *developed* police tradition in Europe, possibly in the Western world'. With its colonial past, it is also a system which has been transposed to its former dependencies (Jammes 1982).

The French police system has also been identified as an example to be avoided! In the eighteenth and early nineteenth centuries, developments in France were cited as warnings of how freedom might be endangered should police be introduced in Britain, a debate many French commentators found difficult to understand (Radzinowicz 1948; 1956b). Nevertheless, France was readily described as a 'police state' (Chapman 1971) and commentators on both the political (Hayward 1983) and police (Stead 1983) structures have accepted that public administration and policing systems are closely interwoven. It is therefore somewhat ironic to find that in the nineteenth century Napoleon III looked to the London Metropolitan Police as a model on which to hang his own reforms (Stead 1983).

The French example is also a useful one because, compared with many other societies, English-language texts are readily available. Most notable are Jammes's (1982) description of the *gendarmerie* and Stead's (1983) account of the policing system as a whole. While both are somewhat descriptive and uncritical, they do – inevitably – locate policing in a broader socio-political framework. Historians have also focused on the emergence of policing in France, with Emsley (1983), for instance, comparing France with England and Wales for the period 1750–1870. More recent evaluations of particular aspects of policing are also available; for example Regan (1984) contrasts accountability in France, West Germany and England and Wales, and Roach (1985) and Bowden (1978) focus upon the control of public order in France compared with other Western European nations. Before going into further detail of the police developments, however, it is instructive to describe briefly the social and political structure of France.

FRENCH SOCIETY

With a population of about 54 million, France is very similar in size to the United Kingdom. However, its area is over twice that of the UK, with the result that its population density, 99.1 inhabitants per square km, is low by West European standards (Lipietz 1983). Indeed, population growth has been relatively slow in France: between 1800 and 1970 the population doubled, while in Britain it increased fivefold. The result of this slow growth – due to distinctive marriage and fertility patterns, exacerbated by wars – was that France urbanized and industrialized relatively late. It was not until the 1930s that a majority of the population lived in urban areas (Birks 1987; Rodgers 1979). By the 1980s 8 per cent of the population still worked in agriculture, and while some 80 per cent of the population lived in urban areas (Lipietz 1983) this reflects the fact that in the postwar period France has had one of the highest rates of urban growth in the world (Ashford 1982), with consequential implications for urban development, planning and crime.

The problems of imposing central control on a sprawling, rural population are reflected both in the turbulent history of the country and in police developments. In the pre-revolutionary period, the French kings appeared to pursue the maintenance of control in the capital, the undermining of the feudal lords in the provinces, and – incidentally – the sale of public offices and responsibilities as a means of raising income. The overall result of these policies was a loss of power among the aristocracy, commensurate with some degree of municipal independence, with *intendants* appointed in the provinces to supervise finance and justice (Ashford 1982). Following the 1789 revolution, and the subsequent *coup d'état* of Napoleon Bonaparte, central–local relations were cemented into a structure of *départements arrondissements* and (at local level) *communes*, 'with central government appointees at each tier so as to set up a chain of command leading from and back to the Ministry of the Interior in Paris' (Roach 1985, 110).

One result of this has been a highly centralized and powerful civil service:

> France's highly centralised administrative institutions, derived from the revolutionary principle of sovereignty of a nation of citizens expressing itself through the state, are staffed by an efficient, elitist and powerful civil service, less controlled by ministers or parliament than its British counterpart. (Rogers 1979, 80–1)

Additionally, the regional structure of France today derives from the Napoleonic period, although more tiers have been added (Gilbert and Guengant 1989). Thus in the 1960s twenty-two metropolitan regions were introduced, each under a *préfet de region* with responsibilities for co-ordination of social and economic planning. Under these are the ninety-five mainland *départements*. Codified under Napoleon, these were, until 1981, headed by *préfets*, who, as agents of central government appointed by the head of state, had wide power as ex-officio members of the central council and local head of the civil service. In 1981 *préfets* were renamed *commissaires de la république* and became advisors to the central council, with authority passing to a locally elected president. Below the *départements* came some 325 *arrondissements*, with responsibilities for co-ordinating policies in the *communes*. There are, in fact, over 36,000 *communes*, varying in size from under 200 inhabitants in the smallest to over a million in the largest. Each *commune* is represented by a municipal council which elects a mayor, a change from the Napoleonic period when mayors were appointed centrally. The municipal council has local responsibility for local taxation policies, law and order and the enforcement of local by-laws. Between the *commune* and *arrondissement* levels lies a fifth tier, the *canton*, of which there are over 3,000. *Cantons* are administrative sub-divisions of the *arrondissements* and form the constituencies for the election of the departmental councils. Additionally though they serve as the bases for the local *gendarmerie* units (Jammes 1982).

The intricacy of the network which links local government with the central state is often epitomized as one which enhances central control. However the position is not unequivocal. One the one hand, as Ashford (1982) argues, the mayors have resisted successive attempts at central government control and in fact the interlinkages also enhance the importance *to* central government of local government officials, especially the mayors, whose national role may be more significant than, say, in the UK. This is especially likely when, as at present, there is a socialist president and a conservative parliament. During the 1980s this balance, termed colloquially *la cohabitation*, has arguably resulted in increased power for local government at the expense of parliament, and certainly one hallmark of the Mitterrand presidency has been a shift towards local autonomy. Moreover, while some areas of policy, such as education, are characterized by central direction, most others evidence considerable diversity and sectionalism (Birks 1987; Rodgers 1979). To argue that France epitomizes the centralized state is thus a simplification, just as, as will be demonstrated later, the image of a police state owed as much to myth as to reality.

CRIME AND THE CRIMINAL JUSTICE SYSTEM

As in many other Western industrial societies, France experienced a rising rate for recorded crime during the 1950s and 1960s (Radzinowicz and King 1977). Van Dijk (1989), introducing the Dutch criminal justice system, compared crime rates in the Netherlands, West Germany, Sweden, England and Wales, and France between 1950 and 1988. These show France to have a rate slightly below that for England and Wales, rising for most of the period but falling in the late 1980s. Recorded data cited by Kalish (1988) show a similar picture. The homicide rate is comparable with that in the UK and well below that for the USA. Corroborating this picture, the 1989 international victim survey suggests that in general crime in France is slightly lower than in England and Wales, especially for assaults as opposed to property crime.[1]

Nevertheless, the increasing recorded-crime rate allied to an increase in fear of crime has ensured that discussions about crime have been high on the political agenda, constantly fanned by media attention. Up until the 1980s, two broad policies for handling the crime problem existed, apparently completely separate from one another. On the one hand there was a preventive tradition, focusing mainly on juveniles. On the other hand there was a 'policy of repression undertaken by the police and the system of criminal justice, which has been reinforced between 1978 and 1981 by a series of legislative reforms' (Liege 1988, 254).

In many respects, the sentences imposed on adults are familiar to a British or North American audience. The prison system, while openly criticized for its poor conditions, inadequate work programmes and lack of aftercare, has in fact been less readily used than that in England and Wales (Radzinowicz and King 1977) and in 1988 some eighty-one people per 100,000 population in France were imprisoned compared with ninety-seven in England and Wales.[2] Probation officers provide welfare (and organize education) services in prison (Birks 1987). They are also responsible for aftercare and probation order supervision, where volunteers are commonly used for client control (Rodgers 1979). Probation is in fact of relatively recent origin; in contrast suspended sentences were introduced at the end of the nineteenth century as a means of limiting the use of imprisonment (Radzinowicz and King 1977).

With regard to juvenile offenders, these are catered for in a variety of ways, reflecting the complexity of social services in France (Birks 1987; Rodgers 1979). There is a range of supervision settings, from community to institution-based, run by community, youth or other specialist social work agencies, most notably *éducateurs spécialises.* Custodial sentences are rare (Hackler 1988).

In the 1980s the socialist government introduced a number of reforms, including the abolition of the death penalty. The most significant innovations, however, followed the setting up in 1982 of an all-party commission of mayors invited to make recommendations on how to fight crime and fear of crime. Its report led to the introduction of correctional service orders and to a series of preventive initiatives. Councils for the prevention of crime were created at national, departmental and communal level to propose and implement a variety of programmes dealing with, for example, drug addiction projects, victim assistance, housing and emergency shelter, illiteracy schemes and recreational programmes for juveniles during the summer months (Liege 1988). The latter, particularly, have been evaluated in some detail by King (1987; 1988), who suggests that they may have contributed to the fall in recorded crime in the mid-1980s. Additionally, though, both he and Liege (1988) argue that the initiative has led to closer relationships between police and welfare agencies and to a greater awareness among public and politicians of the social causes of crime. In particular:

> The contrast with the law and order policies of the Tory party in Britain is striking. No right-wing French politician would dream of denying any causal connection between youth unemployment and crime. Most of them, including the mayors of many large cities, subscribe to a policy which explicitly recognises that social deprivation, family instability, school failure, lack of job prospects and a negative self-image all contribute to a drift by young people towards anti-social and self-destructive behaviour. (King 1987, 15)

Interestingly, the judiciary has also been drawn into the initiative, and Liege (1988, 259) suggests that as a result 'justice is better articulated with the activities of the outside world'. More generally, however, as reviews of the criminal justice system (Radzinowicz and King 1977) and policing (Jammes 1982; Stead 1983) demonstrate, the French judicial system has a number of distinctive features.

The fundamental principles of the legal system were defined following the 1789 revolution, when the independence of the judiciary – in theory if not always in practice – was established. Criminal courts are established on three levels: the *tribunaux de police*, in the *arrondissements*, presided over by a single judge; the *tribunal correctionnel* within each *département* where cases are heard before three judges; and the high court, the *cour d'assises*, again in each *département*, where three judges preside over proceedings and retire with nine jurors to reach a verdict.

The judiciary is in fact entirely professional and quite powerful. Newly trained judges start work in the lower courts and are subsequently promoted to work in the higher courts. A further distinction is made between those who judge cases in court, *magistrats du siège*, and those who act on behalf of the state as public prosecutors (*magistrats debout*) or examining magistrates (*juges d'instruction*). In practice, the public prosecutor is responsible for overseeing the investigation of the case, and will instruct the police accordingly. In particularly difficult or more serious cases the examining magistrate will become involved in reassessing the evidence prior to trial. Overall, though, police investigative work is more closely supervised under the French system than in England and Wales or North America.

POLICING FRANCE: A HISTORICAL OVERVIEW

Any analysis of the French policing system, whether historical or contemporary, must begin with a twofold distinction: on the one hand between the policing of rural and urban areas, and in the latter case between Paris and other cities. The distinction is readily understood if we begin by reviewing police developments under the *ancien régime*, that is until the 1789 revolution and the guillotining of Louis XVI in 1793.

Prior to this, policing in rural France was the responsibility of two very different bodies. On the one hand, there were those elected by individual villages, the *gardes messiers*, or *consuls*, whose principal responsibilities seem to have centred on protecting the harvest, ensuring good order, and supervising the roads (Emsley 1983, 20). On the other hand there was the *maréchaussée*, a highly organized military police (Emsley 1983; Jammes 1982; Stead 1983). The latter appears to have its origins in royal bodyguards and a number of officials within the army responsible for military discipline. Between the thirteenth and fifteenth centuries this body was restructured and became responsible for wider policing responsibilities, with the *maréchaussée* performing these duties in wartime and the *connétablie* fulfilling the same functions in peacetime. In 1520 the two organizations were merged and given particular responsibilities for the pursuit of highwaymen and in 1566 they were placed under the judicial authorities and restricted in their operations to rural areas. The system was modified in 1720 when Louis XV, possibly concerned to control vagrancy in the postwar period, caused them to be reorganized into 520 brigades of five men, with a *provost général* responsible at the provincial level and the Minister of War holding central responsibility.

In Paris, there is evidence of a police system stretching back to the constables of the watch, *guet de Paris*, in the fifth century. The most significant reforms, however, came about in the late seventeenth century when Louis XIV appointed a lieutenant of police for Paris (Emsley 1983; Stead 1983). The responsibilities of the new police were considerable, incorporating the supervision of street cleaning and firefighting, control of the food supply and prices, inspection of markets and lodging houses, and the checking of booksellers and publishers. The city was, for policing purposes, sub-divided into 16 administrative wards, *quartiers*, each under a police magistrate with a staff of public officials or *sergents*.

The police of Paris also clearly had a political role, and indeed the priority given to policing in the capital was related to the police role in maintaining the monarchy. For the same reason, rather less importance was placed on policing in other cities, where a piecemeal system appears to have operated, encouraged by the king's attempts to counteract the influence of the nobility by allowing considerable degrees of municipal independence. Town militia, *milice bourgeoise*, played a significant role, for example, until the eighteenth century. Attempts at standardization in the early seventeenth century included the appointment of an intendant of justice, police and finance in each of the thirty provinces. Then, following the apparent success of the Paris system, Louis XIV raised income by selling posts of lieutenant-general of police in all the larger cities.

It is, however, easy to exaggerate the degree of central control in France under the *ancien régime*. Thus, in the latter case, cities were able to prevent loss of individual autonomy by buying the offices of lieutenant-general and appointing their own officials. Moreover, as Chapman (1970, 27) notes, not only in the country as a whole but even in Paris:

> The internal structure of pre-revolutionary France was so decentralized, with so many sources of competing power that policing, in the English sense of the word, was unsystematic, ineffective and haphazard. The royal corps of men at arms, the Gendarmerie, provided for the safety of the highways, and local communities provided for their own security according to traditional laws and customs. But most eighteenth century literature on the subject stresses the inability of the police to adequately maintain public order, health or morality in the densely populated quarters of Paris, from which the revolutionary mobs were eventually to come.

Indeed despite the policing system (or systems), with an emphasis upon political or high police, revolution was neither prevented nor apparently even predicted. Its result, however, was the abolition of the old system, attacked in the Declaration of Rights of 26 August 1789, although in the case of the *maréchaussée* rebirth was almost immediate, with the *gendarmerie* formed in 1791 on a departmental and divisional basis under the *préfets*. Elsewhere a variety of policing systems were established and indeed responsibility for the police fell on a number of different people in a short period of time. Joseph Fouché, for example, appointed Minister of General Police of the Directory in 1799, was the tenth to hold that office in as many years.

Fouché was, in fact, instrumental in the *coup d'état* which brought Napoleon Bonaparte to power with the First Republic and it is under his influence that France attained particular notoriety as a police state, with priority afforded to the high police, concerned with political affairs. However, although there was a move towards an increased role for the police and the civil service, plus further centralization, Napoleon maintained a balance of power by rejecting Fouché's recommendations that the different policing systems be merged. The *gendarmerie nationale* attained particular importance, and was regularly used on plain-clothes duty in the role of a political police force. Meanwhile, based in Paris, Fouché consolidated his own position within the ministry controlling the *gendarmerie*, the Paris police under their own prefect, and the police in other regions:

> A myth grew up, and has been perpetuated by historians, that Fouché was the all-seeing, all-hearing policeman . . . From his

> headquarters of the Quai Voltaire (now Quai Malaquais) Fouche supervised four councillors of state who, in turn, each supervised a police division of France: the first covered fifty departments of the north, west and east; the second was formed by the south and parts of the east; the third division was the City of Paris; and the fourth the French-occupied departments of Italy. The ministry also had six administrative offices, the most important being the *sûreté* or secret police, the others being responsible for censorship, prison surveillance, food prices and the money market, police accounts and the secretariat which processed the information received. Each day Fouché sent Napoleon a digest of information drawn from his subordinates. (Emsley 1983, 34).

It is, indeed, ironic that such a complex system was not able to prevent the eventual overthrow of Napoleon (Bowden 1978). During the nineteenth century, however, the police presence was extended. Uniformed police, *sergents de ville*, comprising a hundred ex-soldiers, were introduced to Paris in 1829 and although later disbanded they were subsequently reintroduced by Napoleon III during the Second Republic from 1884 to 1870. Napoleon III, with experience of the emerging Metropolitan force in London, emphasized the preventive function of the uniformed branch and instigated a series of reforms which led to the Paris patrol system being modelled on that of London (Stead 1983, 54–72). At the same time, the *gendarmerie* was confirmed as a *uniformed* force and its numbers increased. The political role of the plain-clothes police was not, however, neglected. The railway police system was established in 1855 as a mechanism for collecting information on unrest throughout the country, and the nineteenth century also saw the detective force of Paris, largely comprising ex-criminals, gaining notoriety.

The twentieth century, at least prior to the Second World War, in fact saw few fundamental changes to the system established under Napoleon Bonaparte and Napoleon III. Despite pressure towards centralization, the *gendarmerie* remained separate, and the Paris police were themselves distanced from other policing arrangements, co-ordinated by the *sûreté générale* (renamed *sûreté nationale* in 1934). However the director of the *sûreté* was of lower status than the prefect of police in Paris, and attempts at central co-ordination of the *départements* ran into difficulties. Indeed, central/local disputes over the management of the police characterized the period. Perhaps the most notable single development was the formation of regional crime squads in 1907.

The next major changes in police organization came in the wartime period, 1941–5 (Roach 1985). During German occupation in 1941 the Vichy government created a general directorate of the *police nationale*, responsible for the police in all towns with a population of over 10,000. A further public-order force was created, the *Gardes Mobiles de Réserve*. In 1945 this was disbanded, although a similar mobile police reserve, the *Compagnie Républicaine de Sécurité* (CRS) was formed to maintain public order and quell communist initiatives. Interestingly, because the *gendarmerie* was preoccupied with military affairs the CRS was placed under the Ministry of the Interior. The *police nationale* was retained, with the Paris police remaining separate.

In turning to consider the role of the police in the postwar period, it is perhaps useful to highlight points which have been made in this brief historical overview. First, the intertwining of government and policing is evident, and the role of the police in maintaining (or at least attempting to maintain) the status quo is considerable. Second, the role of the police, both politically and in various administrative capacities, was far wider than in Britain or the US. Third, despite the omnipresence of the police, co-ordination was incomplete. At national level the *gendarmerie* was distinct from other police systems, which themselves were factious, reflecting the traditional autonomy of the Paris force and the jealousy with which other large cities guarded their independence, and it took German occupation during the Second World War to instigate a second centralized force.

THE POLICE IN POST-WAR FRANCE

Perhaps the most significant development in the postwar period, in fact, was the incorporation of the Paris police within the *police nationale* in 1966. This stems from the Ben Barka scandal, where a prominent Algerian dissident was assassinated while visiting France, having been set up by officers of the *sûreté*, providing the government with the *cause célèbre* it needed to instigate changes (Roach 1985). There are today upwards of 123,000 personnel in the *police nationale* (Hudson 1988), which provides a centrally controlled police service for Paris and all provincial towns with a population exceeding 10,000. Training, which has been extended during the 1980s, is quite highly centralized, with recruits carrying out basic training and initial work experience in the Paris area (Hudson 1988; Roach 1985).

The Minister of the Interior, now renamed the Minister of the Interior and Decentralization, has overall control of the *police nationale*. There is a secretary of state in charge of public security and, within the police organization, a director-general based in Paris. There are seven directorates at headquarters level, dealing with general intelligence and gambling, criminal investigation, the urban police, the CRS, counter-espionage, air and frontier police and international technical co-operation. Central intelligence and gambling is further sub-divided on a regional and departmental level, criminal investigations on a regional level. The CRS is sub-divided into ten groups and sixty-one companies. The urban police, essentially the uniformed section of the *police nationale*, is administered on a departmental level, and with reorganization in 1981 is a major responsibility of the *commissaires*, although in the largest cities of Paris, Lyon, Lille and Marseille there is a separate prefecture of police (Stead 1983).

The *gendarmerie nationale*, which is directly responsible to the Ministry of Defence, has some 80,000 officers (Pope 1982). Most of these are deployed within the main organization. The structure in fact mirrors that for public administration as a whole, with *legions* at regional level, *groupements* in the *départements* and *company* in the *arrondissement*. At the local level brigades, living in barracks with their families, are broadly distributed according to canton. Although brigades are no longer found in every canton, there is still a considerable variation in the size of each brigade, covering areas ranging from under 200 to over 20,000 inhabitants. There is also a third force, the *gendarmerie mobile*, stationed in squadrons at the *arrondissement* level, to be called on in emergencies. Additionally a number of specialist units exist concerned with anti-terrorism; state-protection duties; maritime, mountain and air rescue services; and policing in the overseas colonies (Jammes 1982). The overall structure of these two main forces, and their relationship to local and central government are presented in Table 3.1. There is, in fact, a third police faction, comprising the municipal police and rural police auxiliaries, which operate in some towns of under 10,000 and 2,000 population respectively. They are directly responsible to the mayor and financed by the municipality. However, as they have very limited powers, tend to concentrate on minor incidents, and in any case comprise only about 9,000 personnel in all (Jammes 1982), they will not be referred to further here.[3]

The issue of police powers does however raise a further complication. Not only is the French policing system divided vertically into the *gendarmerie nationale* and the *police nationale*, it is also divided horizontally, with different grades of police having distinctly different legal authority. The principal distinction here is between

Table 3.1 ***Political and policing structure***

Area	Civilian authority	*Gendarmerie nationale*	*Gendarmerie mobile*	*Police nationale*
Région	*Préfet de région*	Regional command: legion	Unit	Regional crime services
Départements	*Président*	*Groupement*		Departmental commissaire
Arrondissement		Company	Squadron	
Canton		Brigade		
Communes	Mayor			

officers de police judiciaire (OPJ) and *agents de police judiciaire.* The OPJ have legal authority to hold a suspect in custody. *Agents*, who are generally less experienced or of junior rank, do not have this authority and may also be constrained in other aspects of the law-enforcement process (Stead 1985, 144–7). Only OPJs are entitled to act as investigating officers in a case, and then only on behalf of the *juge d'instruction.*

These variations are related to the complexity of the recruitment process and ultimately to the type of people who become police officers. The *gendarmerie nationale* recruits from amongst those who have completed their national service. Entry is at two levels: as a basic-grade *gendarme* or to the officer corps which accepts non-commissioned officers of the *gendarmerie*, regular officers of the armed forces and reserve officers. In contrast the *police nationale* recruits on five distinct levels. These are, in ascending order: *enquêteur* (a junior officer); *gardier de le paix* (equivalent to a constable in the UK); *officier de paix* (equivalent to an inspector in the UK); *inspecteur* (a plain-clothes officer); and *commissaire* (Stead 1983, 131–3).

However, the literature includes minimal details of the social characteristics of police recruits other than the information that females are grossly misrepresented. In the *gendarmerie* women were first recruited in 1974 but are largely deployed in non-operational posts. In the *police nationale*, similarly, women were only accepted in the early 1970s. Most work as assistants, although the multi-entry system which allows for specialism has meant that a number have been accepted as *inspecteurs*. Women were only admitted as *gardiers de la paix* in 1978 when fifty-one out of 1000 applicants were accepted (Stead 1983, 111–12).

As is evident from a historical analysis, the term 'police' developed in France to encompass a far wider range of administrative tasks and responsibilities than in the UK or USA, a point stressed by Fosdick ([1915] 1969b) in the early twentieth century. Many of these have been taken over by other agencies, as government has become more complex and specialized, a trend accentuated in the 1980s with moves to relieve the police of duties covering visas, identity cards and passports (Roach 1985). Nevertheless the police role, especially *vis-à-vis* public order, is still wide. This is particularly the case for the *gendarmerie nationale*, as Jammes's (1982, 154–62) detailed account illustrates. Thus the *gendarmerie* is concerned with conventional crime but also wider aspects of law enforcement ranging from checking firearms and vehicle licences to fine collection; meteorological data collection; regulation of markets; veterinary services and abattoirs; and the supervision of working conditions of foreign labour. Its military role is, however, its most pronounced feature. It is an integral part of the national defence and, in wartime, is under the complete command of the military. It also has a military police role. For example:

> As an integral part of the Armed Forces, the *Gendarmerie* assists in the enforcement of military law and discipline amongst service personnel and reservists. *Gendarmes* take part in the search for servicemen absent without leave and for deserters. They escort military convoys and carry out the many other duties normally associated with military police units in other armies. When a crime has been committed by military personnel, *gendarmes* conduct all necessary inquiries on behalf of the Regional Officer Commanding and of the relevant military courts. (Jammes 1982, 56).

Clearly, as Stead (1983, 140) succinctly puts it, 'A gendarme is a soldier but a soldier is not a gendarme', and this is reflected in recruitment, training and duties. Equally clearly the role of the *police nationale* is less extensive, but it still comprises a multitude of administrative and political tasks. In the latter case, for example, there is the CRS, the Directorate of Counter-Espionage and the Sub-Directorate of General Political Information which monitors public opinion, internal social conditions and overseas issues (Stead 1983). It is difficult to escape the conclusion that the structure and role of the French police today has been shaped by the priorities of those governing eighteenth- and nineteenth-century France.

THE POLICE AND THE PUBLIC

The police forces of France are political agencies rather than public ones. This is, not surprisingly, more so in the case of the *gendarmerie* where police and their families are accommodated in barracks within areas broadly equivalent to the cantons, and where traditionally rural policing has minimal community overtones, despite the fact that *gendarmes* have, commonly, served in their local area (Emsley 1983, 41).

There have, particularly in the 1980s, been a number of initiatives aimed at modifying this overall picture. Thus councils for the prevention of crime have established new levels of inter-agency co-operation and brought the police involved in various schemes into closer contact with the public (King 1987; 1988; Liege 1988), and the Mitterand government also suggested an increased emphasis on community-based policing. Nevertheless, the 1980s have also seen an increase in police personnel and additional expenditure on technology and weaponry (Hudson 1988; Roach 1985). The French police are, of course, also armed although the use of firearms, particularly by the *police nationale*, is closely regulated (Stead 1983). Other community initiatives involving public–police co-operation, which are common in many other societies, such as neighbourhood watch or volunteer police auxiliaries (Gill and Mawby 1990), are relatively unknown. Compared with the UK, for example, the availability of a third force within both of its central forces (Nelson 1978) prevented the emergence of a volunteer police reserve which may be used later on wider policing duties. Victim services, although now becoming more common, were also late in developing, and the inquisitorial system appears to have given no greater attention to victims' needs than is the case elsewhere (D'Hautville and Bruno 1989; Piffaut 1989). Ironically, the *gendarmerie* has been seen, even by socialist administrators, as politically more reliable than the *police nationale*, which was involved in public protests in 1958 and again in 1983 when 2500 police took part in an anti-government demonstration in Paris (Hudson 1988). Thus:

> Reams have been written on the attitudes of the French public to the police. Traditional mistrust is not based solely on the fact that French policemen are armed, or that members of the CRS and *Gendarmerie Nationale* live in barracks, apart from society. It is based more upon a traditional 'hard' approach to the general public, in which police have been accused of a disinterested, racist and sometimes brutal approach. (Hudson 1988, 173).

This distrust of the police is perhaps extended by lack of public involvement in control of the police. Accountability is, in both forces, dealt with within the organization. This is not surprising in the *gendarmerie* given its military features: 'breaches of military discipline . . . are subject to normal military law and regulations' (Jammes 1982, 64) and public complaints are handled by senior officers, although crimes are ultimately prosecuted by the civilian judicial authorities. Within the *police nationale* complaints are handled by the Inspectorate General, an improvement, according to Stead (1983, 116–17) on the past when there was a reluctance to admit any police deviance in case the creditability of the police in the eyes of the public was threatened!

Regan (1984), in a comparison of police accountability in France, West Germany and England and Wales, argues that it can be assessed in three contexts: the extent of centralization; the scope of police work; and the balance between political control and individual discretion. On the first of these criteria, France is considered 'a formidibly centralised policing system. French policemen are either civil servants or military personnel and their hierarchical lines of command run back directly to the government in Paris' (Regan 1984, 5–6). While Mitterrand has committed himself to a policy of decentralizing power, Regan sees this as unlikely to occur *vis-à-vis* policing, given the strength of traditional structures.

With regard to scope, the political role accredited to the police is seen to undermine its responsibility to a wider public. If the primary mandate of the police is to safeguard the political system, then its accountability other than to that system is likely to be constrained.

Finally, on the level of individual discretion, Regan argues that compared with the UK and West Germany French police have least discretion and, conversely, most hierarchical control. To illustrate he refers to the *memento du gendarme* which *gendarmes* are required to carry, listing the appropriate response to every conceivable situation. Thus the accountability of the police, through the management structure, to the minister and, ultimately, the President is confirmed. Overall, then, 'the police are not representing local community responsibility for law and order but are vested with the authority of the state to undertake their tasks' (Regan 1984, 20).

SUMMARY

Perhaps more than in any other country considered here, the French police system today has been shaped by the past. The police structure under the *ancien régime*, and its re-establishment by Napoleon

Bonaparte and Napoleon III, laid emphasis upon a system which was both relatively centralized and highly pervasive. Occupation during the Second World War, and postwar reorganization, have tended to increase centralization and extend the public-order role of the police. The military and highly disciplined *gendarmerie nationale*, although smaller than the *police nationale*, characterizes police–public relations, with its personnel housed in barracks, a reactive force separated from the general public.

In some respects, however, this model can be overemphasized. While the nature of French policing systems is a partial reaction to political fragility, the fact of political turbulance itself is indicative of the lack of police omnipotence. Moreover, police investigations are under the control of the judiciary and police powers thereby constrained in ways unfamiliar to a British audience. In recent years there have also been attempts to involve the police in community-based initiatives, notably through the creation of councils for the prevention of crime.

Nevertheless, compared with other countries considered in later chapters, the literature on the French police contains a paucity of references to community aspects of policing, and a multitude of references to administrative and political functions. In terms of legitimacy, structure and function, then, the French police system can perhaps still be characterized as the continental model *par excellence*.

4

The Netherlands: Variations on a Theme?

INTRODUCTION

The Netherlands makes an interesting contrast with France, if only because its policing system, at least in peacetime, has been decentralized. It has featured as the subject of considerable debate among those interested in the criminal justice system, having gained an international reputation for its enlightened policies (Downes 1988; Rutherford 1984).

With regard to both policing and the criminal justice system as a whole, the Dutch system is indeed one in which research is welcomed. The Ministry of Justice plays a significant role in initiating and sponsoring research, much of which is published in English. Government-sponsored research is considerable, university-based criminology departments are well established, and the interchange between policy-makers and academics, including radical academics, is marked (Bianchi 1975; Bottomley 1986). Although much material is published in Dutch, and is thus relatively inaccessible to foreigners, some of the Dutch sociology journals are in English, and other journals, like *Police Studies*, contain a variety of articles by indigenous academics, policy-makers and practitioners as well as visiting academics.

That said, most of the research on policing has tended to be sociological (Rosenthal 1984), the most notable by the British expatriate, Maurice Punch (1979; 1985). Punch has been principally involved in three pieces of research in the Warmoesstraat, an inner-city district of Amsterdam: the first an observational study of patrol work; the second a study of police corruption; and the third an evaluation of police management strategies. In a recent, and revealing, account of his personal experiences of researching this particular station, Punch (1989) stresses the openness of the police organization to outside researchers, compared with both Britain and the United States. As he himself has frequently acknowledged, however, inner-city Amsterdam is no more typical as a venue for research than Soho or the red-light districts of San Francisco, and it is therefore important to balance the richness of Punch's work with less detailed accounts of the policing system elsewhere in the Netherlands.

THE SOCIAL AND POLITICAL STRUCTURE OF THE NETHERLANDS

As Punch (1979, 29) points out, the Netherlands, with an area of some 34,000 square km, is only a quarter of the size of New York. Its population of 14.3 million is smaller than all but Cuba and Hong Kong of the countries included in this study and a quarter of that of the United Kingdom. However, with a population density of 387 per square km, the Netherlands is one of the most densely populated countries in the world (Boyer 1983), exceeded only by 'special cases' such as Hong Kong and Singapore. About three-quarters of the population lives in urban areas, which is similar to the United States but rather less than the UK (Ayrton 1983). Its major area of population, the Randstad, include the four major cities of Amsterdam, Rotterdam, the Hague and Utrecht.

Given its geographical position, the Netherlands has been politically vulnerable. The area which is today identified as the Netherlands was part of the Spanish Empire until the late sixteenth century. Following the Union of Utrecht in 1579 and for the next two centuries, the country emerged as a trading nation and colonial power, with territories in the East Indies, South America and the Caribbean. From 1795 to 1838 the Netherlands was under Napoleonic control. Then, following the Treaty of Separation, it was established as a nation with broadly the same boundaries it has today. It was neutral during the 1914–18 War but occupied by the Germans during the Second World War.

By European standards, industrialization was late arriving in the Netherlands, and the country was hard hit by the depression of the 1930s. In the postwar period, however, the economy expanded with membership of the European Community and real incomes and public expenditure increased markedly (Bryant 1981). From being a net exporter of population, expansion entailed immigration, most particularly from its former colonies and later through a migrant workforce (Bagley 1973; 1983; Domingo 1982). Emigration from its South American colony, now named Surinam, had in fact accounted for one-third of the total population of Surinam, amounting to 1.3 per cent of the population of the Netherlands in 1975, with 45 per cent of Surinamers living in the Randstad (Domingo 1982).

Until recently, the most evident social divisions within the country were based on religion. The majority of the population is protestant (principally Calvinist and Lutheran) with about one-third, especially in the south-east, Catholic. For much of the twentieth century, Dutch society has been dominated by 'pillars' or *zuil*, based on religion. Following religious riots in the north in 1848, these pillars allowed for separate development within areas. A range of institutions thus emerged whereby for most people choice of political party, school, union or leisure-based organization – and even television station – was determined by religion. Modifications in the postwar period led, not to the diminishing of such structures, but to extension and refinement, with an additional two secular pillars based on political affiliation (Bryant 1981). Since the late 1960s, expansion and modernization have, as Bryant (1981) and Kramer (1979) note, resulted in a degree of 'depillarization'. Nevertheless, the pillarized structure of Dutch society has been a crucial determinant of its socio-political development.

The Netherlands is a constitutional monarchy with two chambers of parliament. Politicians are elected by a complex system of proportional representation which, given the strong ties between pillars and voting patterns, generally results in a large number of parties, none with a working majority, being represented in parliament. Governments are therefore commonly based on coalitions which are consolidated only after a four- or five-year policy plan has been agreed between the parties. The 1989 general election brought about a change of government, with a Social and Christian Democratic coalition replacing one between the Christian Democrats and the Liberals.

The other major feature of the political structure is the balance between central and local government (Blaas and Dostal 1989). Towns enjoyed considerable autonomy prior to the Napoleonic period, when in the course of centralizing the administrative structure a uniform structure of municipalities was established at local level. On independence the relations between these municipalities and central government were defined and codified, and an intermediate tier of provinces was created, with rather fewer powers. Significantly, by 1865 municipalities were restricted in their collection of revenue; in the interests of territorial justice taxes were collected by the state and subsequently reallocated to municipalities which were then responsible for the provision of public services.

Since the latter half of the nineteenth century the number of municipalities has declined from over 1,200; in 1987 there were 714 municipalities within eleven provinces.[2] Nevertheless, and despite overall central control, there are considerable problems associated with this large number of relatively small local-government areas. Central government has sought to achieve economies of scale by encouraging joint agreements between municipalities, leading to co-operative ventures in the provision of services such as education, public health, traffic and transport, housing and policing. Control at provincial level, and within provinces at a new regional level, has also been expanded. Nevertheless, more radical proposals for a shift of local responsibility to a larger number of smaller provinces, perhaps based around the twenty-one principal cities, have met considerable opposition. Municipalities, governed by directly elected councils chaired by burgomasters, are thus the most significant local-government structures, with a long-established tradition (Blaas and Dostal 1989).

The system of pillarization, *verzuiling*, and the central–local-government relationship are each important in the context of public and social services. Traditionally, these pillars became the basis for the provision of education, health and welfare services (Brenton 1980; 1982; Kramer 1979). In the postwar period, welfare services in the Netherlands have expanded, such that the state is seen as one of the most generous providers of welfare in the industrialized world (Heidenheimer, Heclo and Adams 1983). However, while these services are *financed* centrally, they are *provided* either by local government or by *particulier initiatief* agencies based on the pillars and acting as funded charities (in British terms) or state-financed non-profit-making private agencies (in North American parlance). The results of economic recession and an ageing population have, as in other Western capitalist societies, placed an additional burden on state-funded welfare services, resulting in government attempts to exert more control through evaluation of services and pressures towards rationalization, although according to Brenton (1980; 1982) economies of scale have been sought through the provision of universal services at local level rather than by centralization.

Dutch socio-political structure is indeed complex and perhaps unique. Rather than provide further analysis here it is perhaps most important to re-emphasize the salience of depillarization and central–local relationships, since they have implications for crime and criminal justice policies.

CRIME AND THE CRIMINAL JUSTICE SYSTEM

Official statistics, while notoriously unreliable, suggest that the Netherlands has a crime rate roughly comparable with that of England and Wales (Tulkens 1979). Certainly homicide rates in the two countries are similar (Kalish 1988), and the relatively higher rate of burglary in the Netherlands is more than compensated for by the lower rates of motor-vehicle theft (Downes 1988, 104–5). In a comparison of victim survey data, Block (1987) suggests that the United States has a household burglary rate some three times that of the Netherlands and England and Wales, with the Netherlands having a particularly low rate of auto-thefts and a high rate of thefts from the person. Crime risks increased with urbanization in all three countries, being highest for the inner cities. In an earlier paper, Block (1983), again using victim survey data, shows household burglary rates in the Netherlands to be well below those in the United States, Canada, Israel, England and Wales and Australia, and suggests that much of the difference between the Netherlands and the United States arises from the very low rate of daytime burglaries in the former.[3] With the stringent firearms controls, offences involving firearms are also markedly less than in the US (Colijn, Lester and Slothouwer 1985).

Of equal importance to the level of crime is the question of *trends*. Here we are necessarily dependent upon official statistics. In an extensive analysis of these, Downes (1988, 33–45) shows that while rates for serious offences in the Netherlands and England and Wales were broadly similar in 1950 and 1985, with marked increases between those dates in both countries, there were substantial differences in the *pace* of change. In the Netherlands the crime rate rose only marginally in the 1950–65 period and then rose at an accelerated rate to catch up with that in England and Wales by the mid-1980s.

It is possible to see this later and more rapid rise as the result of more liberal sentencing policies (see below). However Downes (1988) argues that it is more likely to reflect the historically more stable social structure of the Netherlands and the later social upheavals caused by depillarization, expansion followed by recession, and – possibly – an increasingly alienated black youth (Bagley 1983).

Interestingly, while the pillar system may be used to explain crime rates, with the exception of probation (Heijder 1973) it receives practically no consideration in the context of the criminal justice system. Two issues have been stressed in the literature: namely, the *structure* of the system – including the central/local context – and outcome – in terms of pre-court diversion, sentencing policies and prison conditions.

The system of law in the Netherlands is based around sixty-two local courts and nineteen district courts. Juveniles, between the ages of 12 (the age of criminal responsibility) and 17 are dealt with in separate courts, although diversion is the norm (Hoeven 1988; Junger-Tas 1988; Laan 1988).

There has been no jury system in the Netherlands since 1840, decisions being the responsibility of professional judges. The key actor in the criminal justice system is, however, the public prosecutor, *officier van justitie*: 'The prosecutors are empowered to act as the catalysts of policy, with roles that connect them with the judges on one side, the police on another, and the Ministry of Justice and Parliament on a third' (Downes 1988, 13). Their responsibilities cover decisions on whether or not to prosecute, sentencing recommendations (which judges are required to take into account), detention of suspects and bail, sentencing guidelines, and – in consultation with the local police chief and burgomaster – decisions on local policing issues. There are about 240 prosecutors, who provide a crucial centralizing component to criminal justice policy and comprise 'a veritable cache of thoroughly professional decision-makers' (Downes 1988, 15).

Alongside the prosecutors and judges, the probation service provides a professional input *vis-à-vis* sentencing decisions. Founded in the nineteenth century, the service has, along with other welfare services, maintained its separateness from the state, despite being funded by it (Downes 1988; Heijder 1973). As in the UK and USA it is involved in pre-sentence reports, through care, the supervision of community service orders (introduced in 1980), and implementing probation orders, although the latter are not sentences in their own right but are instead combined with a suspended sentence. A small group of paid officers are helped by large numbers of volunteers who are responsible for much client contact (Heijder 1973). As Downes (1988) makes clear, the probation service enjoys more prestige and influence than in many other countries, and has, with the prosecutors and the judges, been influential with regard to sentencing policies and practices. Indeed:

> The Dutch criminal justice system approximates to the Fabian ideal of small, highly trained elites getting on with their jobs without undue public interference (though with a due regard to public opinions and the public interest). (Downes 1988, 76).

There is some suggestion that 'public interest' was less vociferous in the 1960s and early 1970s as the crime rate remained relatively low, and that pressures on tougher sentencing policies, especially with regard to drug-related offences, have come more recently (Downes 1988; Parker 1986). Nevertheless, the Dutch system is still recognized as one in which the decision to waive prosecution is commonly taken and imprisonment is used infrequently, sentences are particularly short, and prison conditions (especially the social environment of prison) are relatively good (Downes 1988; Kelk 1983; Rutherford 1984; Steenhuis, Tigges and Essers 1981; Tulkens 1979). Even where there have been expansionist moves, expressed in the 1985 policy plan *Society and Crime*, these have been characterized as attempts to *contain* that expansion. Both Bottomley (1986) and Downes (1988), in critiques of the policy document, note that it illustrates two notable strengths of Dutch policy-making: a concern by policy-makers to involve a whole range of academics and practitioners in the process of formulating new policy; and a willingness to start from first principles and consider the entire system, rather than, as in the British case, following a narrow incrementalist path.

This is an important consideration in the context of police policy-making. Additionally, though, a brief review of the criminal justice system suggests three other areas of particular relevance. First, the system is one dominated by 'experts', where public involvement – except in the probation service – seems to have been minimal. Second, and dominating the varying elites of professionals, the role of the prosecutor is crucial with regard to both sentencing and policing. Finally, a system whereby prosecutors commonly waive prosecutions has implications for the role of the police, perceptions of justice, and their morale (Punch 1985).

THE HISTORY OF POLICING IN THE NETHERLANDS

The early history of the Dutch police has been immortalized by Rembrandt in his painting of the 'Nightwatch'. These militia units formed voluntary, armed civic guards in the cities from as early as the fourteenth century. By the time of Rembrandt's painting, in 1642, Amsterdam had six companies of guards which patrolled the city throughout the day. (The title 'Nightwatch' is in fact a misnomer added in 1808.)

The militia were under the control of the town governors and regional landowners, and served as an army in times of war. Their policing responsibilities included checking weights and measures, supervising roads and watercourses, publishing ordinances, and policing drinking houses and brothels as well as more specific crime-control duties (Brink and Bulthuis 1979). In addition to the militia, residents were obliged to come to the aid of victims within their neighbourhood, a system known as *maling*, whereby informal justice would be meted out to offenders who were captured (Diederiks 1980).

Until the end of the eighteenth century local responsibility for policing and the sentencing process fell on sheriffs, *schouts*, in the cities and bailiffs, *baljuws*, in rural areas. While in theory responsible to central government, in practice these officials exercised considerable local autonomy. Attempts to modify the system were made under the 1798 constitution and then again in 1806, but were pre-empted by French control, when a centralized system was imposed (Brink and Bulthuis 1979; Shane 1980). However, when Dutch sovereignty was re-established in 1813 there was a return to local control, although in the remoter provinces a French-*gendarmerie*-type force was created, the *korps maréchaussée*. Between then and 1850 control of the police was the subject of considerable debate, with local/central control as one issue and the balance of power between the Ministries of Justice and the Interior as another.

The basis for current police organization was provided in 1851 with two pieces of legislation: the Municipalities Act which confirmed the local nature of municipal forces, under the supervision of the Minister of the Interior, and the National Police Decree which placed the national force under the Minister of Justice. The National Rural Constabulary Act of 1856 then provided for local accountability of the national force to either the public prosecutor or the burgomaster (Brink and Bulthuis 1979).

This balance between local and central accountability was appreciated by Fosdick ([1915] 1969b, 65) when he described it as 'a unique arrangement of local autonomy modified by the firm, centralized control of the government'. While the police were legally under the authority of the burgomaster (with financial control), he himself was responsible to the Minister of Internal Affairs and the senior offices were appointed (and removed) by the Minister of Justice. There was a lateral entry system, and while an attempt to recruit senior staff from the military had been abandoned as a failure, officer recruits tended to be young, educated and middle-class. In contrast, in Amsterdam and Rotterdam at least, recruitment policy *vis-à-vis* the junior ranks favoured former soldiers, who comprised 80 per cent of recruits.

Fosdick ([1915] 1969b) also noted the continuence of the *maréchaussées*, which he likened to the *gendarmerie*. This rural force was expanded in 1935 under a new National Police Decree which extended the duties of the national police to cover all areas and aspects of policing not exclusively defined under the Municipalities Act. The Ministry of Justice remained in control of the national police (Brink and Bulthuis 1979).

From 1940 to 1945, under German occupation, overall control of the police passed to the German police force. However, normal police duties were carried out by the national police, renamed the state police, and the municipal police who remained under the immediate control of the burgomaster. Because of the role of the police in enforcing German control, including the repression of Jews, a postwar commission carried out a major reappraisal of the police organization. New laws were passed in 1945, 1948 and 1957 which aimed to re-establish the local nature of policing and confirm the civilian rather than the military characteristics of the police forces (Brinks and Bulthuis 1979; Shane 1980).

THE CURRENT SYSTEM

Although there have been recent initiatives to change the policing system, the 1957 Police Act still provides the basis for the way the police are organized in the Netherlands. Crucial here is the distinction between the municipal police forces, *gemeente politie*, and the national force, *korps rijkspolitie*.

There are, currently, some 148 municipal police forces (Doornebal 1987; Wiebrens 1989). Towns and cities above a particular size are allowed to form their own force, with the result that population increases have led to an increased number of such forces, drawing responses from central government (in 1957 and 1988) to 'up' the size at which the decision to opt out of the state police could be taken. Following the 1957 Act most (127) of the municipal forces operate in towns with populations of more than 25,000 and the municipal police have in total some 21,500 officers. The size of these forces varies considerably, however, from forty in the smallest force to 3,500 employees in Amsterdam. Rotterdam and the Hague are the only two other municipal forces with more than a thousand officers, and indeed about half the forces employ no more than 150 police (Brink and Bulthuis 1979; Wiebrens 1989). Police within the municipal forces are city employees, although mostly financed by central government, through the Ministry of Internal Affairs, according to the population of the force area (Wiebrens 1989).

The national police force provides policing services in rural areas and all municipalities considered too small to warrant their own force.

There are some 14,500 police employed in the national force, organized, within the Ministry of Justice, in seventeen districts, defined in terms of the provinces or sections of larger provinces. Districts are further subdivided into groups, which provide daytime policing services, 24-hour cover and specialist services being available at district level (Doornebal 1987; Wiebrens 1989). The state police system also manages three other branches: the waterways police, traffic, and aviation. Other nationwide police services are provided by specialist agencies within particular ministries dealing with taxation, public health etc. and the military police force, *maréchaussée*, which guards royal palaces, controls the borders and – since 1967 – has been used as an emergency reserve in Amsterdam (Brink and Bulthuis 1979; Doornebal 1987; Rosenthal 1984; Wiebrens 1989).

There are thus at least two distinct political and administrative structures within which the police operate. The state police are the responsibility of the Minister of Justice, and through him an Inspector General, although at local level there is constant liaison with the burgomaster and prosecutor. Municipal forces, while responsible to the Minister of Internal Affairs, are administered via a triangular relationship between police, burgomaster and public prosecutor. The burgomaster is responsible for maintaining public order; the prosecutor for the detection and prosecution processes (Wiebrens 1989). Apparently many police chiefs operate as the junior partner in the triangular relationship, and in recent years the Public Prosecutions Department has expanded its range of interests to include a variety of police activities other than the judicial (Rosenthal 1984).

Co-ordination between the police and other public services is however, confused:

> There is no link between the police and the administrative machinery of the modern state or between the police and politics at a local or national level. In fact, they are separated from government policy through the control exercised by the burgomaster (mayor) and the public prosecutor and through the powers invested in the police under the law. (Reenen 1985, 94).

The administrative confusion of the system is compounded by the costs incurred by a large number of relatively small autonomous policing units, with the result that pressure for change has mounted. One possibility is a shift towards forces run at the provincial level, more akin to the British system (Reenen 1985; Rosenthal 1984). Another, paralleled in other public services, is for co-operation between smaller forces, in terms of specialist services for example.

Local interests have, it appears, blocked moves for more radical changes than this although some specialists within the Ministry of Justice feel that greater centralization is both evident and likely to increase. Moreover, in the light of escalating recorded-crime rates in the 1980s, and government unwillingness to sanction expansion in police personnel, the government has attempted to control growth and rationalize levels throughout the different forces. The reallocation exercise, described in detail by Wiebrens (1989), is important in at least two respects. First, at the policy-making level, it illustrates the willingness of the Dutch government to work from first principles and involve a range of expertise in seeking solutions, and also the degree to which factional interests may block the more radical proposals. Second, in terms of outcome, the evaluation's conclusions are that there should be a shift in resources away from the state police and the smaller municipal forces towards the medium-sized municipal forces. Using a range of indicators measuring police-work practices and socio-demographic data, the review demonstrates the will to challenge incrementalist assumptions of appropriate police levels in different areas.

At present, however, considerable variation still exists. Individual forces vary according to the extent to which they provide specialist services, and at what level. Most larger forces, for example, have specialist juvenile divisions, but smaller forces may be limited to one juvenile specialist (Hoeven 1988; Laan 1988). Some services are provided nationally within the Ministry of Justice (Shane 1980). The latter include the National Criminal Intelligence Service and the Forensic Science Laboratory (Doornebal 1987).

In terms of the management of a municipal force, Punch's (1979; 1985) account of the Amsterdam force, while scarcely typical, is enlightening. Moreover, the distinctive management structure which he describes, and indeed sees as partly accountable for the corruption scandals, is a feature of national policy. Essentially, the Dutch police operate a two-tier entrance system, with no mobility from lower to management ranks, described by Punch (1979, 194) as 'highly ascriptive and elitist'. The division between the lower ranks and management is compounded by the fact that the latter are office-bound and work only office hours, and even the sergeants, as in the United States and Britain the hub of the policing machine, are practically confined to the station. This situation allows lower ranks even more autonomy on the streets than in other countries, and leaves the system open to corruption and other forms of mismanagement.

Punch (1979, 117–48) describes policing the Warmoesstraat as involving a considerable amount of discretion. In an area where pro-active policing is especially common, and order maintenance, peacekeeping, and conflict resolution dominate everyday priorities, this is inevitable, although Johnson (1984) argues that the police may widen their use of discretion as a cynical response to what they see as over-leniency on the part of public prosecutors, and Punch (1985) also suggests that police corruption may be a spin-off from an over-lenient (in police terms) system. Undoubtedly, as Punch (1979) himself recognizes, the police role in the red-light district invites comparisons with British and North American studies, with an emphasis on the action components of policing and a hostility towards health and welfare services and the range of social problems with which the police are left to deal. Equally, the police in the Netherlands, as elsewhere, have been drawn into a series of public-order confrontations. The Provo movement of 1965–7 and the riots over Metro developments in 1973–5 in Amsterdam saw the municipal police (aided in the latter case by the *maréchaussée*), caught in the middle of political conflict and vainly attempting to define their role as public servants rather than as agents of government repression (Reenen 1981).

As in many continental forces, the Dutch police have traditionally had responsibility for a number of administrative tasks concerning public health and economic and work conditions (Shane 1980). Also, and surprising in the wider context of the criminal justice system, they have been identified as a paternalistic and militaristic organization (Punch 1987; Tjepkema 1984). There were some attempts to move towards a more community-oriented approach in the late 1960s (Tjepkema 1984). However, the main impetus for a shift in priorities and practices was heralded by a major review, when in 1975 the Ministry of Home Affairs, together with the Chief Commissioners' Committee, set up a project group on organizational structure (POS). The POS report highlighted the Amsterdam riots of 1966 as heralding a change in police–public relationships and argued for a better developed police role in providing help and assistance for the public:

> A community-integrated police force will lead to police work that is characterized increasingly by conflict prevention whereby policemen play an active mediating role while conflicts are still in an early stage and while people are still ready to negotiate . . . the integration of police services is the second major condition for skilled and socially just police work. Effectiveness, in our opinion, requires that the police service be provided by geographically decentralized, comparatively small units that become associated with social groupings in the city or region

> and that will be responsible, in a relatively independent fashion, for providing overall policing services in their territory. (Nordholt and Straver 1983, 40–1).

This quote is important partly because it is indicative of what the police were *not*, and thus counters rather glossier accounts like that by Shane (1980). It is also important because it indicates an attempt which largely failed. On one level, moves towards larger forces counter the decentralization initiatives. On another level, moves towards team policing and a more problem-solving, welfare-oriented police service seem to have faltered in the face of police hostility (Broer and Vijver 1983; Outrive and Fijnaut 1983; Punch 1987).

This point should perhaps not be overemphasized. Arguably, Dutch evaluations have been more open in identifying internal resistance than have their equivalents in the UK and USA. Neighbourhood policing teams still feature strongly in Haarlem (Dijk 1989), where they involve the police in co-operation with victim services, health agencies and the schools. In Amsterdam a new decentralized police structure was introduced in 1985 (Visser and Wierda 1987). Impetus was given to these more recent developments by the 1983 Roethof Committee which focused on means of preventing much petty crime within urban neighbourhoods and advocated inter-agency co-operation as well as target hardening and functional surveillance by public employees (Dijk 1989; Junger-Tas 1987).

The difficulties faced by the police in such initiatives is well illustrated in the account by Vissier and Wierda (1987) of police/public conflicts in the Staatsliedenbuurt, a section of the Warmoesstraat. Change is, however, also resisted by police culture. Police prioritization of crime, excitement and action is reflected in Punch's (1979; 1985) work, with little evidence of value being placed on a service or welfare role. Equally, despite the initiatives of the Attorney General and police approval of victim initiatives, Hauber and Wemmens (1988) found little emphasis on 'victim-mindedness' among officers, and Dijk (1985; 1988) implies a broad similarity with the situation in Britain and North America (Gill and Mawby 1990b, 78).

This slant is perhaps not surprising, given that police work is male-dominated. Despite its liberalism in other respects, the Netherlands has, by European standards, a low rate of female participation in the workforce, which is reflected in policing both directly and indirectly. Thus as Poel and Punch (1981) note, there was a reluctance to employ *any* female officers in some areas such as like Warmoesstraat and even elsewhere numbers were low (Shane 1980). Few other details of the social characteristics of the police are available in the literature, although the two-tier entry system has important implications. Many senior officers have had fathers in the police while lower ranks appear to attract upper-working/lower-middle-class recruits looking for a secure job with a reasonable salary (Punch 1979). Interestingly, though, given the importance of the pillar system, there is practically no discussion of religious or other pillar enclaves within the police, although union affiliation apparently varies according to the pillar system.[4]

POLICE AND PUBLIC

Public attitudes towards the police were, as already noted, influenced by the role of the police during the Nazi occupation, and Punch (1985) suggests that this was one of the reasons behind the public's enthusiastic response to the corruption scandals. Shane (1980, 128) argues that the scars of wartime experiences have healed and that: 'Police generally are respected by and give respect to the public'. However, as Punch (1979, 124–5) notes, police/public relations vary according to the nature of the 'public' involved. In Amsterdam, the police, largely recruited from *outside* the city, apparently consider Amsterdammers to be 'volubly and spontaneously against authority'. In the Warmoesstraat district, police/public relations were punctuated with conflict, minor violence, hostility and rudeness (Punch 1979, 78–85).

In other countries, the barrier between police and public is often compounded by a police subculture which prioritizes the action components of the job, provides comradeship and support, and insulates the police from public influence. One might anticipate that the dual-entry system prevalent in the Netherlands, producing a corps of police who can never aspire to promotion, might intensify identification with a subculture, at least for the lower ranks. However, the evidence on this is ambiguous, and in the context of his researches on everyday policing of the inner city and, subsequently, on reactions to the corruption scandals, Punch (1979; 1983c; 1985) implies that subcultural affiliation is relatively weak, with schisms and internal divisions endemic. Thus while the individual officer may prioritize those aspects of policework associated in other societies with a police subculture, this was not generally the case:

> Basically the policemen I talked to seemed more 'privatised', less prejudiced, more able to step out of their police role, less

> identified with the police outside of work, and less given to crude anti-liberal statements . . . What did emerge from the interviews was a degree of withdrawal from the police culture and the police identity outside of work. (Punch 1979, 38–40).

Despite the failure of many team-policing initiatives, this at least suggests a potential for stronger ties between police and public, perhaps more so away from the inner city. Ijzerman (1987), for example, described a recent initiative in the small city of Enschede which involves crime prevention, inter-agency co-operation and decentralized police structure. However, while evaluation of the neighbourhood initiatives in the Staatsliedenbuurt of Amsterdam is largely an acceptance of a failure to improve relations with the community in the heart of the inner city, the fact that an attempt was made is indication of management's commitment to such policies (Visser and Wierda 1987).

Unlike in a number of other countries, including the UK (Gill and Mawby 1990a), the use of police auxiliaries is of relatively recent origin.[5] In the postwar period police reserve units were formed within both state and municipal police systems to act as emergency support to the regular police, but only in the 1980s has this role been expanded to incorporate a broader range of activities. Currently there are approximately 2,500 auxiliaries attached to the state police and 3,500 working with the municipal police. Applicants receive evening training for two years and undertake examinations before being attached to the regular police. They are paid for their duties, which include patrol work, traffic control and duties at fetes, carnivals etc. but exclude detective work and attendance at serious traffic accidents. Other than these they have the same powers as regular officers, and are similarly armed.

Because they are paid, auxiliaries are not strictly speaking volunteers or civilian representatives of the community, although there are some moves afoot to abolish the reserve and replace it by a volunteer force. In other respects, the involvement of the community in the policing process is similarly low. For example, crime prevention initiatives tend to have focused more on professional/employee involvement than on the role of private citizens, and neighbourhood watch initiatives have only recently emerged, based on experiences in the United States and Britain (Dijk and Junger-Tas 1988). Nevertheless, neighbourhood watch has been a singular failure in the Netherlands, with little public enthusiasm for the idea, provoking one Ministry of Justice official to note that it was 'hard to convince a Dutchman that he has a community responsibility'.

Instead, government crime-prevention initiatives in the 1980s have tended to shift towards alternatives that do not require the same level of community involvement. Functional surveillance, where paid employees are accorded crime-prevention responsibilities, is an idea borrowed from the Home Office in London (Mayhew *et al.* 1979). Specifically Dutch initiatives, described briefly by Junger-Tas (1987) and Dijk (1989), include tram and underground police (SIC or VIC), and city guards. The former are government-funded appointments to work on the transport systems in the cities as part of a job-creation scheme. Uniformed, and under the supervision of the police, they are expected to prevent vandalism and act as a deterrent to possible fare dodgers. City guards, a recent innovation, are part of a job-creation scheme for the long-term unemployed, formed by the Ministry of Social Affairs. Following a small pilot project in Dordrecht, 250 city guards were due to be introduced in Amsterdam in 1990. Again uniformed and under the control of the police, city guards have limited powers of arrest and are employed for one year, with the expectation that they might then gain employment in the private security industry. Significantly, their work is focused on commercial and shopping areas, and there are no plans to deploy them in residential areas.

This brings us to the other side of police/public relations; the extent of control that the public have over their police. At first sight, the plethora of smaller forces, with the role of the burgomaster pronounced at local level, suggests a high degree of public involvement. However this may be misleading. Although a public inquiry followed the Amsterdam riots, the riots themselves were partly attributed to a failure of consultation between police chief and burgomaster (Rosenthal 1984), and Brink and Bulthuis (1979) argue that the burgomaster has little autonomy over the municipal police and may, indeed, in reality differ little from burgomasters in areas covered by the state police:

> With regard to the performance of police duties, the burgomaster of a municipality with a municipal police force has much the same powers as the burgomaster of a municipality with a national police unit . . . There are only a few municipalities in which the municipal council, by means of a committee, exercises a certain control over the operations of the police and hence indirectly over the burgomaster's work as head of the local police. (Brink and Bulthuis 1979, 17).

Similarly:

> Although the central government bears the costs of the municipal police, there are no inspection powers or powers regarding fulfilment of the police task. The local council approves the police budget but has no direct influence on the functions of the police. It thus appears that by function and operation the municipal police are quite independent. (Shane 1980, 127).

To some extent, this is a reflection of the low profile of civil rights and watchdog agencies in the Netherlands (Punch 1979, 195). Partly, as in other areas of the criminal justic system, it is indicative of the exclusion of the public from decision-making processes. Nevertheless, given the rise in recorded crime, restrictions on police expansion, criticisms of the ways in which the police operate and moves towards larger forces, clearly the question of accountability to the public is crucial:

> The nub of the problem now is how to reorganize the police in the Netherlands in such a way that democratic control by the local authorities is preserved while the police are enabled to operate as efficiently as possible. (Brink and Bulthuis 1979, 21).

The burgomaster is, in theory, the representative of the local authority (Steenhuis 1979). However, in practice to see him as such is misleading, a point that is compounded by the tendency to translate 'burgomaster' as 'mayor'. In fact he is no such thing. The burgomaster is a cross between a civil servant and a politician, appointed by the Ministry of the Interior for a minimum of six years. Although the provincial government must agree to the appointment, and the local council may hold him or her accountable, and may control the budget, the latter has no control over the appointment or continuance in office of the burgomaster. Moreover, since burgomasters are frequently former politicians who see their future career moves in terms of either cabinet office or as burgomasters of larger municipalities, they are likely to be influenced more by central than by local government.

The chief of police is nominated by the burgomaster and the appointment needs to be ratified by the Minister of the Interior on the advice of the Minister of Justice. In many cases, then, he may be seen as the burgomaster's 'man', although where the chief pre-dates the burgomaster there may be a clash of personalities. In Breda, for example, there was apparently a long-running conflict between burgomaster and police chief. In general, though, it appears that while the large number of municipal forces suggests some closer local accountability, in practice police operations are relatively autonomous of local government. Moreover, future trends are likely to expand the influence of central government.

SUMMARY

The Netherlands provides an interesting contrast with France. With its prosperous cities in the Middle Ages, the Netherlands avoided the centralization associated with much continental government and policing, and at various times the extent of central control over its police has been the subject of controversy. However, the localized nature of its police structure is not all it seems. On the one hand, the national force provides an equivalent, if less militaristic, service to that of the French *gendarmerie*. On the other hand, central government influence, through the procuracy and through initiatives aimed at rationalizing and improving the efficiency of the police, has undermined local influence. Moreover, as in many other areas of the criminal justice system, public involvement in the system is minimal. This is reflected in the participation of the burgomaster alongside police chief and prosecutor in the administration of the municipal police. While in theory the representative of local government, burgomasters are more closely attuned to the needs of central government, such that local accountability is restricted.

In many respects, central government initiatives in the last twenty years have prioritized a more community-oriented role for the police, although many of the policies adopted have faltered in the face of police hostility. Moreover, levels of public participation, for example in neighbourhood watch, have been low and a disappointment to government, and crime prevention initiatives that have been pursued most vigorously have tended to centre on inter-agency co-operation and job-creation schemes.

It is, consequently, difficult to characterize the Dutch police system. Officers are routinely armed, and carry out some general administrative tasks, and recruitment is on a two-tier basis, in line with the continental model, but in many other respects there are parallels with policing in the UK. Thus while amalgamations have occurred and central government influence has increased, the police system remains distinct from those of its neighbours.

5

Canada: Between Britain and the United States

INTRODUCTION

Canada, as a Western industrialized country, is of particular interest from a policing perspective because of its diversity: of population, policing systems, and outside influence, for example. After early French influence, its police system was then moulded in Britain, but on both English and Irish models. The Royal Canadian Mounted Police (RCMP) owes its ancestry to the latter, and symbolically (Walden 1982) dominates discussions of Canada and its police. There have, consequently, been a myriad of accounts of the 'Mounties', although most have, until recently, been romanticized and uncritical. For example, having criticized the 'romantic nonsense' of most accounts, one author concluded:

> What, however, may justly be said of its record of sixty-five years service is that always its members have been incorruptible; unswayed by public clamour; unswerving in work for the public weal; tenacious to breaking-point in bringing the wrong doer to justice; the sure shield of the weak and oppressed; arbitrators, administrators, diplomats; unbeatable trail-breakers into the untrodden regions, torch-bearers of order and justice to peoples hitherto beyond the law! (Douthwaite 1939, unpaginated).

Other accounts of policing, most notably by practitioners like Kelly and Kelly (1976), are also limited in their lack of a critical edge. In complete contrast, political scientists (Weller 1981), historians (Morrison 1985), and sociologists (Taylor 1986) have been scathing of Canadian police practices.

Many of these more recent critiques have been written by Canadian academics, where policing is assessed in the context of the North American tradition, with some reference to the British situation. The most notable of such writers are perhaps Ericson (1981; 1982) and Shearing and Stenning (1983). Accounts by outsiders are less common but include a review by the political scientist Brian Chapman (1978) (which is surprisingly uncritical) and the more sceptical review of Ian Taylor (1986), a British sociologist working in Canada at the time. Compared with most other countries covered in this study, then, details on Canada, particularly sociological studies, are readily available.

THE SOCIAL AND POLITICAL STRUCTURE OF CANADA

Covering an area of over 3,850,000 square miles, Canada is larger even than China. Its size is, indeed, frequently expressed in tourist brochures which boast that the maximum distance across it is greater than the distance from the UK to its eastern coast! Yet with a population of less than 25 million (less than half that of the UK or France), it is one of the 'smaller' countries considered in this study. Combine the two statistics, and Canada has a population density of a mere 2.5 people per square km. The United States has a population density 10 times that, China 40 times, while the population density of the Netherlands is 150 times that of Canada.

Such figures are somewhat misleading, given that 85 per cent of Canadians live in the far south, within 200 miles of the US border (Torczyner 1987) and 76 per cent live in urban areas (Latouche 1983), setting the conditions for the very different police systems which emerged in the metropolitan areas compared with the central plains, Yukon and North-West Territories.

Another distinction with far-reaching socio-political implications concerns nationality – Canada was settled in the seventeenth century, first by French, then British. Today this is reflected in the ethnic diversity of its population (Loree 1985). While overall British law prevailed, in some respects, especially in the province of Quebec, the French influence has continued, culminating on the one hand in an (unsuccessful) referendum on independence, on the other in a series of terrorist campaigns. Today, while 70 per cent of Canadians speak English as their first language, in Quebec French is the first language of 80 per cent of the population; in two of Montreal's four universities French is the language for study.

The Canadian Constitution was originally established in the British

North America Act of 1867 and most recently modified in the Constitution Act 1982, at which time the Canadian government also adopted a Charter of Rights and Freedoms as a part of constitutional law. The 1867 Act, following the 1841 Union of Upper and Lower Canada, provided the basis for a federal government with considerable local autonomy delegated to provincial government. Thus while the national parliament, based in the capital Ottawa, is responsible for passing laws for the whole country, provincial legislatures have broad powers over, for example, education, civil rights, hospitals, housing and justice.

Partly as a result of this, public welfare services were much slower to become established in Canada than in Britain and are less comprehensive, and there are enormous variations in provision between the provinces (Guest 1984; Torczyner 1987). Another factor here is the conservative nature of national and some provincial governments. Power nationally had tended to be held predominantly by the Liberals and to a lesser extent the Conservatives, with the leftwing and more recently formed Democratic Party picking up about one-fifth of the votes. Canada has, in fact, become much closer politically and economically to the United States in recent years, with consequent implications for public policy (Ratner 1986), and with the abolition of trade restrictions they are likely to increase.

What then of the provinces? Canada comprises ten provinces stretching from Newfoundland and Novia Scotia in the east to British Columbia in the west. However only four provinces have populations of more than 2 million: Ontario (9 million), Quebec (6.5 million), British Columbia (nearly 3 million) and Alberta (2.5 million). At the other extreme Prince Edward Island has a population of only some 130,000. Additionally, one-third of the Canadian land mass is not incorporated within the provincial structure, being defined as two territories, headed by commissioners appointed by the federal government. These are the North-West Territories with about 50,000 inhabitants for 1.3 million square miles, and the Yukon with 23,000 inhabitants for 200,000 square miles.

Canada is, consequently, a country of variety, where the federal structure allows for the continuance of much of that variety. This is evident if we turn to consider the criminal justice system and the structure of policing.

CRIME AND THE CRIMINAL JUSTICE SYSTEM

In terms of its crime levels, Canada is more like the UK than the USA. Its homicide rate, although slightly higher than that in England and Wales, is only a quarter of that in the US. In other respects, recorded crime levels are not too dissimilar from England and Wales. Burglary rates are now slightly lower and car thefts considerably lower for example (Kalish 1988). While official data are open to various interpretations, victim-survey data also allow comparisons beween Canada and other Western industrialized nations (Block 1983; Mayhew 1987; Waller and Okihiro 1978). Although in Canada more readily available for the major cities than for the country as a whole, these again suggest that levels of crime are broadly similar to England and Wales. Mayhew (1987), for example, suggests that in the early 1980s the household burglary rate in Canada was some 15 per cent higher than in England and Wales, with the US rate some 25 per cent higher still. Both crime statistics and victim survey data also suggest a rise in crime in the 1970s and 1980s (Taylor 1986).

Comparisons between the Canadian and English criminal justice systems are more direct. With British settlers to Canada eventually predominating, the legal system is based on the common-law tradition. Originally, however, the common law of medieval England sat alongside *le droit civil*, the Roman-law tradition introduced by the French, and civil law in Quebec is still based on the latter, illustrative of the extent of provincial autonomy.

The 1867 Act made the federal government responsible for the criminal law, and provided for a judiciary, but provinces have always been responsible for the *administration* of justice, including law enforcement. Within each province there is a two-tier system of courts, the (lower) provincial courts and the superior court, with a third tier, district or county courts, sandwiched between them in some provinces. The ultimate court of appeal is the Supreme Court of Canada. The jury system, while imported from England and distinct from the French alternative, has its own characteristics. Trial by juries is available for more serious crimes, normally those imprisonable for five or more years; and findings have to be unanimous. The size of the jury is twelve in each of the provinces but six in the territories. Eligibility criteria for jury membership also vary between provinces. Although the 1982 Charter of Rights and Freedoms provides national conditions for the implementation of justice, in fact it does allow some degree of modification by individual provinces (Ratner 1986). One national requirement of the charter, however, distinguishing it from the British experience, is that courts are required to exclude any evidence obtained illegally.

The federal government provides overall guidance and some financial support in terms of the criminal justice system. The head of the Department of Justice is a minister, who traditionally doubles as the Attorney General. The department has been behind a number of initiatives regarding, for example, legal-aid provisions and help for crime victims (Department of Justice Canada 1986). The Canadian Sentencing Commission (1987) also raised a number of national concerns easily recognizable to an international audience, for example *vis-à-vis* victim services and use of imprisonment.

Victim services have received considerable attention in recent years (Rock 1988), having developed along similar lines to those in the US (Mawby and Gill 1987). Early initiatives covered services for rape victims and homes for spouse-abuse victims, known as transition houses in Canada. Attempts at services for wider categories of victims, for example in British Columbia by the penal reform group, the John Howard Society and the Probation Department in the early 1980s, faltered. An alternative model, in Vancouver, British Columbia, began in 1984 based within the police system but deploying volunteers (McClenahan 1987). This and many other schemes, most integrated into the police organization, are funded by the Department of the Solicitor General.

Just as victim services have developed in similar ways to the US, so the use of imprisonment has been applied as readily by the courts, and indeed Canada has on occasions had the higher rate of imprisonment, although since the early 1960s there has been a decline (Lowman and Menzies 1986). There is, however, still an overwillingness to imprison offenders, and considerable sentencing disparities between provinces (Canadian Sentencing Commission 1987).

The federal government has a role in the *administration* of the prison system, since it runs federal penitentiaries for those sentenced to two years or more in prison, the provinces running jails for those serving lesser sentences. In other respects, however, some non-custodial sentences have been introduced to provinces independently.

Considerations of non-custodial alternatives, such as community service orders, and a more recent development, electronic monitoring, in fact demonstrate three features of the Canadian criminal-justice system: the variation between provinces, the balance between British and US influences, and the importance of the 'private' sector. For example, decisions to implement tagging were taken first, and independently, by British Columbia on the basis of the US experience,[1] and community service orders, introduced by Ontario judges as a condition of probation, appear to have been influenced by both the British model and US alternatives (Menzies 1986; Vass and Menzies 1989). Clearly tagging has involved the private sector in its administration. In other respects, though, private and voluntary sectors appear to figure significantly (Ericson, McMahon and Evans 1987). This is in fact one marked difference between the operation of community service in Canada and Britain, with services in the former contracted to agencies like the John Howard Society and the Salvation Army (Vass and Menzies 1989).

THE HISTORY OF THE POLICE IN CANADA

The emergence and form of policing in different parts of Canada varied according to the time of settlement, country of origin of the settlers, and the particular problems requiring some form of control. Among the first areas to develop readily identifiable early police systems were the French settlements of Quebec and Montreal (Chapman 1978; Kelly and Kelly 1976; Morton 1986; Whittingham 1981), in the latter case partly as security against a hostile indigenous population. Responsibility for these early police was taken by the richest landlords, who acted as magistrates and formed town militia to keep watch at night, guarding against not only crime and outside attack but also fires. Police regulations for the 'New France' were drafted by the governor, Count de Frontenac, as early as 1673. Although the British wrested control of these areas by the mid-eighteenth century, responsibility for law and order was originally left in the hands of the French. Thus even when full-time paid police forces were established in the 1830s and 1840s, French influence continued (Kelly and Kelly 1976) and today provincial and municipal police structures in Quebec are distinctive (Chapman 1978; Statistics Canada 1986).

In British Canada the pattern was somewhat different. The governor of Newfoundland appointed unpaid constables from as early as 1729. In Halifax the problems caused by sailors provoked the governor to adopt a similar system in 1749. In Upper Canada (later Ontario), parliament in 1793 provided for the appointment of high county constables for each provincial district, responsible for the appointment of unpaid volunteers in the towns and parishes to act as nightwatchmen (Kelly and Kelly 1976). It was, however, no coincidence that paid police forces were introduced in the wake of the early English initiatives. Thus York (later Toronto) established a six-man paid police force in 1835, which by 1859 had increased to 42. The 1858 Municipal Institutions of Upper Canada Act authorized towns and cities to establish their own forces under police boards, and the 1867 British North American Act, in making the provinces responsible for their own justice administration, encouraged the provincial governments to police areas not covered by municipal forces. British Columbia in fact had already established a province-wide force in 1866; Quebec followed suit in 1870 and Newfoundland in 1871, the latter, significantly, being modelled on the Royal Irish Constabulary (Kelly and Kelly 1976).

This was in fact not the first adaptation of the Irish model to provincial Canada. In the 1850s the colonial authorities in British Columbia, faced with threats from the United States intensified by the discovery of gold, requested police support. In response, the British colonial secretary sent a sub-inspector from the Irish Constabulary to establish a similar force to maintain order (Chapman 1978).

Two other federal forces were established during this period. The later of the two, the dominion police, was created in 1868, and although having national jurisdiction was based in Ontario and Quebec to protect parliamentary and other government buildings, including the dockyards (Chapman 1978; Kelly and Kelly 1976). Of considerably more significance was the force subsequently to be named the Royal Canadian Mounted Police (RCMP).

This traces its origins to the 1845 'Act for the Better Preservation of the Peace, and the Prevention of Riots and Violent Outrages at and Near Public Works, while in Progress of Construction'. The mounted police force subsequently formed was deployed to maintain order among labourers employed on the construction of the Welland and St Lawrence canals, and later to quell political unrest in Montreal in 1849 (Kelly and Kelly 1976; Statistics Canada 1986). Based on the Irish system, this formed the model for the establishment of the North-West Mounted Police Force (NWMP) in 1873, responsible for enforcing the law in the central plains and later the Yukon and North-West Territories. For the next twenty years, the NWMP established bases across the central plains, from which it acted as a frontier patrol against US incursions, collected customs and prevented whisky trading, while allegedly acting in the national interest to protect the natives, control buffalo trading and maintain law and order. In so doing, as Macleod (1976) demonstrates, it both operated as a military, regimented political police force and itself initiated government policy in many respects.

The Yukon gold rush of 1897 brought additional responsibilities for the NWMP, shortly followed by its deployment in bringing order to the whaling communities of Hudson Bay, the exploration of the MacKenzie delta and, in the 1920s, the Arctic archipelago. In all of these ventures, the police found themselves involved in a far wider range of roles than other forces based on the English *or* Irish models. In the Yukon, for example:

> In many respects of their work the NWMP found themselves to an increasing extent involved in affairs that had little or nothing to do with keeping the peace. Sometimes they were apparently selected for tasks because they were best qualified to do them; in other cases, such as the customs service, they were likely to be picked merely because they could do the job with little cost to the government . . .
>
> The list is impressive: for the Department of Justice they kept the penitentiary prisoners and the lunatics and frequently acted as magistrates and justices of the peace. They looked after the welfare of the Indians and ran the Yukon postal service. They acted as land agents and mining recorders for the Department of the Interior. They acted as coroners and as returning officers at elections. They helped the health officer of the territorial government and isolated diseases among animals for the federal Department of Agriculture. (Morrison 1985, 38, 50–1).

As in the plains, the NWMP was also responsible for interpreting law, reinterpreting it, and formulating it where no law existed, in the name of order. In the Yukon senior officers on occasions closed stores, and refused access to the territory to those with 'inadequate' means of support; in Hudson Bay the export of musk-ox skins was prohibited to prevent the extermination of the species (Morrison 1985). In imposing its own version of Canadian law and order, the NWMP in effect achieved two ends. On the one hand, it negated any alternative interpretations of the law: from the Indians of the plains or Inuit of the north; by foreign prospectors or whaling crews; or by private organizations like the Hudson's Bay Company. On the other hand, it asserted Canadian sovereignty against possible incursions by the US in the Yukon or Denmark in the far north. As Morrison (1985, 136) observes: 'Nothing establishes sovereignty over an area more clearly than effective policing of it'.

Unlike developments in the municipalities, the NWMP was a military-style force, disciplined and administered accordingly, organized to impose British/Canadian control in areas where it was a minority force. To quote Morrison (1985, 2) again:

> The role of the police will be familiar to any student of the British colonial system. The Mounted Police were, in a certain sense, the Canadian equivalent of those forces of imperialism – the British Army, the Royal Irish Constabulary, and the various colonial police forces – which brought British law and civil administration to the wild corners of the Empire. The difference in the Canadian case was that the colonial power was in Ottawa rather than in London. As agents of this central power, the police imposed on the Canadian north a system largely alien to it, a system which originated elsewhere, in a different culture, and which was designed not to express the aspirations of the north, but to regulate and control it.

This is particularly significant for two reasons; first, symbolically, as already noted, the RCMP is identified as *the* police system of Canada; second, practically, the period from the 1920s saw an expansion of the NWMP from its origins in the plains and north. Thus in the period following the First World War it took over responsibility for policing federal laws across the whole country, absorbed the smaller and insignificant dominion police, was renamed (in 1920) the Royal Canadian Mounted Police, and moved its base from Regina in the prairies to Ottawa, the seat of federal government.

The interwar period also saw two other significant expansions. On the one hand, the RCMP continued the policy of taking on a wider range of responsibilities; in 1932 it became responsible for all customs and excise work, and by 1937 had its own marine and aviation sections. On the other hand, it took on additional provincial responsibilities (Kelly and Kelly 1976).

This expansion was not in fact unbroken. During the First World War the Royal North-Western Mounted Police[2] withdrew its services from the provinces of Saskatchewan and Alberta and provided minimal cover in the Yukon and north, as it concentrated more on security and counter-espionage services. Saskatchewan and Alberta in fact were compelled to form their own provincial forces (Chapman 1978). In 1919 the force lost considerable national popularity, though proving its worth to the government, when it figured prominently in breaking the Winnipeg general strike. Horrall (1980), in a detailed account of the period, notes that the RNWMP, faced with a postwar shrinkage in its influence, reacted by demonstrating its value to the government. One key aspect of this was in its involvement in undercover work to undermine the 'national threat' of strikers and 'communists'. Another was its advantage in offering a non-unionized force at a time when local police forces were becoming unionized and police militancy abroad was headline news. During this period it also took over responsibility for enforcing immigration laws and for the customs services, which had been the subject of scandal over corruption (Chapman 1978).

Fuller involvement of the RCMP in provincial policing, however, commenced in 1928 when Saskatchewan reverted to its original policy of subcontracting responsibilities to the RCMP. Alberta, Manitoba, Nova Scotia, New Brunswick and Prince Edward Island followed suit in 1932 (Statistics Canada 1986). Its security work became more important during the Second World War, especially with early US neutrality and the defeat of France, and at one point it infiltrated a Nazi cell in Quebec (Weller 1981).

In the postwar period it assumed provincial policing responsibilities for Newfoundland and British Columbia. The inclusion of British Columbia is of significance in at least two respects, regarding process and precedence (Chapman 1978). In 1949 the Attorney General of the province, himself under investigation by the provincial police for alleged corruption and spurred on by moves towards unionization within the force, apparently took the initiative, unbeknown to many of his cabinet colleagues, of negotiating a new contract with the RCMP. When the latter took over responsibilities for provincial policing in 1950, most of the old provincial police, excluding senior officers and the secretary of the police federation, were incorporated into the RCMP.

The precedent set by this takeover was an involvement of the RCMP in municipal policing. From 1924 municipalities had been allowed to subcontract police services to the provincial police. Thus when the RCMP took over responsibilities in British Columbia it also took over some municipal contracts. By the 1950s, then, the RCMP had federal police responsibilities; responsibilities for policing the Yukon and North-West Territories; responsibilities under contract for policing eight of the ten provinces; and some contractual arrangements *vis-à-vis* municipal policing.

POLICING IN CANADA TODAY

Nevertheless, the RCMP accounted for only 27 per cent of the public police in Canada in the mid-1980s (Statistics Canada 1986). At provincial level, although the RCMP has contractual arrangements with eight provinces, the two largest, Ontario and Quebec, provide their own provincial forces. At municipal level, the RCMP has contracts with 32 per cent of the municipalities but since these tend

Table 5.1 ***Major policing arrangements in each province or territory in 1985 (Percentage in Each Category)***[3]

Municipal police (%)				Federal/provincial police (%)	
RCMP	MDP		Numbers	RCMP	Own provincial
0	70	Ontario	18,662	6	22
0	61	Quebec	14,187	7	30
31	30	British Columbia	5,875	38	0
13	57	Alberta	4,292	29	0
7	53	Manitoba	2,156	36	0
11	42	Saskatchewan	1,985	46	0
4	48	Nova Scotia	1,485	45	0
6	51	New Brunswick	1,239	28	9
5	0	Newfoundland and Labrador	943	55	39
7	34	Prince Edward Island	181	59	0
0	0	North-West Territories	247	100	0
0	0	Yukon	116	100	0

to be the smaller cities it has responsibility for only 9 per cent of municipal police officers. As can be seen from Table 5.1, the form of policing varies markedly between areas. In the Yukon and North-West Territories the RCMP has direct responsibility for police services, and in six provinces it monopolizes provincial policing. In Newfoundland, the Royal Newfoundland Constabulary – confined mainly to the city of St John's – shares provincial responsibilities with the RCMP; in New Brunswick the New Brunswick Highway Patrol, created in 1978, complements the work of the RCMP. Finally, in Quebec and Ontario the provinces have retained responsibility for provincial policing, with the role of the RCMP restricted to federal policing.

The picture is quite different with regard to municipal policing. Except for Quebec and Ontario, the RCMP has contracts with municipal governments in all the provinces; however, only in Newfoundland and British Columbia is this presence significant, with most municipal forces in the other provinces being autonomous. Given the relative size of the municipal forces, then, the RCMP actually only provides a majority of the police services in four provinces: British Columbia (69 per cent), Prince Edward Island (66 per cent), Newfoundland (60 per cent), and Saskatchewan (57 per cent).

The local autonomous forces tend to be of two kinds. Some are confined to one particular municipality, but others have been formed by amalgamation to create regional municipal forces, like the one researched in Ontario by Ericson (1981; 1982).

We might briefly pause here to consider the four largest conglomerations of public policing in Canada today: the RCMP, Ontario, Quebec and British Columbia (Statistics Canada 1986). The RCMP is formed into four 'activities': administration (which includes recruitment and training); a section dealing with federal laws, involving for example drugs, customs and excise, and security services for government property and foreign diplomats; police services under contract to the eight provinces, two territories and 191 municipalities which currently subcontract their police responsibilities; and Canadian police services, a specialist support for all the country's forces, including specialist aid in forensics, fingerprinting and firearms.

The Ontario police, with a strength of 18,662 in 1985 (approximately one per 490 population), is dominated by its 116 municipal and nine regional police departments, which in 1985 employed nearly 13,000 police personnel. The provincial police employed approximately 4,200 officers, in comparison, plus 147 other officers in 13 small municipalities which subcontracted the police service to the provincial police. The provincial police force is regulated to some extent by the Ontario Police Commission, which also oversees municipal services, which may additionally have their own boards of commissioners.

In Quebec the postwar period saw a continuation of the French model, with a judicial police, *gendarmerie*, traffic police, and somewhat idiosyncratic liquor police. In the 1960s, in the light of some glaring inefficiencies, the services were reorganized in line with the RCMP and Ontario (Chapman 1978), although some French terms remain. In 1985 the police strength of 14,187 (approximately one per 475 population) was largely employed in municipal police departments (61 per cent) or by the *Sûreté du Quebec* (30 per cent), with a staff of 4,250 officers based in nine policing districts. The municipal police are based in 166 municipalities employing some 4,300 officers, and the Montreal Urban Community Police Department with about 4,400 officers. The Quebec Police Commission, established in 1968, has overall authority over both the provincial and municipal forces, although the latter may also be accountable to the municipal councils.

British Columbia is worth brief consideration because of the more significant role played by the RCMP, which provides provincial services and slightly over half the municipal police, in 43 of the 55 municipal forces. In 1985 overall police strength was 5,875, one per 490 population, similar to that in Ontario and Quebec. Autonomous municipal police forces are accountable to boards of commissioners, whereas those municipalities with a subcontracting arrangement and the provincial force are responsible to the provincial Attorney General and the British Columbia Police Commission.

Specialist services may be provided at municipal, provincial or national level (through the RCMP), or by specialist agencies. At municipal level, for example, many forces operate specialist units dealing with juveniles, domestic violence etc. (Leeson and Snyder 1981; Sewell 1985). At national level, there has, since 1984 and following a number of scandals (Weller 1981), been a security intelligence service separate from the RCMP and subject to the Inspector General and the Security Intelligence Review Committee (Statistics Canada 1986). The ports police and railway police are also federal agencies, but with longer histories. The railway police force is responsible for policing on the Canadian National Railway, but the privately owned Canadian Pacific Railway has its own private force (Statistics Canada 1986). While the role of the private sector in policing is long-established in Canada, recent changes – for example in government policy and in the organization of private property – have led to a dramatic expansion of the private police, now considerably outnumbering the public sector (Shearing and Stenning 1983).

While the organization of the police in Canada appears unique in a number of respects, sociological studies of police work produce few surprises, with research indicating similar patterns to those of Britain and the USA. For example, in considering community policing initiatives in Toronto, Murphy (1988, 399) describes changes in policing patterns which have been reproduced in most Western industrialized societies:

> In pursuit of more organizational autonomy, centralized organizational control and rational administrative efficiency, urban police departments have systematically closed neighbourhood police stations, abandoned foot patrol, minimized police–citizen contacts, narrowed the police role, and limited local political influence through formalized police commissions. Modern police decision-making and operational strategies are determined by the technology and logic of the telephone, computer-aided despatch, response lines, patrol allocation models, mobile response, and equitable case loads.

The emphasis upon mobile patrols is central to Ericson's (1982) study of police patrol work in a regional municipal department in Ontario; here again, the role of the police in non-crime work, and conflict between plain-clothes and uniformed branches (Ericson 1981; 1982) will be familiar to outside audiences. Ericson (1981) also identifies the extensiveness of police discretion, both in terms of the decision to intervene and in terms of whether or not to take official action. In the former case, he suggests that pro-active policing may be more prevalent in his research than elsewhere, although the picture is blurred by the (not unexpected) predominence of pro-activity in traffic situations and minor incidents. In the latter case, he demonstrates how police decisions to pursue a formal charge are determined by the demeanour of the suspect, with those who challenge police authority most likely to be charged.

Ericson (1981; 1982) also identifies the extent to which 'real' police work, involving excitement and action, is preferred to service- or welfare-related roles.[4] Not surprisingly, then, police work is a male-dominated occupation. Given the distinctive historical role of the RCMP, women were in fact only admitted into the RCMP in 1974, although their place in other forces was established considerably earlier (Linden 1983). In other respects, police officers appear to be drawn from distinctive subgroups of the population. Despite formally stated official policy (Loree 1985),[5] the RCMP has recruited predominantly from those of British ancestry, and is underrepresentative of French, Indian and Inuit as well as black and Asian minority groups (Weller 1981). While information on other forces is less readily available, a range of authors has identified the police with the political right, with racist views and punitive philosophies on issues such as capital punishment (Ericson 1982; Jackson 1979; Lee 1981; Taylor 1986; Weller 1981). Two immediate implications of this are worth noting here. First, there has been considerable criticism of police partiality in the enforcement of laws against, for example, racial minority or gay groups (Lee 1981; Weller 1981) and radical political groups (Weller 1981). Second, the police may come to identify themselves as a 'beleaguered minority' (Taylor 1986), strengthening police subculture. Emphasis on 'real' police work and loyalty to one's colleagues, being features of the police subculture elsewhere, are emphasized by Shearing (1981), and epitomized to varying degrees in the working styles of those he calls 'wise officers' and 'real officers'. Identification with and loyalty towards other officers, of course, has implications for police–public relations.

POLICE AND PUBLIC

Possibly because it is essentially Canadian, the RCMP has attained symbolic importance (Walden 1982), and despite controversies the police in Canada tend to enjoy high public esteem. However, although government philosophy is that Canada is a multicultural society, as Taylor (1986) points out urban communities are demarcated in race and class terms. Thus just as the police differentiate between respectable and suspect communities (Ericson 1982) so police–public relations differ markedly between neighbourhoods. In observing that the police are responsible for more public deaths than vice versa, Lee (1981) argues that the police scarcely value some 'publics'. Equally, Taylor (1986) notes that police killings, fatal motor accidents caused by police vehicles, and an increasingly sophisticated police weaponry indicate scant regard for community values.

Steps have, however, been taken to improve community relations. Murphy (1988), for example, describes a recent community policing initiative in Toronto which aims to place more emphasis on locals' definitions of the communities' problems and put more police back in the area. Also following US initiatives, neighbourhood-watch and crimestoppers schemes have become more common. The role of the public as uniformed police volunteers has also expanded recently, although unlike in Britain there is no long-standing tradition in this respect (Gill and Mawby 1990a; Willett and Chitty 1982). Nevertheless, as Taylor (1986) notes, such initiatives are police-orchestrated and police-controlled, and are dismissed by their critics as public-relations exercises or ways in which control of the community *by* the police is extended.

The extent to which the police are controlled by the public raises the question of accountability. Here we need to draw a distinction between the RCMP and provincial and municipal forces.

As a centralized, semi-military force, the accountability of the RCMP (and to whom) has been the subject of numerous controversies, most notably in the context of its role in policing political protests. Until 1984 the RCMP was responsible, through its security and intelligence branch, for political policing. The revelations which forced a change followed an incident in 1974 when Robert Samson, a corporal in the branch, injured himself when acting as an *agent provocateur*, planting a bomb outside the Montreal home of a supermarket executive (Dion 1982). Subsequent investigation, particularly of the role of the branch *vis-à-vis* the Quebec separatists, unearthed a considerable number of illegalities, many of which were established departmental practices rather than isolated incidents by 'overzealous' officers. They included the illegal opening of private mail, burglary and arson. For example, during Operation Ham in 1973 the RCMP broke into commercial premises to gain information about the Parti Quebecois and in 1972 it was responsible for burning down a barn scheduled as the site for a meeting between Quebec activists and American Black Panthers. The subsequent inquiries revealed a disturbing lack of central accountability of the RCMP, either to the responsible minister or parliament. Former Solicitors General denied that they were fully informed of security operations, and Prime Minister Trudeau appeared to accept that he did not wish to be kept informed (Weller 1981). The changed structure of the security apparatus is partially an attempt to strengthen such accountability.

Of wider significance, however, is the local situation. On one level, for example, it was clear that in some operations municipal and provincial police colluded with the RCMP in illegal operations. For example, burglary of the headquarters of the Agence Presse Libre du Québèc in 1972 involved the RCMP, the Montreal urban community police and the Quebec provincial police (Dion 1982).

The latter two forces were clearly held accountable at provincial level. However, while the federal inquiry, the McDonald Commission (generally considered to be a half-hearted attempt to uncover the facts), required RCMP co-operation, the Quebec inquiry under Jean F. Keable was consistently hampered by the refusal of the RCMP to be held accountable at provincial level (Dion 1982). Weller (1981, 7–9) argues that this confusion has been exploited by the RCMP on a number of occasions. While in theory the RCMP is subject to the provincial Attorney General when it is under contract to a province, in practice accountability to the province is minimal. Thus the Laycraft Commission in Alberta experienced difficulty discovering the relationship between the RCMP and tax officials; on another occasion the Alberta Supreme Court ruled that the province could not investigate internal RCMP operations and decisions; elsewhere, in Ontario, the Krever Commission failed to get the RCMP to reveal how it gained access to confidential medical files.

How accountable then are local police? In a detailed assessment of municipal police accountability, Stenning (1981) traces the origins of police boards and commissioners to the mid-nineteenth century when control of the local police passed gradually from justices and mayors to municipalities acting on behalf of provincial government. Police boards, developed on the US model, generally had between three and five members. While Stenning (1981) and Hann *et al.* (1985) suggest that boards are composed of respectable, middle-class, white members, in fact the ways in which members are appointed vary enormously. Thus:

> In terms of their composition alone, it is possible to identify no fewer than thirty eight different models of police boards during

> the institutions' 122-year history in Canada, ranging from boards whose members were all appointed by the provincial authorities, through boards whose members were all chosen by and/or from among the members of the local council, to boards whose members were chosen through direct public election to office. (Stenning 1981, 176).

The operation of boards is equally diverse. However, because they are composed of part-time members and meet infrequently their control over police policies is minimal. Increased police professionalism also appears to have dampened the influence of the boards.

Whether provincial police boards, which have become more influential in recent years (Stenning 1981), will operate any differently is difficult to say. However, it seems that, despite the controversies that have surrounded the RCMP, and more recently the expense of local policing (Stenning 1981; Taylor 1986; Weller 1981), the public's demand for a more accountable police is muted, or limited to minorities within the public. Local accountability does not appear to exist for the RCMP, even when under contract to provincial or municipal government, and there does not seem to be any strong evidence that smaller, more localized forces are significantly more accountable to their communities.

SUMMARY

Like the Netherlands, the structure of policing in Canada is difficult to categorize. It has been influenced by the French, British colonial and American systems, with the result that different structures emerged in British- and French-dominated urban areas, and a different pattern again in the central plains, Yukon and North-West Territories.

Moreover, although Canada, like the US, has a federal structure, the early dominance of the RCMP led many provinces to subcontract their police administration to this 'national' force, which had been created on paramilitary lines and owed its second phase of growth in the interwar period to its loyalty to central government. Consequently, while in the two largest provinces – Ontario and Quebec – and in many municipalities local police forces operate and are accountable in ways which are somewhat similar to the US, the RCMP provides a more militaristic, centralized structure and has resisted attempts to hold it accountable to local government.

Again, while initiatives with regard to community policing and neighbourhood watch have clearly been influenced by developments in the US, the RCMP has no direct equivalent south of the border and would undoubtedly be unacceptable in a country dominated by local forces, be they at state, county or city level. The Canadian policing system is perhaps best characterized as one where the local decentralized principle predominates, but where local areas have the opportunity to opt for a centralized system. In so doing they may save financially but undoubtedly their control over policing is weakened, and the accountability of the RCMP has been the subject of controversy in the last twenty years. Moreover there is little evidence of wider public involvement over the decision to subcontract. It is, therefore, particularly appropriate to turn here to policing in Hong Kong, the scene of a less equivocal colonial policing system.

6

Hong Kong: Colonial Capitalism

INTRODUCTION

Hong Kong is included here for two reasons. First, it is an example of a colonial police force. Its force is indeed still the general responsibility of the Inspector General and Commonwealth Office (Stead 1985, 104). Second, with its future, from 1997, firmly linked with China, comparison of its police system with that of Communist China is of timely relevance and the subject of renewed controversy after the Tiananmen Square massacre.

In one sense, a review of Hong Kong is relatively easy. Despite the fact that the majority of its population speaks Chinese as a first language, English is the 'language of government' and internal reports and reviews in English are readily available.[1] On the other hand, its police system has not been subject to any detailed academic scrutiny. Jeffries' review of colonial police systems, while providing a useful background, only briefly and superficially mentions Hong Kong (Jeffries 1952, 83–7). Indeed, the main accounts of its police, by Crisswell and Watson (1982) and Sinclair (1983), were written by a police officer, local historian, and crime reporter respectively. Perhaps the most critical theoretical appraisal is that by Tsui (1979), a Chinese student who assesses the changing face of the Hong Kong police from a colonial to a community-based service, largely following the model developed by Jeffries. Interestingly, it is this latter emphasis on community participation that has attracted the attention of British police representatives such as Alderson (1981a), May (1981) and Pope and Hui (1984).

Nevertheless, as current controversies over reunification illustrate, Hong Kong is not a democracy; it is a colony in which the interests of the majority have been accorded minimal consideration. The place of the police within such a political structure must thus be considered in terms of how the changing nature of policing is perceived in the light of a political system which has changed marginally.

SOCIAL AND POLITICAL STRUCTURE

The territory of Hong Kong was first claimed by the British in 1842 when Hong Kong Island was ceded under the Treaty of Nanking. The Convention of Peking in 1860 added parts of Stonecutters Island and the Kowloon peninsula, and in 1898 the New Territories were acquired on a 99-year lease, due to run out in 1997. Although the whole of Hong Kong covers only 412 square miles, with a population of about 5.25 million it is extremely densely populated, with over 5000 people per square km. Ninety per cent of the population, not surprisingly, live in urban areas: about 40 per cent live on Hong Kong Island itself, a third in New Kowloon and a quarter in the New Territories where a series of new towns have been built (Lacoste 1985; Lloyds Bank 1986).

Under the 1984 Sino-British agreement, China will resume sovereignty over Hong Kong in July 1997. Hong Kong will then become a special administrative region (SAR) of China. While China will dictate defence policy and foreign affairs, the agreement allows for considerable autonomy for Hong Kong, with the capitalist system protected for the next fifty years, and Hong Kong responsible for its own economic and political system, including its legal system. The SAR government may continue to employ British and foreign nationals in the public service, including the police, but not as heads of major government departments (Lamb 1985). Current controversies also suggest that dual passport holders will not be eligible for these senior positions.

British possession of Hong Kong originated in the ending of the First Opium War and was maintained against considerable opposition from the indigenous population, at times drawing support from mainland China. A general strike in 1925, for example, lasted for sixteen months. During the Second World War Hong Kong was occupied by the Japanese. Following the war, Britain re-established control of Hong Kong against opposition from Chinese nationalists and, later, the Communist government. There were Communist-led strikes in 1949. However, Communist support waned in the 1960s after the Great Leap Forward in China (when many Hong Kong immigrants heard of the hardships suffered by relatives in China) and Maoist-inspired strikes in 1967, followed by a bombing campaign, did not draw widespread support (Benton 1983).

Indeed, the population density in Hong Kong to a large extent reflects emigration there from Communist China and Vietnam. At the end of the Second World War there were nearly 600,000 Chinese in Hong Kong. By the end of the 1970s there was a 4 per cent growth per annum, provoking revisions to immigration policy and subsequently controversy over refugee status and the repatriation of the boat people. The rapid growth due to immigration has had a significant effect on the characteristics of the population. While 98 per cent are Chinese (by first language), only 57 per cent were born in Hong Kong, and only 23 per cent are aged under 15 (Benton 1983; Lloyds Bank 1986).

Immigrants are attracted to Hong Kong by its financial success. It is a key centre of international banking and finance, with relatively full employment, a normally buoyant economy and strength in the manufacturing sector, notably for export. Textiles and clothing account for some two-fifths of exports, and there have been recent growths in the electronics and plastics industries (Benton 1983; Ismail 1989). However, while the colony is largely self-financing, for example funding its own administrative structure, expenditure on welfare has not expanded at an equal rate (Hui 1989). Although the unemployment rate has been low – 1.5 per cent in 1988 – unionization is weak, security of employment is minimal, and social security benefits low. Educational facilities are, however, generally available and free. Primary education, free since 1971, is universal, although children commonly spend only morning or afternoon at school. Health care is good. Housing conditions, previously very poor, have necessitated rather more government intervention in recent years, with public housing and subsidized rates, new buildings on Hong Kong Island and new towns in the New Territories. A large part of such development is high-rise (Benton 1983; Ismail 1989). There is also a Social Welfare Department which provides family welfare, income maintenance and probation services (Ismail 1989). According to Starak (1988) this began in the late 1940s in response to the problems which arose in a period of increased migration from China.

While this migration is often portrayed by the British government as a move from dictatorship to freedom, Hong Kong's *laissez-faire* economic system is scarcely matched by a democratic political system. Neither is it a colonial state controlled from Britain:

> For all its lack of democracy, Hong Kong is a colony only in a technical, legal sense, and though constitutionally its government could take the form of a dictatorship, in reality it does not. Constitutionally it is under the Crown, but it acts more like a semi-autonomous city-state, free since 1974 even from the financial controls that London once exercised over it. The colonial government – dominated at the top by British

> expatriates – decides its own internal affairs largely independently of Whitehall and in consultation with local conservative elites, pressure groups and business lobbies who are in frequent contact with the decision-makers. (Benton 1983, 30–1).

In fact, it was only in the 1980s and the run-up to 1997 that Britain declared an interest in a democratic Hong Kong. Even though there have been changes, however, the voice of the population in decision-making is severely marginalized. There are, in fact, three levels of government. At the apex of the system is the governor, representative of the Queen in Hong Kong, head of administration and Commander-in-Chief of the British Forces. On the second level, and presided over by the governor, are a number of councils and committees. The most important of these are the executive council and the legislative council. The former comprises four ex-officio members and (since 1988) ten appointed members; it meets in private and addresses the governor on general policy matters. As its name implies, the legislative council is responsible for the enactment of legislation, although again the governor has to agree to any changes. The legislative council has fifty-seven members, of whom twenty-six are elected by various restricted constituencies. The third level of government comprises urban councils, the regional council and district administration. The latter, with largely advisory responsibilities, is the only group where elected members form a majority. Urban councils and the regional council, with mixtures of appointees and elected members, operate very much like local authorities in England and Wales, having responsibilities for a number of local services, including street cleaning, restaurant and shop regulations, and leisure facilities (Hong Kong Link 1985; Ismail 1989; Lloyds Bank 1986).

In many ways then, Hong Kong is a classic example of unregulated capitalism. Policy is in the hands of an elite, and legislation restricting the private market is minimal. Consequently, when the economy is healthy, internal inequality is matched by prosperity compared with much of Asia; in periods of recession, the problems of inadequate housing and income support become manifest:

> There is an extraordinary degree of inequality in Hong Kong and appalling poverty and suffering in the shanty towns and squatter areas, where well over half a million people live without running water or legal electricity. Yet when industry and commerce are flourishing and the labour market is buoyant, the ways of those who have work are far better than those of mainland workers, and in Asia are second only to wages in Japan. (Benton 1983, 19).

Nevertheless: 'Whereas Hong Kong's economy has become increasingly sophisticated . . . its political development has been lethargic' (Hong Kong Link 1985, 2).

CRIME AND THE CRIMINAL JUSTICE SYSTEM

To the visitor who has sampled both China and Hong Kong, the difference is marked (Alderson 1981a). In the latter's densely populated high-rise accommodation and commercial and tourist sectors, crime is of Western proportions but tainted with Eastern flavours of secret societies, corruption and drug trafficking. The change has been made since the British took Hong Kong in 1841, and the flotsam of the Chinese ports drifted south, allegedly to benefit from a more liberal penal system (Sinclair 1983). The history of Hong Kong indeed contains an acceptance of the high crime rate, the product of corruption, closely associated with gambling, narcotics and vice in the control of the Triads, Chinese secret societies which are the Asian Mafia. Today, emphasis is still placed on the problems caused by the Triads. Additionally, commercial crime and the narcotics industry – with supplies arriving direct from the Golden Triangle of Laos, Thailand and Burma – are stressed alongside the traffic problems in a country where many roads were built for rickshaws rather than cars (Sinclair 1983).

Official statistics for 1987 show the crime rate at about 4,100 per 100,000 population (Royal Hong Kong Police 1988). Interestingly, the homicide rate is not high: there were seventy-two cases of murder or manslaughter in that year, few using firearms, given the restrictive firearms regulations (Sinclair 1983). While shoplifting had been increasing, robberies (including those involving firearms) and burglaries had decreased. Violent crimes comprised 19 per cent of the total, burglaries 14 per cent and drug offences as much as 11 per cent. Although official statistics must be treated with caution, in many respects these figures suggest less crime than in Western capitalist society. Overall rates, for example, are well below the rate in England and Wales, and burglary figures particularly low; homicides are comparable with the UK. Data on known offenders revealed a marked increase over the decade in crimes by those aged under 16 and 41–50 with the latter having the highest crime rate, followed by those aged 51–60 (Royal Hong Kong Police 1988).

If these crime patterns are somewhat surprising, how does the criminal justice system compare? We might expect a system similar to that of England and Wales. In many respects this is so, but there are notable variations. English common law applies, as does the Justices of the Peace Act of 1361 and the Habeas Corpus Act of 1679, although, with a view towards 1997 the 1985 Hong Kong Act provides for the development of separate legislation (Ismail 1989, 41). The courts of justice include the Supreme Court (incorporating the court of appeal and high court), the district court, magistrates courts and a juvenile court. A jury system operates for the high court only, with a jury of seven to nine members. Majority verdicts are possible. Lay assessors sit in as advisors to newly appointed overseas magistrates. There are also ten 'special magistrates', local, unqualified people who deal with minor cases in the magistrates courts (Ismail 1989, 41–8).

Other features of the system have British origins: the legal aid system and criminal injuries compensation for example. Nevertheless, there are distinct differences, most apparent in the administration of non-custodial sentences. The probation service, for example, was originally part of the police force and then the prison system, but is now part of the Social Welfare Department (Lee 1973). A probation order is available for offenders of all ages, including juveniles, and volunteers are commonly deployed. Community service orders, available for all offenders (aged 14 or over), and introduced in 1987, are attached to a probation order. A pre-court assessment panel was established in 1987, to advise the courts on appropriate action regarding younger offenders, aged 14–25. This young offenders assessment panel comprises staff from the Social Welfare Department and the Correctional Services Department (Ismail 1989, 167–71).

The latter, as its name implies, is responsible for the administration of the penal system, including aftercare responsibilities (Commissioner of Correctional Services 1988; Ismail 1989, 244–9). In recent years it has been subject to considerable expansion and a widening of responsibilities with the containment of Vietnamese refugees prior to their forced repatriation. Thus by 1989 it employed some 6,700 staff responsible for 11,314 'conventional' inmates and 17,724 Vietnamese boat people. The pressures on the system caused by such refugees and other illegal immigrants has considerable implications for policing today. In contrast, in the past, immigration was considered a police problem more in terms of the undesirable characteristics of newcomers, who were allegedly responsible for the crime problems of the area.

THE EMERGENCE OF THE POLICE

Prior to the 1840s the Island of Hong Kong was subject to Chinese administration, similar to elsewhere on the mainland, save that its isolated position made it vulnerable to pirates and brigands. Magistrates had formal responsibility for upholding the law, but in practice order was maintained within the isolated villages by village elders (Crisswell and Watson 1982). This changed with British control. On the one hand, the indigenous population of 5,000 was joined by a medley of Chinese criminals, discharged sailors and soldiers, shipjumpers, and the vice industry that traditionally accompanied a military station. On the other hand, law and order was conceived as necessary to protect the European middle class, responsible for trade and administration. The police system that developed, as elsewhere in the colonies, was based on the Irish experience, with the police a paramilitary force responsible to the government in the person of a British-appointed governor. In contrast with police forces in England and Wales,

> in Hong Kong, as in other colonial territories, the police were obliged to impose an alien system of law on an indigenous population who regarded them as no more than agents of the colonial government which, of course, they were. Consequently, from the first, colonial forces adopted certain military characteristics alien to the English police system, for example they habitually carried arms and were quartered in barracks. The model for the Hong Kong force was not so much Peel's Metropolitan Police as the Irish Constabulary . . . Hong Kong's authorities initially saw the police as a para-military gendarmerie enforcing the ordinances of the colonial government, these ordinances being formed principally to protect the expatriate business community. (Crisswell and Watson 1982, 8, 149).

A close review of the texts revals the emergence of this force from 1841 (Crisswell and Watson 1982; Sinclair 1983). Additionally, though, we are reminded that colonial policing cannot necessarily be equated with military precision. The force that was shaped was haphazard, subject to considerable change, the object of criticism and controversy and neither omnipresent nor particularly effective.

The original force, which combined responsibility for the prison system and firefighting, was under the command of a former army officer. This practice of appointing the 'captain superintendent' from the military was continued until suitable candidates were available through the cadet system, introduced later as a means of ensuring the availability for senior office of gentlemen with relevant policing experience. There was, interestingly, no tradition of appointing at senior level officers from other colonial forces. However, the first chief police officers had considerable power, also operating as senior magistrates, where they had a role in deciding the guilt of defendants and appropriate sentences.

Thirty-two police officers were initially appointed, comprising eleven Europeans, including a sergeant and two corporals, and twenty-one Chinese. The latter, deployed in separate units, were largely responsible for policing the Chinese quarters, which were originally segregated from the respectable European housing areas. The emerging Chinese middle class was encouraged to operate, and pay for, an additional nightwatch system. Order was maintained by these various units, overseen by a larger number of magistrates (forty-four in number by 1843) and curfew restrictions against the Chinese community.

As Hong Kong expanded its crime problems expanded with it. Triad groups, corruption facilitated by the gambling and prostitution businesses, and piracy, added to the conventional crime problems of the day. Equally, the new police were clearly incapable of coping with the situation. Recruitment was a problem: the Chinese, with divided loyalties, were unreliable, the local Europeans equally so, comprising many discharged from the military as unfit for active duty. At various times attempts were made to improve the service, while ensuring its loyalty. Two methods that were adopted were to recruit officers from the United Kingdom, possibly on secondment, and to establish an Indian section. The former approach began in 1845 when a superintendent and two inspectors were appointed from the Metropolitan police.

The establishment of an Indian section does seem to fit a colonial model of relying on marginal ethnic groups at basic level. In the first few years some Indians were recruited from among the locals, sometimes discharged servicemen. By 1845 the force numbered 171, of whom seventy-four were European, fifty-one Chinese and forty-six Indian. By the 1860s more Indians were recruited from the colonial army. In the mid-1860s, 150 Indians, mostly Muslims, were recruited from Bombay and the British Native Infantry, and shortly afterwards a corps of fifty Sikhs arrived. The latter were identified as particularly successful, being loyal and reliable. In 1867 there were eighty-nine Europeans, 132 Chinese and 377 Indians in the force. Nevertheless, the force was scarcely a byword for efficiency. In 1867 the new governor, Sir Richard Macdonnell, who had considerable colonial experience, remarked that 'he did not remember ever seeing, in any colony, a body of men so inefficient in proportion to numbers and so corrupt generally as the Police Force which he found in Hong Kong' (Crisswell and Watson 1982, 49).

As the result of pressure from the magistrates a commission of inquiry was established in 1871. Despite the fact that there were at the time 644 police, or one per 193 residents, its report was highly critical of the way the force was administered. The next governor, Sir Arthur Kennedy, acted on the recommendations of the commissioner by splitting the police from the prison service and transferring the Indian contingent to the latter. Police were armed more routinely than in the past, and a renewed effort was made to recruit from the UK, especially from the Scottish and Metropolitan forces. Again, however, it does not appear to have been common practice to recruit men as officers from other colonial forces. At the same time, the Chinese became more integrated into the police.

Kennedy is in fact accredited with the establishment of a more efficient and disciplined force, which, while subject to periodic corruption scandals, could at least be relied on to maintain order on behalf of a European contingent that at no time numbered more than about 4,000. Such discipline was particularly necessary later, as war and strikes caused additional problems in the colony. As in Britain (Gill and Mawby 1990a) a special constabulary was sworn in as an emergency reserve during the First World War. Specials were also used during the 1911 riots, sparked off by revolution in China. The most notable public order situation, however, arose in 1922 with the seamen's strike, when new laws, an expanded police force and further reliance on specials were used to contain and eventually crush the strike.

In fact, during the strike the loyalty of Chinese officials was questioned, and in its aftermath the force was reorganised and expanded by some 15 per cent. In 1923 the Criminal Investigation Department was formed and in 1925 an auxiliary Chinese detective force, named the Labour Protection Bureau, was established temporarily to counter worker intimidation during further strikes. Also at this time, street committees, *kai ching*, were formed to provide the police with information on neighbourhood disorder.

By the 1920s, clearly, the role of the police was more explicitly defined in a public-order capacity, notably to protect the colonial government from disorders originating from the disenfranchised Chinese majority. With the growth of Communism in mainland China, a more explicitly political role for the police was added in the 1930s with the creation of the Anti-Communist Squad, forerunner of the Special Branch.

During the Second World War, Hong Kong was occupied by the Japanese. In the aftermath of the war, Britain again established control, in the face of American opposition, and, with Communist influence from China, public order continued to be a police priority. Perhaps significantly, the new police commissioner, Duncan MacIntosh, had considerable colonial policing experience in Ireland, Malaya and as acting commissioner in Singapore (Sinclair 1983). In 1949 the government initiated mass deportation of Communists and expanded numbers in the police (Benton 1983, 14). Ironically, the first major riots, in 1956, stemmed from nationalist celebrations marking the anniversary of the 1911 Chinese revolution. Tear gas was used by the police (Sinclair 1983). Police riot squads were also deployed in the 1956 Star Ferry riots and the 1967 riots in response to the Cultural Revolution in China. The importance of the police in putting down this major threat to law and order has been described as the 'finest hour' of the force, and led to the prefix Royal being attached to its title (Sinclair 1983). It also, ironically, heralded the second major feature of postwar policing in Hong Kong, the extensiveness of corruption within the force, which had indeed been endemic since the outset. Exposure of corruption among senior officers, with one, Chief Superintendent Peter Godber, alleged to have 'earned' over HK$4 million, provoked an inquiry and the setting up of an independent commission against corruption with no less than 600 investigators. The result was a loss of morale within the force, culminating in a petition signed by over half its members and an inquiry in 1977 into the force's management structure by a three-man British team (Mangold 1975; Sinclair 1983).

Behind the gloss of somewhat partisan publications, it is clear that the Hong Kong police force has faced considerable problems over its history. In one respect, it has been tainted with corruption, not surprisingly given the centrality of sex, drugs and gambling to the colony. In another respect, it has been transformed from an unprofessional force somewhat incompetently looking after British interests into a more efficient agency of social control.

THE ROYAL HONG KONG POLICE IN THE 1980s

In the late 1980s the force comprised some 27,000 officers, plus 5,800 auxiliary reserves and a similar number of civilian support staff. With one full-time officer to every 213 citizens and twenty-five officers per square km of territory, Hong Kong is clearly a heavily policed society.

The commissioner, who is responsible to the governor, is assisted by three deputy commissioners responsible for operations, the Special Branch, and management, personnel and training, and a civilian police administration officer. Headquarters houses five departments: operations (A); Special Branch (B); personnel and training (C); management and inspection services (D); and civil and administration (E) (Royal Hong Kong Police 1988). 'A' department incorporates four specialist 'wings': traffic, operations, support and crime. The operations wing deals with national security, illegal immigration and contingency planning for major disasters and incorporates the police tactical unit of approximately 1,000 officers, drawn in rotation from pools in the individual regions. Since immigration laws were tightened, the role of the police in policing the border has expanded. Currently some 785 officers are employed daily on sea and land border patrols and in 1988 an average of sixty-eight illegal immigrants were arrested daily (Ismail 1989, 234). At the time of writing they work in conjunction with the military, but in the build-up to 1997 are scheduled to take over total responsibility for border policing in late 1990.

The support wing deals with licencing regulations, and provides central administration for the auxiliary police. It also specializes in community relations and public-relations work with the media, combined in a police public relations branch. Finally, the crime wing, formed in the early 1980s, includes ballistics, a commercial crime bureau, the narcotics bureau and an organized and serious crime bureau.

Day-to-day policing is also the responsibility of 'A' department, but is delegated to four regional commands, which are largely autonomous in operational matters. One of the four, the marine region, established in the nineteenth century, is one of the largest of its kind in the world with sixty-four heavy launches and eighty-three smaller craft (Ismail 1989). The three land regions are further divided into twenty districts, one of which covers the underground system and another the airport. Specialization also occurs at regional level; for example, each region has its own traffic and detective units. Regions are further subdivided, with police stations, reporting centres and neighbourhood police offices providing more community-based centres for police patrols. As Sinclair (1983) describes in some detail, the nature of policing at local level varies considerably between areas: for example between the commercial and red-light districts, areas of high-rise accommodation, and more rural borderlands. The village penetration unit in Tap Mun, for example, on patrol for days on end, includes within its responsibilities the eradication of dangerous wild boars as well as the search for illegal immigrants.

The Special Branch, riot-control duties, and border policing represent the three major facets of public-order policing. Clearly the policing of illegal immigrants is of increasing importance, and in addition to border patrols involves spot checks on citizens, who are all required to carry identification cards. In fact in 1987, 22,425 illegal immigrants were arrested entering Hong Kong and 4,298 arrested later of whom about one-third were detected after being arrested for a routine crime (Royal Hong Kong Police 1988, 10). Add to these some 11,000 from Vietnam and the importance of this part of police work is starkly evident.

What, then, of other features of everyday police work? As already noted, the police were originally responsible for prison administration and the fire service. They were also traditionally called out to help with public-health emergencies (Crisswell and Watson 1982). However, while the police force is now by far the largest sector of colonial administration, its current role in these wider services appears minimal. The exception, perhaps, is its responsibility for checking and registering societies requiring licences under the Societies Ordinance, and, notably, the registration of private watchmen, of whom less than 2 per cent are licenced to carry firearms (Royal Hong Kong Police 1987, 12).

Information on recruitment is less readily available. The force is now predominantly Chinese, although Europeans comprise a larger proportion of senior ranks. Notably, though, European recruits to the junior ranks tended in the past to be of lower class and poor calibre (Crisswell and Watson 1982), and the dual-entry system of recruitment is likely to sustain this. Currently some 16 per cent of new recruits join at the inspector grade. In 1987, 16 per cent of new constables but only 6 per cent of new inspectors were female (Royal Hong Kong Police 1988, 17).

Despite this, women have played a significant role in the force since 1949 (Calderwood 1974), a situation largely provoked by the need for specialists to work with women and children, the latter especially drawn from refugees. However, women took part in crowd-control tactical training as early as 1971, currently work in the police tactical unit, and are integrated into most aspects of police work (Calderwood 1974; Mishkin 1976; Sinclair 1983).

POLICE AND PUBLIC

The expanding place for women and Chinese in the police reflects moves since the 1970s to shift the basis of legitimacy of the police from a colonial to a consensus or community model. This reflects Jeffries' (1952) original thesis, as developed in the Hong Kong context by Tsui (1979). The extent to which the role of the police has changed is to some degree dependent upon the role of the public in the policing process. At least three aspects of this have been identified in the literature: the 'Junior Police Call' initiative, the role of the public in neighbourhood-watch-type activities, and the importance of the police auxiliary.

Junior Police Call (JPC), launched as a five-minute television programme in 1974, is frequently cited by outside commentators (Alderson 1981a; Pope and Hui 1984) and official sources (Ismail 1989, 235; Royal Hong Kong Police 1988) as the major success *vis-à-vis* police/public relations. A club for those aged between 9 and 17 was formed which aimed to improve police relations with juveniles and involve the latter in helping to clear crimes. By early 1975 it had attracted 93,000 members. Television and radio coverage was increased and a JPC council established in each district, and in 1976 a 'leaders club' was added for those aged 18–23. Satellite clubs were introduced to schools in 1979 and by 1983 there were 284 school clubs. Currently JPC attracts some 3,000 applicants per month.

The origins of neighbourhood watch are, perhaps ironically, to be found within the colonial model, where the Chinese were encouraged to become involved in policing their own communities. It also seems likely – although the texts do not state as much – that the influence of the Japanese during occupation provided a model for community policing as it did elsewhere in the Far East (Austin 1987; Ismail 1987). Certainly it pre-dates similar initiatives in Britain (Alderson 1981a).

Linked in to the neighbourhood policing units and particularly common in high-rise flats, mutual-aid committees form their own patrol groups engaged in internal security and crime-prevention initiatives (May 1981). By 1989 there were 2,818 groups involving 29,056 households (Ismail 1989).

The special constabulary also had its origins in the nineteenth century. Established as a police reserve during the public-order turmoil of the 1850s (Sinclair 1983), it also featured significantly during the seamen's strike of 1922 and the two world wars. In the postwar period it was re-established as an emergency support unit. Then in 1973 it was reformed during the 'Fight Violent Crime Campaign', since when specials have worked alongside regular officers and performed similar duties (Gill and Mawby 1990a). Currently the reserve has some 5,700 members.

The reserve has a strong community orientation. Its policy is that auxiliaries should patrol in the areas where they live or work, and recruitment is oriented towards community representation in the reserve. However, in many respects the special constabulary differs from the current British model and is more closely allied to a colonial system. This is reflected in the range of duties carried out by auxiliaries, including stop-and-search anti-crime sweeps, stop-checks directed at illegal immigrants, and specialist units. It is also evident in laws which require employers to release auxiliaries for duty when necessary. However, most notable is the fact that auxiliaries are paid; indeed their hourly or daily rate of pay is equivalent to that of a regular officer of the same rank and in 1987–8 the cost of deploying the reserve reached HK$81 million.

While JPC, neighbourhood watch and the reserve are illustrations of community involvement in the policing process, there are others that might be added. For example, a school liaison officer scheme was introduced in 1989, and community policing has received considerable emphasis in recent years. While such initiatives may be seen as means by which the nature of police/community relationships are changed, however, in some respects they are quite compatible with an intrusive policing system, a point made graphically by Austin (1987) in his analysis of current policing patterns in Singapore.

The ultimate test is whether or not moves towards community policing have incorporated any role for the community in the way in which policing is carried out. In fact, control of the police, police accountability and the investigation of complaints against the police can all be understood in terms of the wider forms of colonial administration. The police force, as the largest client in the public service, is directly accountable to the governor via the civil service branch of the government secretariat. With regard to penal policy, the governor is advised by a fight crime committee, chaired by the chief secretary, which incorporates nineteen district committees (Ismail 1989). As a result of the 1973 commission of inquiry into corruption an independent commission against corruption was established, under a civilian commissioner, which reports directly to the governor. Other complaints against the police are dealt with by an internal complaints and internal investigations branch, which is responsible to a police complaints committee comprising members of the executive and legislative councils and magistrates (all of whom are nominated by the governor) and the Attorney General (Over 1982; Royal Hong Kong Police 1988). There is also an internal inspection services wing responsible for reviewing all sections of the force except the Special Branch.

The overall picture is thus one of police accountability on one of three levels: internally; externally to a committee appointed by and responsible to the governor; and externally to the governor directly. This is not surprising, and parallels the Hong Kong administrative system as a whole whereby government is in the hands of a nominated (rather than elected), fairly small group of influential businessmen and public figures. The lack of public accountability of the public service is, however, compounded by the lack of any true democratic process whereby the views of the majority of citizens have any significant impact on policy. The result is a system of policing which is clearly identified with the needs of the colonial administration, whether or not these are benign. In such a context, there is clearly the danger, as in Singapore, that police involvement within the community becomes an alternative means to achieving the same ends, rather than a radically different form of policing. More explicitly than in Western capitalist societies, the community becomes an extension of the police rather than a control over policing.

SUMMARY

To appreciate the role of the police in Hong Kong requires an understanding of its colonial past and its colonial present. Hong Kong was developed by the British as a strategic harbour, with a colonial administration bent on maintaining law and order principally in the interests of the European community. The police force that emerged reflected this, being an armed force with its senior officers drawn from the UK, and a militaristic structure, dual entry, and a chain of command centralized through the colonial administration and ultimately answerable to the British government. This is not to say, however, that the model is an exact replica of that suggested by Jeffries (1952) and Tobias (1977). For example, the force lacked military precision and efficiency, was fundamentally corrupt, and does not appear to have explicitly recruited its senior staff from other colonial forces.

Moreover the move towards a democratic force has been somewhat erratic. While there is clear evidence in the postwar period of community-based policing initiatives, political conflicts and threats posed by Communist China, priority accorded to controlling illegal immigration, and the continued problems of vice, drugs and organized crime, have each contributed to the continuance of a repressive police system. The balance between different policing priorities is well illustrated by Tsui (1979, 33, 36), quoting from the annual reports of two commissioners of police. In 1956–7, A. C. Maxwell noted that the force was 'designed to function as an efficient civil force in a sophisticated, cosmopolitan environment, as a sympathetic village constabulary and also as a highly disciplined gendarmerie, trained on para-military lines, should occasion arise'. Six years later, H. W. E. Heath acknowledged that, contrary to the Metropolitan model, in Hong Kong 'the policeman may frequently appear to individual members of the public as someone far removed from being their "servant or guardian" '.

Hong Kong's system of *laissez-faire* capitalism, with its marked inequalities, co-exists alongside a political system which allows the public little say in the operation of government. Thus, as an agency of the government, directly accountable to the governor, the police force is the principal agency charged with the task of maintaining the current political and economic system. In this context, moves towards greater community involvement may be interpreted, as in Singapore (Austin 1987), as mechanisms for extending control *of* the community, rather than as opening up the police, or indeed the government, to public accountability. While there is no inevitable link between democratic government and democratic police, in Hong Kong it seems unlikely that the police system can be changed significantly without fundamental changes in the political system, changes ruled unlikely in the run-up to 1997.

7

Japan: Gemeinschaft *Capitalism*

INTRODUCTION

Japan is the second Asian country to be considered here. Unlike Hong Kong, however, its policing policy has been the subject of numerous studies, not only by Japanese academics but also by outside commentators. Some of the latter, like John Alderson (1981a), are police practitioners attracted by Japanese policing practices which epitomize close ties between police and community. Not surprisingly, this theme has also featured centrally in academic analysis. In other respects, though, the work of outside academics, most commonly from the United States, invites some interesting contrasts. In perhaps the best known text, Bayley (1976) analyses Japanese policing systems through the eyes of a criminologist, drawing direct comparisons with the United States. Parker's (1984) text is on similar lines. Clifford (1976) also describes Japan through Western eyes, but because Clifford is concerned with the criminal justice system as a whole the reader is more able to make sense of police policies and practices in a wider context. In contrast to both, Ames (1981), a Japanese-speaking anthropologist, spent three years on field work with the police in a number of different areas of the country, and is thus able to provide a picture which, while lacking much comparative insight *vis-à-vis* policing elsewhere, both allows police work to be put in a societal context and more successfully teases out the distinction between the reality of police behaviour (*honne*) and the myth which describes how ideally the police should behave (*tatamae*).

While an outside observer who has only visited Japan briefly can scarcely expect to have surmounted such a methodological obstacle, the following sections attempt to draw from the lessons of these writers by considering policing in Japan within a brief review of Japanese society.

JAPANESE SOCIETY

Japan is widely recognized as the most successful and most completely industrialized nation in Asia. Its population of some 120 million is approximately twice that of the United Kingdom and half that of the United States (Ayrton 1983). As in the United States, about three-quarters of the population live in urban areas (rather less than in the UK). However, its urban characteristics are well illustrated in the population density, some 312 people per square km (Ruel 1983). Moreover, about two-thirds of the population live on Honshu Island, where the density level averages an incredible 2375 per square km (Rose 1985).

Until the latter half of the nineteenth century Japan was largely insulated from outside influences. From the twelfth century it was ruled by the *shogunate* system, the power of the emperor declining particularly during the Tokugawa *shogunate* of 1603–1867, immortalized in James Clavell's *Shogun*. During this period, a feudal bureaucracy emerged, headed by samurai warriors, a system described by Fulcher (1988, 231) as a 'successful feudal monarchy', a bureaucracy without a centralized administrative structure. Trade with the outside world, which expanded following moves by the Americans in 1853, accelerated under the Meiji dynasty of 1868–1912. During this period, Japan looked to Western Europe and North America for ideas and pursued military expansionist policies in an attempt to build a modern industrial state capable of competing with the West (Fulcher 1988). The policy ultimately led to Japanese intervention in the Second World War, defeat, and postwar reconstruction under the influence of General McArthur, Supreme Commander of the Allied Powers in the Far East.

The postwar period in fact saw a further diminution in the power of the emperor, with power vested in two houses of parliament. The Liberal Democratic Party has enjoyed a majority throughout most of the period although, as Fulcher (1988) argues, the relative weakness of the party structure and the influence of the civil service since the Meiji period has resulted in a continual power struggle between competing bureaucratic elites within the Liberal Democratic Party well illustrated in the period prior to and following the 1990 elections.

The close relationship between the government departments and vast business empires, *zaibatsu*, has been a feature of Japanese industrial progress (Fulcher 1988; Pinker 1986). As Lee (1987, 245) notes: 'The Japanese never relied upon the invisible hand of market forces. Instead they depended upon the very visible hand of the central authoritarian government.' To a large extent, employers are an important part of the paternalist authoritarian state, with loyalty to one's occupational group underpinning a variety of other social relationships (Dore 1973; Nakane 1981).

Japan's postwar 'industrial miracle' owes much to the relationship between individual, company and government, although it was initiated by American policy, concerned to stem the advance of communism in Asia, and the demand generated by the Korean war (Fulcher 1988). As a result, the late 1970s and 1980s saw Japan with an enviable balance of payments, a healthy annual growth rate, low inflation and low unemployment (Ruel 1983). By August 1989 the Economic Planning Agency in Tokyo proudly announced that, in terms of natural assets, Japan had become the richest nation in the world. Taxation levels are also low.

Partly as a result of this low taxation, Japan's performance on a series of welfare indicators is mixed (Lee 1987; Maruo 1982; Pinker 1986; Rose 1985; Takahashi and Someya 1985). On the one hand, Japan has one of the lowest rates of infant mortality in the world, and the longest life expectancy (74 for males, 80 for females). The values placed on education are also indicated in the high proportion of the population participating in higher education. On the other hand, Japan rates poorly on other health indicators – deaths among pregnant women and mortality caused by tuberculosis for example – and on many aspects of quality of the environment, including housing conditions and urban green-area amenities.

Public expenditure on welfare – initiated during the Meiji period – is extremely low, even allowing for low levels of unemployment and a relatively young population, and tends to operate as a safety net rather than a universal system of provision. Instead, more is expected of the family and immediate local community – including, more recently, formally structured consumer co-operatives (Crump, 1987) – and especially the occupational and private sectors.

Occupational welfare is comprehensive, applying to employees and their families. It may include the provision of company housing, supplementary family allowances, health care and sickness benefits (Lee 1987; Pinker 1986). The voluntary sector is also considerable, incorporating both voluntary organizations, many of which are financed by central government, and the principle of volunteering, which Pinker (1986) estimates at twice the United Kingdom level. The principle of voluntary-sector involvement has a long history, with public-welfare services in the early twentiety century being administered by volunteer officers, *hohmen-iin*, succeeded by the *minsei-inn* system in the postwar period (Takahashi and Someya 1985) which Pinker (1986) equates with the Charity Organisation Society of Victorian Britain.

The extent to which the individual is enmeshed within a series of relationships – with kin, local community, employer and ultimately the state, is the key to an understanding of social order and social control in contemporary Japan. Within the economic sector, worker mobility is minimal and loyalty to the company near-absolute (Nakane 1981). Within the public sector, central government was originally structured to incorporate a network of local neighbourhood groups.

In feudal times groups of five families, *gonin-kumi*, acted as the lowest administrative tier, providing mutual help and law and order. These groups were abolished under the Meiji dynasty but reincarnated as neighbourhood teams of ten families, *tonari-kumi*, during the Second World War (Clifford 1976). Above these, and maintained during the Meiji restoration, were larger neighbourhood groups known as *buraku kai* in the villages and *chonaikai* in urban areas, which provided a link between the individual and central administration. Because of the role of such groups in promoting the war effort the formal links were severed under postwar American influence, but the village residents' associations and city neighbourhood associations have continued as local community focal points, providing meeting halls and a forum for recreational and cultural activities. Under the umbrella of individual associations a number of specialist groups thrive – women's associations, children's groups, clubs for the elderly, a sanitation subsection, a fire protection division, and crime prevention associations. On a more localized level, groups of some 20–30 households, *hans*, have responsibilities for public services such as drain clearing and rubbish collection (Ames 1979; 1981; Bayley 1976; Clifford 1976). The significance of such community bands is stressed by one outside commentator:

> however similar the associations and councils may appear to their western counterparts, they usually have immeasurably greater influence. Counselling or guiding a person is not helping him with his personal problems only, it is bringing to bear a great force of family, neighbourhood, and sometimes employer opinion that is not to be ignored easily by anyone, young or old, who expects to go on living within the local society . . . they represent a power of public guidance and sanction far beyond anything implied by its name, which was probably borrowed from the west. The substance of public participation in Japan is far more than its form. (Clifford 1976, 99).

In this sense, Japan is an urban society without the culture associated in the West with such developments. According to Maruo (1982), while European countries moved gradually from semi-feudalistic societies characterized by *Gemeinschaft* and a lack of democracy to *gesellschaft*-type democracies, Japan has developed quickly to a democratic society without shedding its *Gemeinschaft* qualities. It is a society founded upon acceptance of inequality, and submission, dependence and loyalty to those in authority. Confucian emphasis on loyalty to the group and lack of emphasis upon individuals and their rights is used by Nakane (1981) to illustrate employees' loyalty to their firm. The low priority given to the individual, and the extent of dependency, is well illustrated by Clifford (1976, 165):

> the Japanese is born in debt. From birth he owes something to his family, his teachers, his classmates, his friends and associates, his superiors, his local society, and ultimately his emperor (although modern developments would appear to have greatly diluted this last obligation). He grows up in a context of duty more than right, and he continues, even in modern urban conditions, to be motivated far more by the expectations of others than by his own expectations of others.

It would be surprising indeed if these conditions were not influential in affecting the level of crime or, indeed, the form which penal policy has taken.

CRIME AND THE CRIMINAL JUSTICE SYSTEM

On one matter, at least, Western observers are agreed: Japan has a low crime rate compared with the rest of the industrialized world (Ames 1981; Clifford 1976; Kalish 1988). Of course, official statistics are open to criticism, but such conclusions are supported by the casual observer: inner-city streets appear remarkably crime free and the more visible signs of crime, such as vandalism, are a rarity.

Official statistics in fact suggest that while juvenile crime has fluctuated in the postwar era, with a rise in the late 1970s, adult crime has fallen steadily in the same period (Ames 1981; Fenwick 1983; Kazuhiko 1981). There is some indication of a rising rate in the 1980s (Nakayama 1987; National Police Agency 1984). Additionally some deviant groups do stand out: 'automobile gangs', radical students, and crime-prone indigenous and immigrant minority groups like the burakumin and Koreans are cited (Ames 1981). Equally, homicide rates, while fairly low (Bayley 1976; Kalish 1988), evidence high levels of infanticide (Clifford 1976; Lunden 1976; Research Committee on Female Crime 1986). Organized crime has posed a rather different (if persistent) problem (Clifford 1976; Ames 1981) and certain aspects of Japanese culture increase the likelihood of some types of fraud (Matsumoto 1986).

These examples notwithstanding, crime is not as evident, or indeed perceived to be as problematic, as in most Western societies, and there are consequent implications for the operation of the criminal justice system in general and policing in particular.

If we turn to consider the criminal justice system, outside influences are immediately apparent. The Meiji period of government saw the most significant move towards a formalized system, with the first comprehensive criminal code drafted in 1870 by a French advisor to the government, and the Ministry of Justice created in 1871. Following the French model, a Roman-law system was adopted and a public prosecutor introduced (Nakayama 1987; Westney 1982). Judicial independence was established in 1889, by which time German influence was most notable. More recently, postwar reconstruction has been significantly influenced by American and British ideas (Clifford 1976).

The system is, however, distinctly Japanese in at least three respects. First, and despite the availability of the death penalty, the judiciary is notably lenient with regard to sentencing, with fines being the most common sentence. Indeed, it appears that judges hold more lenient views on sentencing than does the general public, whose influence is muted (Ishimura 1985; Rutherford 1984). Interestingly, as in the Netherlands, with a similar reputation, the jury system does not exist, having been suspended after a brief period of operation from 1928 to 1943 (Clifford 1976). Moreover, a considerable degree of discretion to avoid prosecution has been built into the system since 1885. Japanese law allows prosecution to be withdrawn at a relatively late stage, and prosecutors are encouraged to see formal court action as the last rather than the first resort. Dando (1970), for example, reported that prosecution of 25 per cent of those aged 20–25 and 65 per cent of those aged 71 or more was suspended. Second, and related to this, is the prioritization of mediation rather than prosecution, a policy pre-dating the Meiji period, when duties and obligations underpinned the philosophy of justice, and rights were unheard of (indeed, the term 'rights' had no equivalent in the Japanese language) (Ishimura 1985). Third, and somewhat differently, the criminal justice system is characterized by considerable private- and voluntary-sector involvement, the latter including women's associations for rehabilitation aid and voluntary guidance hostels for juvenile delinquents (Clifford 1976).

These features are well illustrated if we consider various aspects of the penal system. Imprisonment, for example, has been used sparingly by the courts, although for those sentenced to imprisonment sentences tend to be relatively long. Nevertheless, in the postwar period the use of imprisonment declined, and indeed fell more quickly than the crime rate (Rutherford 1984). For those in prison, regimes operate according to a philosophy of 'benevolent authoritarianism' (Clifford 1976, 93). Classification and staged progression are accorded priority, with belief in rehabilitation – characterized for example in the 1960s in the *naikan* method of treatment through meditation (Clifford 1976) – still evident. Many prisons also operate as factories, indeed many are profitmaking, and in the postwar period voluntary prison visitors have featured as a significant aspect of the rehabilitation process (Clifford 1976).

The probation service emerged in the early part of the century with responsibility for operating halfway houses for discharged prisoners. Probation in an Anglo-American sense is a postwar innovation, though even now it is used primarily in conjunction with a suspended prison sentence rather than as a sentence in its own right (Clifford 1976; Ishimura 1985; Rutherford 1984). Moreover, most client contact is undertaken by volunteers, known as *hogoshi*, who tend to be elderly, middle-class males, whose relationship with their client is a uniquely Japanese one characterized by duty and obligation framed within paternalistic authoritarianism (Gill and Mawby 1990b; Hess 1970).

Probation work is primarily concerned with juveniles, defined in Japan as those aged under 20, who come under the jurisdiction of the family court. Again, the discretion to keep juveniles out of court is important, with the police involved at this stage (Clifford 1976). The use of volunteers is also particularly important, not just within the probation service but in a much wider sense. Thus in 1962 over 150,000 volunteers were commissioned to take part in 'street guidance' activities with juveniles. Ames (1981) describes these volunteers in the Kurashiki district as tending to be predominantly male and middle-class, with an average age of 49.

With regard to the deployment of volunteers, clearly the criminal justice system reflects some of the key features of Japanese society described in the first section. Equally, in turning to consider the police in modern Japan, it is evident that policing shares many of the features already described.

THE HISTORY OF THE POLICE IN JAPAN

Details of some form of policing, as part of social control in feudal Japan, are available from the end of the twelfth century, with primary responsibility for the handling of crime falling to the provincial military governors, the *shugo*. However, it was during the Edo period (1600–1867) that a more elaborate policing system was constructed (Ames 1981; Clifford 1976). This was codified in a uniform set of criminal laws, the *Kujigata Osadamegaki* in 1742.

Below the *shogun* were the feudal lords, or *daimyo*, with overall responsibility for maintaining order through either civil or criminal law or, preferably, informal mediation arrangements. Below the *daimyo*, samurai magistrates served as judges, prosecutors and police chiefs, aided by various other levels of police officer, mostly lower status samurai. The lowest level of police, the detectives – *meakashi* or *okappiki* – armed only with a metal truncheon, were often outlaws who had been spared by their lords and thus bound in loyalty to the interests of their superiors. This official structure was then supplemented on a neighbourhood level by the *gonin gumi*, or five-family associations, whereby citizens assisted and were held responsible for their neighbours. In the urban areas and at the intersections of major roads watch points were established which were staffed either by hired guards or local residents.

This system survived until the Meiji period (1868–1912) when Japan looked to western Europe for ideas on how to develop its public and social services. Influential at the time were Li Pen Chu Yun, the Japanese ambassador to France, Fu Tse i Chi, who was appointed in 1869 to evaluate European policing systems, and Kawaji Toshiyoshi, who was sent to Europe in 1872 to gather first-hand experience. During the 1880s the government also employed a number of expert advisors from both France and Prussia. A police system on European lines was consequently introduced first to Tokyo and then throughout the country (Ames 1981; Clifford 1976; McKenzie 1984; Westney 1982).

Under an Act of 1875 the new police system was centralized under the Ministry of Justice. In common with its precursors in continental Europe, policing was organized on a national basis and responsibilities covered a wide range of non-crime-related affairs. For example, the police were responsible for the supervision of hospitals, the enforcement of public health regulations, factory inspection, and the supervision of the labour force (Ames 1981; Westney 1982; Winant 1972).

However, while the system was centrally controlled, it contained a strong local element. All police jurisdictions were divided into areas. Within rural areas police residences, *chuzaisho*, were built; in the cities, where this was impractical, small neighbourhood offices, *koban*, were established. *Chuzaisho* were also often established next to large factories. Companies paid for the building of the police houses and paid the officers' salary. The policemen became, in effect, company guards whose job involved protecting company housing and other buildings as well as helping to thwart labour disputes. Interestingly, this system resembles in many respects that of the 'additional constables' of nineteenth-century England described by Steedman (1984). By 1912 there were 13,353 *chuzaisho*, including these privately-funded ones, and 2,473 *koban* (Ames 1981, 23).

The integration of centralized control and local policy continued until the 1940s, and indeed was reinforced in the 1920s and 1930s as Japan sought national approval for its expansionist policies. Thus the 'special higher police' were established in 1928 to regulate publications, cinemas, political campaigns and other group activities, reporting directly to central police headquarters. With the outbreak of war with China in 1937 the police were given additional responsibilities for regulating business activities for the war effort, mobilizing labour and controlling transportation. The various neighbourhood groups, including the *gonin gumi*, were also activated (Ames 1981; Winant 1972).

The political role played by the police, including that of the secret police, became the impetus behind policies pursued by the United States, through General McArthur, in his postwar reconstruction of the police system. Essentially McArthur attempted to establish localized policing, modelled on the American system, and to abolish the centralized system which had been constructed on European lines (Ames 1981; McKenzie 1984; Winant 1972).

Lewis J. Valentine, former police commissioner of New York City, and Oscar G. Olander, commissioner of the Michigan State Police, were brought in as advisors. Partly as a result of their investigations, the political, economic and general administrative roles of the police were curtailed under a new law of 1947. The police system was decentralized and 1600 independent municipal forces were established in all towns with more than 5000 people. A national rural police force, organized at a prefectural level, was responsible for the remaining rural areas. Local police accountability was introduced through locally based public safety commissions.

The system was not a success. It was criticized as financially wasteful, inefficient, and open to corruption. Perhaps most tellingly, from a comparative perspective, it failed because it was not compatible with the socio-political structure of the society:

> The new system was based on an ideological concept of democracy drawn from one culture and forced upon another. It followed an extreme policy of decentralisation of authority which was not in accordance with the natural traditions of Japan and did not suit the natural psychology or culture. (McKenzie 1984, 2418).

Revisions in 1951 and 1952 allowed for smaller districts to opt for central control and introduced a degree of central funding, and a new police law was passed in 1954 following the withdrawal of the United States in 1952. This forms the basis for the current policing system.

THE POLICE TODAY

In fact, the 1954 law, while widening the role of the police and strengthening central control, maintained a degree of balance between prewar and American models, as is well illustrated if we consider the organization of policing and the operation of day-to-day police work.

The system is centralized through the National Police Agency, which has overall responsibility for training, equipment, statistics and operations involving inter-area co-operation. Some 10 per cent of the police budget is funded centrally. It has a national headquarters and seven regional bureaux (Ames 1981).

At prefecture level, each of the forty-seven prefectures has its own headquarters, responsible for area policing policies, although the most senior in the prefectural police are appointed and paid by the National Police Agency. Prefectures are then divided into districts, each with its own police station, which may vary in size from a staff of sixteen to 500 in districts of Tokyo and Kita-Kyushu. Large cities have several stations. Police stations come under the sole jurisdiction of the prefectural headquarters and are unconnected to local government. The area covered by a station is then divided further. Within urban areas *koban* serve as the base for a group of officers with a sergeant in charge; rural areas are covered by residential offices, the *chuzaisho* (Ames 1981; Bayley 1976). In all there are some 200,000 police officers in Japan, or one to approximately 580 people.

The work of the police at the local level has been the main focus of research by outside commentators. Ames (1981, 17–22), for example, details the work of individual officers based in *chuzaisho*. Here officers are relatively isolated from the main station, to which they may report no more than weekly. Consequently, they are more dependent upon their wives for back-up support, and the local community for co-operation, points raised in the British context by Cain (1973). Ames (1981) also describes the role of the local officer, the *chuzai san*, as embodying status and power, symbolizing the authority of the state at this local level, and argues that officers are regularly transferred to prevent their becoming too close to – and under the influence of – local residents. The essence of rural police work is well described by Ames (1981, 27):

> The important point is that the *chuzai san* relies on his personal knowledge of the people in his jurisdiction in performing his police work, and not on formal police records. His effectiveness in investigating crimes and other problems when they occur in the tightly knit hamlets stems from his knowledge of all the local residents. The extensive personal knowledge and the ability to elicit information from key village informants when necessary is the essence of the closeness to the community that is considered an ideal by the police. It is an instrumental relationship and does not necessarily imply universal affection by the villages for the resident police officer.

Nevertheless, he continues by describing the wide range of personal and local issues brought to the local officer:

> Because he is available, all sorts of problems are brought to him. One *chuzai san* referred to himself as a *yaoya* ('jack of all trades'). People sometimes come to the *chuzai san* to discuss personal problems, such as plans for a job, schooling or marriage, or to seek his counsel about marital splits or parent–child quarrels. (Ames 1981, 27).

But what of urban policing patterns? Ideally the *koban* is the urban equivalent. It acts as office for a number of officers, assigned there on a shift system. Shift arrangements also require that some officers sleep in the *koban*. In consequence: 'A *koban* is not simply a place of work; it is a home where officers eat, sleep, and relax' (Bayley 1976, 25).

Police work centred on the *koban* is described in detail by Ames (1981, 34–55) and Bayley (1976, 13–32). Essentially the *koban* provides a base from which the police patrol and to which community groups and individual residents can relate. As in the countryside, officers are encouraged to maintain close contacts with the community. As well as routine patrol work, *koban* officers are required to carry out surveys of all homes within their jurisdiction on a twice-yearly basis and collect information on all local citizens. This and other data is kept in the *koban*. These extensive local records include lists of locals who work late at night, people owning guns or swords, the mentally ill, elderly people who require periodic visiting, neighbourhood organizations, local criminals, bars and restaurants etc. They provide details which enable the police, especially newcomers, to operate more efficiently in the area, and records for members of the public who see the *koban* as the place to go for local information. Citizens may call at the *koban* for advice on addresses, local hotels etc., or to maintain closer links with the police. Local shopkeepers, former police officers, the elderly, or those with specific problems will see the *koban* as a local resource: 'The *koban*, like the elementary school, thus becomes a hub of traditional village solidarity and identity in a modern urban context' (Ames 1981, 37).

Not surprisingly, then, the police are involved within the *koban* in providing help and assistance in a host of non-criminal matters (National Police Agency 1984). One of these, following tradition, is an emphasis on mediation and counselling: indeed, within the station and prefecture specialist staff are assigned to counselling duties (Bayley 1976; National Police Agency 1984). Clifford (1976, 80), in describing police involvement with a variety of citizens' and neighbourhood problems, including debt, pollution, housing, divorce, poverty and employment, concludes:

> The Japanese police are service-oriented. They spend much time and energy providing assistance and services to the general public. They are constantly supplying geographical information to people lost or trying to find particular premises; and they search for young runaways and provide a regular counselling and guidance service at the police stations and by telephone. People are encouraged to bring any problems at all to the police. Everyone knows to 'dial 110' if he has a problem, and every police station has a counselling section, some especially for juveniles.

Bayley (1976, 18) describes *koban* officers as 'the front line of police response'. They are nicknamed *omawari san*, 'Mr Walkabout', and according to Bayley a considerable amount of time out on patrol is spent questioning the public, using street knowledge and interviewing skills to uncover deviant behaviour. In such a context the amount of discretion invested in the individual officer is considerable. Similarly, following tradition, the police as well as the prosecution system extensively use this power to 'no crime' minor incidents or take informal action *vis-à-vis* juvenile offenders (Bayley 1976; Clifford 1976).

Emphasis upon the police at *koban* level should not, however, serve to ignore other aspects of police operations. Thus Bayley (1976), decribing policing in the early 1970s, noted that the role of the foot patrol was declining as cars became more significant in police work; this was part of a tendency towards centralization of personnel, with *koban* and especially *chuzaisho* being closed down. Equally, in line with Western experiences, work in the *koban* or *chuzaisho* is less popular with officers than that in crime prevention or criminal investigation (Ames 1981, 191).

This raises the issue of how far certain aspects of policing are administered at a more central level. Centralization is certainly a feature of the security branch, with its section at station level linked directly with prefectural and regional headquarters, displaying a militaristic influence (Ames 1981, 142–8). The riot police, *kidotai*, although comprised of regular officers specially trained and seconded for two or three years, are also deployed more centrally, at regional or prefectural level. Modelled on the Japanese army, officers are trained in kendo and judo but carry no individual weapons. However, with riot shields, water cannon, tear gas and military vehicles, the *kidotai* present an image of Japanese policing far removed from that of the *chuzai san* (Thornton 1972).

Interestingly, other specialist agencies like the detective branch are located at station rather than *koban* level and, although detectives do use *koban*, arrests and charges take place at the station (Bayley 1976). Detectives, *keiji*, are of course intimately connected to neighbourhood bases through public co-operation and *kikikome*, 'tips from local residents about what they saw or heard before, during or after the occurrence' (Ames 1981, 65). The extent to which detectives build up contacts with informants, however, while in many respects familiar to a Western audience, has less of a sordid feel to it and is instead well endowed with typically Japanese rituals surrounding obligation and dependence. This to some extent explains the fact that while on the surface interrogation methods used by detectives parallel those from the West, the success rate – in terms of signed confessions – is considerably higher (Ames 1981, 130–8).

What then of the police themselves? Traditionally the police were drawn from among lower-status, rural samurai, and in some senses this tradition has been maintained. Thus they appear to be upwardly mobile in social-class terms, better educated than the general population but not drawn from college graduates, and predominently rural. Politically they are conservative, and only a small percentage are women (Ames 1981; Bayley 1976). There is thus little to suggest that the police are more representative of the overall population than in Western society. This raises the question of the relationship between police and public.

POLICE AND PUBLIC

How far, then, is Japan a community-policing ideal?

> the present police establishment in Japan is an imperfectly blended amalgam of the authoritarian, powerful, and highly centralized prewar police system and the 'democratic' and decentralized postwar system. The prewar system was based on a continental German and French model of a national police force on a level above the people, and the postwar system was patterned after an American or British model of small-scale police forces on the same level with the people. The former is closer to the *honne* (reality) of the police system, and the latter is ultimately a mere *tatemae* (facade). (Ames 1981, 215).

Nevertheless, with a comparatively low level of police personnel, Japan relies on public co-operation, and there is a counter-argument, most cogently expressed by Bayley (1976), that the *koban* epitomizes the *honne*:

> A *koban* is an active force in community life; it is not simply a passive source of police assistance. In the United States the justification for contact between police and citizens, apart from criminal activity, is overwhelming need, and initiative belongs to the citizen. An American policeman is like a fireman, he responds when he must. A Japanese policeman is more like a postman, he has a daily round of low-key activities that relate him to the lives of the people among whom he works. (Bayley 1976, 91).

As in the United States, Japanese police are armed; equally there has been a move towards greater use of vehicles and closure of some neighbourhood substations. However, there are a number of points to support Bayley's contrast of police styles. For example, a 1972 opinion poll, cited by Bayley (1976, 157), revealed that 41 per cent of respondents felt that they would recognize their local police officers, 86 per cent said they knew where their local *koban* was located, and overall attitudes towards the police were positive. A follow-up survey in 1979 revealed little change (Parker 1984, 182). This to some extent reflects the importance placed by the police organization on community relations, with specialist committees operating within both the prefecture and the *koban* (Ames 1981). However, the most notable evidence concerns the involvement of the public in helping the police maintain law and order.

There are two aspects to this. One, which has been discussed in some detail elsewhere (Gill and Mawby 1990a), is the part played by formal volunteers in the policing process. As already noted, voluntary work is very common in Japan, and the police are no exception. Volunteers tend to be recruited to work with specific organizations associated with the police, for example on traffic duty or as youth assistants.

On a wider level, crime-prevention work is a central feature of the residents' associations which thrive in both rural and urban areas. Although also involved in conflict mediation work, in other respects community crime prevention is more akin to neighbourhood watch as it has recently developed in the west. There are contact points in the streets where the public can get information on crime prevention, call for police assistance, or pass on information to the police. Associations also organize street patrols, where members may wear identification armbands.

Clearly, as in other countries, such levels of public co-operation vary according to the sectors involved. As Ames (1981, 94–104) notes, community relations are weaker in areas dominated by the Koreans and the indigenous outcasts, the *burakumin*, and Bayley (1976, 96) accepts that co-operation is greater among the elderly, males, and more conservative factions in the community. Nevertheless, there can be no doubt that the public play a considerably greater part in the policing process in Japan than in most capitalist Western societies.

But does this mean that the public have more control over *policy*? It would appear not. Even in the early stages of police development the lack of local control was a source of conflict (Westney 1982), and this has continued to be the case. Bayley (1976, 97) accepts that 'The police are undoubtedly the dominant partner in the relationship with the crime prevention associations', and in both *koban* and *chuzaisho* police personnel are transferred every two or three years to prevent local ties becoming too well established (Ames 1981; Bayley 1976).

If the police are not accountable to the neighbourhoods within which they work, to whom are they then accountable? Two possible alternatives relate to the informal and formal levels, respectively.

Informally, the importance of police occupational culture must be stressed. Such occupational cultures have featured in sociological analyses of policing in Western societies (Holdaway 1983; Maanen 1975; Manning 1987). There is, however, good reason to believe that

Japanese social structure enhances the prevalence of a police culture. As already noted, Japanese workers develop close bonds with the organization; loyalty is expected and given, and the culture and structure of the working environment operate to cement these ties, a fact recognized in the policing context by Bayley (1976, 71). Occupation-based housing, medical provision and insurance thus co-exist with shared leisure pursuits to enhance solidarity which in other respects – a macho/action-oriented focus – shares many features with its Western equivalents (Ames 1981, 151–93). Undoubtedly, then, police officers feel greater obligations and loyalties towards their colleagues than the public, a feeling established in the early days of the police when a professional culture emerged earlier than in other countries (Westney 1982).

In a rather different way, formal processes of accountability are also located within the police organization. Bureaucratic accountability is in fact a key feature of Japanese socio-political structure, and is evident *vis-à-vis* the police. Public safety commissions operate at both national and prefecture level and include lay representatives, although these tend to be elderly, conservative males, and 'In reality, the police are totally independent of effective formal external checks on their power and operation' (Ames 1981, 13).

Ames (1981, 215–22), in an extended discussion of the issue, argues that according to *tatemai* the police are politically independent and publicly accountable. But the *honne* is that the police are insulated from the public influence and, on a senior level within the National Police Agency (NPA), closely tied to government. Thus the head of the NPA appoints his own successor, who is likely to have previously been seconded as NPA secretary to the prime minister. There is, therefore, within the police organization, close line accountability extending to the top of the NPA and ultimately – if informally – to the government:

> The question remains as to who controls the police. The answer is simply that the police are totally autonomous in a formal organizational sense: they control themselves and are ultimately responsible only to the head of the National Police Agency (the *honne*). (Ames 1981, 219).

Undoubtedly police–public relations in Japan are much more firmly established than in most other capitalist societies. Nevertheless, it seems that this partnership is controlled, and its parameters defined, by the police and that public involvement should not be equated with public control.

SUMMARY

Outside commentators have looked with envy at the Japanese economic and social systems. Equally, within police studies, academics and practitioners have written approvingly of both the close relationships between police and public and the apparent outcome of present practices, a low crime rate.

This is, however, only half the story. While the crime rate does appear extremely low, whether this is due to the police system or the wider social and cultural structure is a moot point. Moreover, societal norms, with assumptions and expectations *vis-à-vis* duties and obligations and the transcendence of group interests above those of the individual, hold implications for both crime levels and social relationships which underpin community involvement in law-and-order initiatives. One consequence of this is that the social costs of such a system, in terms of loss of freedom of choice, privacy etc., must be balanced against the gains of a low crime rate. Another is that it is asking the impossible to model Western policing on Japanese lines when the gulf between cultures is so vast.

Moreover, the community aspects of the Japanese police structure must be balanced against the fact that the police system that was created during the Meiji dynasty was a professional, highly centralized one, chosen because of its emphasis upon the political and control-oriented functions of the police (Westney 1982). And despite the influence of the United States in the immediate postwar period, the centralized structure remains a feature of the Japanese police. Thus it is possible to see community-based police initiatives as the tips of the tentacles, with control centralized, rather than as evidence of community control.

The same might be said of China (see Chapter 9) and indeed, despite the very different political systems, there are close similarities between local structures in Japan and China, and to a lesser extent Hong Kong. However, while at various times the Chinese police have been open to local influence, government policy, police operational practices and organizational structures which enhance occupational loyalties combine to isolate the Japanese police from public influence. In this context, the description of Japan as a society of *Gemeinschaft* capitalism is particularly apt. While we may value many aspects of *Gemeinschaft* systems, no one pretends that their peasant populations were endowed with many rights or much power.

8

USSR: Centralized Communism

INTRODUCTION

Inclusion of the USSR in an introductory text such as this might be considered essential. As the first society to establish a (self-defined) communist political system it served as a model for Eastern Europe, and while there are considerable differences between countries of the Eastern bloc (Perger 1989; Pravda 1986; Waller and Szajkowski 1986), these together have presented a more centralized, bureaucratized and industry-led structure than have Third World communist regimes (Deacon 1983; Kowalewski 1981). Moreover, changes accelerated by the moves towards *perestroika* and *glasnost* within the USSR and its allies, with the subsequent reactions from social-control agencies such as the largely autonomous secret police, make it of topical relevance.

That said, however, a detailed analysis of Soviet police systems is near-impossible. Admittedly the KGB and its predecessors have been the subject of considerable attention, largely from popular Western writers or defectors such as Myagkov (1976). But more serious research, even including basic data on the numbers of police, crime rates etc., is lacking, despite early texts on the police (Conquest 1968) and legal system (Hazard, Shapiro and Maggs 1969), Juviler's (1976) critique being an honourable exception.

There is some English-language material available by Soviet practitioners, perhaps the best being by Karpets (1979) from the Ministry of Internal Affairs. O'Connor's (1964) analysis of community initiatives, although now dated, provides an excellent example of research based on secondary material and illustrates the advantages of being a Russian linguist and legal scholar!

There are however, at least two particular difficulties, already noted in Chapter 1. One is that the material is scarcely comprehensive, much of it is dated, and therefore it is difficult to provide an up-to-date picture of the multi-faceted Soviet policing system. The second is the extent to which one is dependent upon official statements which portray the formal aspects of law; that is, how the system is said to operate, rather than what actually goes on. An excellent exception, which undermines much of the other available material, is provided by Solomon (1987) in a critique of the role of the procuracy and judiciary. Where other writers have stressed the importance, in Soviet legislation, of due process, the acceptance of 'innocent until proved guilty', and the impartiality of the system, Solomon shows how a national commitment to demonstrate that the system is both fair and efficient has resulted in pressure being applied on both procurates and judges to produce a conviction rate of nearly 100 per cent. In some ways the system operates as an equivalent to plea bargaining as commonly acknowledged as fundamental to the US criminal justice system. The key issue, however, is that while the average undergraduate criminologist or law student is aware of plea bargaining and other informal processes, the equivalent data on the Soviet system are rarely available.

This is likely to change in the near future. Already some basic data is available for the late 1980s on officially recorded crime and sentencing patterns, but none yet on the police.[1] However, the new era of openness, while expressed in press releases and newspaper articles, has not yet found its way to academic writings (Farish 1990). Thus even Los's (1988) recent text on crime and the legal system, admittedly delayed in publication, refers only to the period prior to Gorbachev's presidency. Consequently, with rare exceptions the following analysis is of the system in operation up to the mid-1980s. Nevertheless, given the distinctiveness of East European communist societies, this is not necessarily a weakness since we can at least assess police structures under such political regimes as they exist (or existed).

THE SOCIAL AND POLITICAL STRUCTURE OF THE USSR

With a land mass of over 8.5 million square miles, the USSR is well over twice the size of Canada, the USA or China. Its population, approximately 270 million, while greater than that of the US, is barely a quarter that of China. Consequently it has a low density of population, with only eleven inhabitants per square km. However, there are – not surprisingly – considerable variations across the country. While 20 per cent of the active population work in agriculture, 64 per cent live in urban areas. Although Russian is the national language, only 58 per cent of the population speak it as a first language, and there are in all 112 officially recognized languages (Sapir 1985).

The USSR is in fact composed of fifteen republics, including Russia (RSFSR) itself, ranging from Estonia and Latvia in the north-west to Tadzhikistan and Kirghizia in the south. This federal structure allows for considerable regional autonomy, although, as recent protests indicate, there are growing demands for complete self-government. Republics were originally designated according to the ethnic and cultural composition of the population. They have traditionally been allowed considerable cultural autonomy, but economic planning is centrally controlled. There was a move under Brezhnev to limit this autonomy, for example involving a short-lived attempt to make Russian the sole official language (Hazard, Butler and Maggs 1984). However, 'leadership drift' during the latter stages of the Brezhnev period (Shoup 1989) and more recent commitment to *perestroika* and *glasnost* have encouraged further moves against central control.

The regional structure is the basis for political control, although, following Lenin, the Communist Party itself does not have a decentralized structure and is nationally organized (Hazard, Butler and Maggs 1984; Miller 1986). Generally speaking, policies are determined nationally and republics feature as the first stage in the administrative structure. Four republics are further subdivided with one or two autonomous provinces or republics within them; additionally, the RSFSR itself is subdivided at this level into thirty-one district units. The lowest levels of local government below this are respectively the 3,224 major cities and administrative districts and the 47,454 smaller cities, city districts and rural soviets (Hazard, Butler and Maggs 1984; Ushkalov and Khorev 1989). As Echols (1986) notes, while class inequalities in the Soviet Union are less extreme than in capitalist societies, income inequalities between republics are considerable and have received little government priority, fuelling current ethnic unrest.

The collapse of the tsarist system in 1917, leading as it did to the Bolshevik reconstruction, introduced the first (self-defined) communist society. However the ideals that state intervention would be minimal and democracy decentralized were shelved as the Bolsheviks attempted to suppress dissent (by both reactionary elements and other socialist groups) (Los 1988, 1–25), 'educate' the population towards accepting communism, and increase industrialization:

> If the consolidation of the revolution had brought about the authoritarianism which a situation of social dislocation invites, the ensuing task of economic and cultural disadvantage produced, in fact if not necessarily, a continuation of authoritarian rule. (Waller and Szajkowski 1986, 11).

In comparing the emergence of communism in the Soviet Union and China, Kowalewski (1989) argues that differences can be identified in the pre-revolutionary and revolutionary periods that influenced the key features of the two systems as they developed. Compared with China, he stresses that prior to revolution Russian government exerted far more effective control over the population; then, in Russia, the revolutionary period was characterized by less popular support, less peasant involvement, and a greater role for the police than the military. As a result, communism in Russia was founded on a party elite, centralized social control, a centralized economy, and an emphasis upon industrialization and modernization, with more importance accredited to material rather than moral incentives.

The Soviet Union has tended to prioritize growth rather than equality but, as Echols (1986) notes, class inequalities are less than in the West. However, the system is, as already noted, highly centralized, and while this is acknowledged in the phrase 'democratic centralism', it is scarcely democratic. The parliamentary system was until recently monopolized by the Communist Party; other parties were barred, and one could only vote against the (sole) candidate by striking off his/her name from the ballot paper (Miller 1986; Pravda 1986). Power was therefore determined by nomination *by* the party, where membership *of* the party was closely restricted (Miller 1988).

While the influence of the party over public and social administration is considerable, in other respects state agencies, operating as enormous bureaucracies, evidence many of the features to be found in capitalist societies. In a critique of the welfare system, for example, Deacon (1983) identifies six criteria by which one might compare socialist/communist with capitalist societies: priority, control, agency, relationships, rationing and sexual divisions. While he argues that the USSR allocates more resources to welfare services, in most other respects he sees little evidence of superiority, with services based in bureaucracies rather than community centres and controlled by party and professionals rather than citizens. This he contrasts with Third World communism as illustrated in China and Cuba. The role of the party, state bureaucracies and central control are thus key features of East European communist societies, and find reflection in the criminal justice system and police organization.

CRIME AND THE CRIMINAL JUSTICE SYSTEM

As Connor (1973) noted some years ago, it is difficult to assess the level of crime in the Soviet Union. Despite a growth in internal and external reviews of crime and deviance, official crime data have not been readily available, and the exceptions are often difficult to interpret. Thus Connor (1973) was unable to provide annual national or regional figures for homicides, although his review of secondary sources suggested that homicide patterns, in terms of offender characteristics, victim/offender relationships, offence location etc., were similar to the US. Juviler (1976, 130–40), while equally cautious, suggests that crime may have decreased during the Brezhnev 'law-and-order' drives, and argues that while property crimes are less common than in the US crimes of violence are *more* prevalent. One is left therefore to choose between official interpretations of a decrease in crime since 1917 (Savitsky and Kogan 1987; Timoshenko 1977) and more lurid accounts of the Soviet crime problem (Feofanov 1988; Marsov 1988; Tsirlin 1988). Shelley (1980) in fact produces some more recent figures on known offenders which suggest that the crime rate is between one-sixth and two-fifths of that in the US, although her data are somewhat ambiguous.[2]

Comparisons are further confused by the wider interpretation of crime in the USSR. As Los (1988, 286) notes, 'efforts to establish total control over the behaviour and life styles of citizens lead to broader, more flexible definitions of deviance and crime'. Thus the most common crime 'hooliganism' (intentional acts violating public order in a coarse manner and expressing clear disrespect towards society) has no obvious equivalent; nor have 'speculations' (the buying up and reselling of goods by individuals for the purpose of making a profit), or 'leading an anti-social parasite way of life' (Armstrong 1967; Berman and Spindler 1963; Juviler 1976; Los 1988; Savitsky and Kogan 1987; Zeldes 1981).

Some crime or deviance problems, such as juvenile delinquency and alcohol abuse (Connor 1970; 1972), have been openly acknowledged for some time; others less so. Berg (1983), for example, estimated a homicide rate midway between that in most Western capitalist societies and the USA, and recent official figures support this while indicating a rise to about six homicides per 100,000 population.[3] Moreover the recent revelation that there are on average sixteen to twenty homicides in Moscow each month,[4] and concern over official corruption – in the public eye following the arrest of Yun Churbanov (Brezhnev's son-in-law) – and organized crime (Feofanov

1988; Loshak and Dyomin 1988), suggest that serious crime has scarcely been eliminated. In other respects, Lampert (1984) assesses the pressures towards the opportunities for 'economic and official' crime within state bureaucracies and Los (1988) describes how patterns of public ownership may increase the likelihood of crime related to scarce resources but restrict household-property crimes. Further, Shelley (1980) argues that one might expect to find lower levels of criminality, given the much greater degrees of control to which citizens are subjected. For example, an internal passport system is utilized to control residence, travel and employment, and released prisoners may be subject to considerable restrictions on where they may live. One result of this is that population shift in the largest cities has been controlled, and with it crime levels, and it is in the medium-sized cities and areas of population expansion that crime is most prevalent.

This serves to remind us that wider public policies can significantly affect crime. But what of the criminal justice system? In many respects, the Soviet legal system shared a Roman-law tradition (Smith 1980), although many have argued that it is quite distinct from both common and Roman law (Cole, Frankowski and Gertz 1987). The theoretical base for such an assumption is the Marxist-Leninist perspective on the role of law in capitalist societies and the need for minimal government in communist societies. Law would therefore be basic and administered at local level by the people; there would be little need for the legal apparatus of courts, prosecutors, police and correctional services (Hazard, Butler and Maggs 1984).

In the immediate post-revolutionary period there was indeed an attempt to focus on neighbourhood (or workplace) justice. However, Bolshevik concern to maintain order led to the establishment of legal principles and the development of a formal court structure, initially a temporary arrangement to cover the period between socialism and communism. Nevertheless, by the early 1920s there was an 'increasingly complex, centralized, bureaucratic and permanent system of laws and justice' (Juviler 1976, 28). Under Stalin there was a further shift towards a central, specialist legal framework, although political crimes were dealt with separately by special tribunals, with a wide mandate, strong powers, and little external control. With Stalin's death the special tribunals were disbanded. The Khrushchev period saw a shift back towards neighbourhood justice (Juviler 1976, 78–82). People's guards, introduced as a volunteer support for the police, will be discussed later. Two other policy shifts at this time involved comrades' courts (Berman and Spindler 1963; Los 1988, 65–77) and the Campaign against Parasites (Armstrong 1967; Los 1988, 78–104).

The former, introduced in 1969, were non-professional tribunals staffed by volunteers and localized in housing apartments or factories to deal with petty offences, such as drunkenness, minor thefts or domestic disputes. Courts could use persuasion to bring about conformity, but were also empowered to fine, evict, or sack the offender if necessary. Comrades' courts were also used in the Campaign against Parasites, initiated by Khrushchev in 1957 to discourage prostitution, loafing and drunkenness. By 1963, however, cases were predominantly handled in the more formal courts.

This court structure, essentially established between 1922 and 1924 (Juviler 1976), is described in detail by Hazard, Butler and Maggs (1984) and Savitsky and Kogan (1987). At the head of the system is the Supreme Court of the USSR; each republic and autonomous republic then has a Supreme Court; below these come provincial and district courts. The basic provisions of criminal law are contained in the Fundamentals of Criminal Legislation, but each republic has its own codes which may differ from the blueprint, reflecting geographical or ethnic distinctions. For example, victims' rights to participate in court, the age of criminal responsibility, and the maximum sentence vary between republics.

Key figures in the courts are the judges and the people's assessors, or lay judges. Judges are elected for five-year terms, although as with the general electoral system, in practice this means they are nominated by the party and unopposed. Most judges are party members. In other respects the system results in a rather different profile for the typical judge compared with Western experiences: in 1982 a majority were aged under 40, and over one-third were women (Savitsky and Kogan 1987). People's assessors, two of whom sit alongside a judge in less serious cases,[5] have similar backgrounds, but are elected by a show of hands at citizens' meetings.

The other key legal institution, and perhaps the most important of all (Smith 1980), is the procuracy. This is again organized on a national, republic, provincial and district level, although the whole system is more centralized than the court structure. The procurator is responsible for the execution of the legal process, from the police investigation through to a review of the sentence.

In theory, since Khrushchev's reforms, both the judiciary and procuracy have been free of party influence. In practice, however, this has scarcely been a reality, not least because of the dependency of judges on party support and the fact that judges and procurators tend to be party members (Hazard, Butler and Maggs 1984; Smith 1980). Moreover, as Solomon (1987) notes in a critique of the near-absence of acquittals, party pressure during the 1940s led to the procuracy being unwilling to drop cases once they had gone to court, and resulted in judges being reluctant to give not-guilty verdicts. Acquittal was defined as a failure of the system and equated with a failure of the system's key operatives:

> As employees of bureaucratic agencies Soviet legal officials were influenced by the way their bureaucratic and political superiors assessed their performance. To accommodate the criteria used in assessing that work, these officials developed a set of informal norms of conduct that governed the handling of criminal cases. Substituting other measures for acquittals turns out to have been one of those norms. (Solomon 1987, 531).

Open criticism of this practice gathered momentum in 1986. However, the new spirit of *glasnost* will not necessarily bring dramatic changes at grassroots level (Harasymiv 1988). Interestingly, as Huskey (1988) describes, the professional/party link has been maintained at the higher levels of the procuracy, only the form of knot changing. Thus, while under Stalin the party sent its members into procuracy posts, current policy is to transfer procurates to fill posts in the party bureaucracy and later reassign them to legal positions where they can maintain party influence.

The sentencing alternatives open to the courts are also distinctive. The repressions of the 1920s and 1930s are well known. By 1927 the prison population was greater than at any time prior to revolution, and by 1933 labour camps housed 5 million (Juviler 1976; Los 1988, 105–43). The Khrushchev and Brezhnev periods also featured an emphasis on a punitive penal system. Juviler (1976, 106) estimates that by the early 1970s the USSR had a rate of imprisonment two to three times that of the USA and ten times that of Sweden. Reforms between 1977 and 1982 resulted in a confirmation of the 'need' for severe sentences – including capital punishment – as a deterrent, balanced with a re-emphasis upon 'depenalized' justice for minor offences. Sentences thus range from the death penalty – also available since the 1960s for large-scale thefts of state property (Los 1988, 209) – imprisonment, exile, and restricted residence on the one hand, to corrective labour (without deprivation of liberty), restriction of civil rights, fines, or limited (up to fifteen-days') detention on the other. As with the example of the comrades' courts it is notable that most non-custodial alternatives imply a degree of restriction on freedoms which would be considered unacceptable in most Western societies. At the other extreme, capital punishment has been widely applied (Berg 1983), prison and labour-camp conditions are appalling (Los 1988, 105–43), and current figures suggest that imprisonment is used by the courts for as many as one-third of offenders.[6] These draconian qualities of the criminal justice system set the agenda for a review of policing patterns.

PRE- AND POST-REVOLUTIONARY POLICING STRUCTURE

To a large extent the Russian political system mirrored its Prussian neighbour in the emergence of a police state (Raeff 1975). A political police force had been established by Tsar Ivan by the late sixteenth century. Known as the *oprichnina*, it quickly established a reputation for brutality and terror (Bayley 1985, 195; Terrill 1989). However, much of its early emphasis was on the nobility, with the assumption that any threat to the tsars was likely to originate in that quarter, and it was not until 1881, with the assassination of Tsar Alexander II, that policing was organized on a comprehensive level. The Ministry of Internal Affairs was created at that stage as a central authority for the co-ordination of both the regular and political police. The latter, subsequently named *Osoby Otdel*, focused on potentially disruptive groups, widely defined to include students, teachers and urban workers, and was instrumental in the suppression of radical groups in the 1880s and 1890s. It was reorganized at provincial level in 1902, and also contained an overseas section (Johnson 1975). Its power provided both justification for an alternative secret police in the post-revolutionary phase and the model on which such a force might be designed:

> In Russia, not only did the Tsarist secret police terror prompt Bolshevik counter terror as a mode of party survival, but the Bolshevik Party also had ample occasion to acquire an intimate familiarity with the terrorist operations of the Tsarist police and adapt them to its perceived advantage . . . Thus the Bolshevik Cheka (Extraordinary Committee or secret police) not merely displayed continuity with post Russian regimes; the *okhranniki* had unwittingly proved good teachers in the school of terror as well. (Kowalewski 1981, 291).

The role of the *Cheka* and its successors has been dramatic, and has inspired considerable outside review, and it is thus appropriate to begin an account of post-revolutionary policing with the state security forces (Conquest 1968, 13–29; Los 1988, 3–14; Terrill 1989).

The *Cheka* was created by the Council of People's Commissioners in December 1917 with a mandate to control the border and to prevent counter-revolutionary activity internally. To do so it adopted wide-ranging powers, being responsible for summary trial and execution of those considered a national threat. Its notoriety led to its official disbanding in 1922. However it was effectively reborn as the State Political Administration (GPU) under the chairmanship of Felix Dzerzhinsky, founder of the *Cheka*. Originally subject to the People's Commisariat for Internal Affairs (NKVD), by the mid-1920s it gained relative autonomy under the Unified State Political Administration (OGPU) and expanded to become the 'master of the largest pool of labour in the Soviet Union' (Kowalewski 1981, 295). In 1934 it was absorbed within a newly structured NKVD but during the Second World War was again separated off under the People's Commissariats for State Security (NKGB). In 1946 when people's commissariats were restructured as ministries it became the Ministry of State Security (MGB). On the death of Stalin in 1953 it was temporarily absorbed into the Ministry of Internal Affairs (MVD) until it was reconstituted as the Committee for State Security (KGB) in 1954, with responsibility for counter-intelligence, espionage and border activities. At this stage it became accountable directly to the Council of Ministers.

The *Cheka* was not, however, the only policing initiative of the revolutionary government. The regular police force, the workers' militia, was formed in November 1917, with dual accountability to the Commissariat for Internal Affairs and the Soviets of Working People's and Soldiers' Deputies, giving it some degree of local accountability (Karpets 1977). For most of the period from then to the present, the militia has come either under the Commissariat for Internal Affairs (NKVD) or, since 1946, the Ministry of Internal Affairs (MVD), later temporarily renamed the Ministry for the Presevation of Public Order (MOOP). For a period in the early 1930s, though, it was absorbed into the Unified State Political Administration (OGPU) and in 1953, when the MGB was merged with the MVD, it effectively came under the influence of state security for a short time when Lavrenti Beria, former *Cheka* officer and head of MGB, was appointed the head of the MVD (Conquest 1968; Terrill 1989). With Beria's arrest and execution the following year, however, the militia was again separated from the security forces. It has remained centrally organized under the Ministry of Internal Affairs since then, except for a brief period in the early 1960s when the ministry was decentralized and control was transferred to the separate republics.

In addition to the state security force and the regular police, there has been a third arm to Soviet law enforcement, involving the general public in law and order activities (Juviler 1976, 78–82; O'Connor 1964). As early as 1917 Lenin called for the creation of supervisory units in the factories. Workers' control units were formed to perform a range of administrative and management roles, including security work. Longer-term and more specialist citizens' police units were established in rural areas in 1924, named rural executors, and in urban areas with the formation of citizen assistance units in 1926. The latter were reorganized under local party and administrative control in 1928 and renamed societies for assistance to the police, and by 1930 there were 2,500 groups involving 26,000 citizens in the Russian republic alone. In 1932 the societies were again reorganized and came under the control of the militia; these brigades, or *brigadmili*, effectively served as police auxiliaries. O'Connor (1964) notes that by 1958 there were 182,000 citizens involved in brigades in the Ukraine.

Various other community groups were formed with a policing function. In the 1930s street or block committees were established, with general responsibilities including supervision of maintenance and sanitation, surveillance of child education, and other local public-order matters. In the 1950s party youth groups, the *komsomol*, were formed with a more specific law-enforcement mandate. Then in the late 1950s people's guards, *druzhiny*, were created as part of Khrushchev's initiatives for expanding the role of the local community in the policing process, to provide citizen patrols which were distinct from the state police organizations and thus able to provide community integration more effectively.

The policing of the Soviet Union today can thus be categorized broadly under these three developments, each now operationally distinct. In the following section, the police organization will be considered with particular reference to the militia, although the KGB will be briefly described. Then in assessing police/public relations emphasis will be placed on the *druzhiny* and other community initiatives.

THE SOVIET POLICE SYSTEM SINCE KHRUSHCHEV

The distinction between the militia and KGB has been maintained since the former was returned to central control in 1966. Before concentrating on the militia, however, it is appropriate to refer briefly to the operation of the KGB, or state security police.

The KGB is a centralized force with responsibility both internally and abroad. It is organized into a number of directorates, specializing in work abroad, foreign nationals in the USSR, border security, security of government officials, and policing of the military (Barron 1985; Conquest 1968; Myagkov 1976). The Fifth Directorate operates, in effect, as a state censorship agency; the Second Directorate deals with internal control and security, charged with uncovering 'state criminals'. Methods include phone-tapping, interception of mail, routine checks on released political prisoners and the use of psychiatric hospitals for dissidents for whom the formal penal process is deemed inappropriate.

While the work of the KGB is secretive, the organization and operation of the regular police is more explicitly defined (Conquest 1968; Karpets 1977; Terrill 1989). Its structure is essentially militaristic; ranks are equivalent to those in the military, and officers sign on for two years' duty initially. It is organized on a national basis under the Ministry of Internal Affairs, alongside the procuracy, with units at various levels within the republics, districts and local areas. Each unit is divided into four departments, entitled the Criminal Investigation Department, the Department for Combating the Misappropriation of Socialist Property, the Passport Department and the State Automobile Inspection and Traffic Control Department.

The Criminal Investigation Department has a rather different brief from that associated with the term in the West. On the one hand, it incorporates the Child Welfare Office, with responsibility for juvenile offenders and neglected minors, and works closely with schools and community groups. On the other hand, it is responsible not merely for the investigation of reported cases, but also for crime-prevention work. One aspect of this involves helping to find employment for those released from prison.

The Department for Combating the Misappropriation of Socialist Property is concerned with theft and bribery within trade and industry. Again, its role encompasses both detection and prevention: it is responsible for passing on crime-prevention advice to factories, for example. It works closely with people's volunteer brigades within industrial work units.

The Passport Department is again distinctive from a Western perspective, having responsibility for the control and monitoring of the internal passport system. This provides, through the militia, a means by which the population can be counted, changes registered, and population movements monitored. It can clearly also be used by the police as a means of monitoring those with prior convictions; for example, enabling them to 'investigate reports that a person who has been released from a correctional institution is evading socially useful work' (Karpets 1977, 36).

In comparison with the first three departments, the State Automobile Inspection and Traffic Control Department is more easily recognized. Nevertheless, its role is also in part preventive. For example, it works closely with motor vehicle manufacturers *vis-à-vis* safety, and it is involved in public-education sessions which take place in housing blocks or schools. It also liaises with specialist transport sections of volunteer brigades.

While these are the main departments, the militia is further subdivided into specialist sections according to the demands of particular areas. Details on this are sparse, but in Moscow at least there is a specialist murder squad of some fifteen officers under a chief inspector.[7]

Clearly the militia has a very wide role, notably regarding crime prevention and passport regulations, but also licensing duties re weapons, explosives, printing facilities etc. (Conquest 1968, 32–3). In some such respects it shares some features with the continental police system discussed in Chapter 2. It also has some involvement in the punishment of offenders, being able to levy fines and liaise with comrades' courts and participate in community-based sentences which entail restrictions on liberty. While crimes may be investigated by the militia, in more serious cases the procurator is responsible for further investigation, and the militia is also subject to the procurator's office *vis-à-vis* arrests and detention of suspects in custody, again suggesting parallels with, for example, the French system. That said, it appears that the militia have considerable powers concerning the interrogation and remand in custody of suspects (Conquest 1968). More recent evidence is unavailable, but the homicide suspect in the documentary, 'Murder in Ostankino Precinct',[8] for example, is detained, questioned, and then held overnight before he is informed of the offence for which he has been arrested!

Less is known of recruitment policies, although Conquest (1968, 36, 66) noted that most recruits were drawn from the main party or the party youth groups, the *komsomol*, and officers were appointed from the party or the internal or frontier guards. In at least one respect, though, the system contrasts with that of the continental model, namely the importance placed on community involvement. Ironically, there seems to have been at least as much written about citizen involvement in policing as there is more specifically on the militia.

POLICE AND PUBLIC

The balance between a centralized police system and a prioritization of community initiative reflects two strands in communist political structures: on the one hand a perceived need for strong government to lead the new socialist nation towards industrialization, prosperity and full communism; on the other hand, the original ideological focus on minimal state involvement. Somewhere between the two lies the possibility of community-based control mechanisms being used in the interests of the centralized state. In this sense, the role of the party in mobilizing the community is not unexpected.

In fact, the role of the public in crime control appears both wideranging and sustained, incorporating alternatives that we might term neighbourhood watch, vigilante groups, police auxiliaries, community liaison groups, and community courts. The situation in the mid-1970s in the Belorussia republic, for example, was described euphorically in terms of both its extent and effectiveness:

> We have recently devised a new and more progressive form of participation by the working people in the prevention of crime, namely, the law enforcement support units established in urban micro regions, which are responsible for implementing a wide range of crime prevention measures of an individual and communal nature. They comprise all the voluntary public organizations within a given micro region. Thousands of people of widely different ages and occupations are helping us to track down and prevent crime . . .
>
> Action by the masses to preserve the legal order finds its expression in the formation of various voluntary organizations which watch over Soviet legality: the People's Volunteer Brigades for the preservation of social order, the Comrades' Courts, the crime prevention councils in enterprises, collective and State farms, and others. There are 7,348 People's Volunteer Brigades in the Republic, comprising more than 250,000 voluntary guardians of law and order. The most massive form of participation by the working people in the preservation of law and order is the extensive patriotic movement for model social order and a high level of culture in the daily life of the inhabitants of towns and villages. This movement covers eighty per cent of the population centres in the Byelorussian SSR. It is largely responsible for the fact that the Vitebsk region, for example, not a single crime was recorded in eighty eight per cent of the population centres. (Timoshenko 1977, 39, 41).

While alternative forms of community participation emerged at different times from 1917 onwards, it was undoubtedly the Khrushchev initiatives which provided the greatest impetus. At this time, numbers in the secret police and militia were reduced, and the role of the community in policing and sentencing expanded (Juviler 1976).

The people's guards, or *druzhiny* (Bakhanskaia 1974; O'Connor 1964), were perhaps the most notable development on the policing front. Early experiences had suggested that where citizens' groups were subordinate to the police, their local influence was limited. Therefore the *narodnaya druzhina* were established as separate units to assist the police in the struggle against hooliganism, drunkenness and public-order offences. Organized on a neighbourhood or factory basis, members carried identification cards and handbooks and were easily identified by wearing red armbands. While methods of recruitment varied, a majority tended to be activists as members of the party or, more likely, the *komsomol*. Although units maintained close contact with militia and procuracy, and indeed were sometimes divided into specialist groups equivalent to militia divisions, they were closer to the party than to the regular police.

At one extreme, guards might be assigned to conventional patrol duties, sometimes replacing the militia. For example: 'As a result of Guard patrols in Leningrad, police posts were removed from the vicinity of a number of clubs, and at one factory settlement the precinct police station was eliminated' (O'Connor 1964, 595). To aid in such duties, guards, while unarmed, had considerable legal powers. However, while they could pass on suspects to the militia, or even directly to the procuracy, the emphasis was originally more on preventive roles and community-based informal sanctions, at which level the influence of the party was considerable. Thus their work incorporated primary prevention through 'educational work amongst the populace on conformity to the rules of socialist community life and the prevention of anti-social infractions', patrol work, and, where deviance was discovered, a mandate 'to influence the violator first of all by means of persuasion and "warnings" ' (quoted in O'Connor 1964, 601). Where warnings were not considered sufficient, informal action could involve public denouncements or victim restitution. Guards were also involved in supervising those given community-based sentences by the courts.

As with other community initiatives, the people's guards featured most notably in the Krushchev period, especially from 1958 to 1962. Indeed, by 1961 their subordination to police and procuracy was being stressed and by 1962 they often patrolled in the company of regular police. O'Connor (1964, 613) noted that they were 'changing from a *civic* into a *public* agency'. By 1966 it had become conventional wisdom that the role of the community had been overemphasized, and crime-control policies shifted towards increased expenditure on the militia and more punitive sentencing (Juviler 1976, 787–82). Thus, while Bakhanskaia (1974) suggests that the *druzhiny* was still operating as an autonomous unit in the early 1970s, Karpets (1977), describing the same period, gives a more ambiguous account and refers to community involvement in terms of brigades rather than people's guards. It seems likely, then, that citizen participation has been rechannelled into auxiliary policing units, integrated with the militia, rather than left on the perimeters of the formal structure.

This is relevant in the context of police accountability and here again the position is ambiguous. Whereas the KGB and its predecessors are centrally, and secretly, accountable, the militia, since its inception, has been defined as jointly accountable. On the one hand, it is internally accountable centrally through the organization and ultimately to the Ministry of Internal Affairs. Allegations of corruption levelled against the militia and other agencies in the criminal justice system in the 1980s, for example, led Andropov to instigate internal investigations (Los 1988, 173–4). On the other hand, it is accountable at district level, with divisional inspectors of the militia appointed by the deputies of the local soviets and then made members of their local executive committees (Karpets 1977). Without further detail of how this works in practice it is difficult to draw any conclusions. In a recent article, Russian academic B. N. Gabrichedze (1987) has argued that local soviets exert considerable (and growing) control over law-enforcement agencies, but the examples given are drawn mainly from ancillary agencies and he admits that they have little influence on the procuracy. At most, one might suggest, given the importance of the party in determining elections, that this makes the militia accountable centrally to the ministry and locally to the party. In either case, it is unlikely that citizens *in general* have any control over the regular police. Even during the heyday of the people's guards, these appeared to operate autonomously of the police but under party influence; in no sense did they exert any control over local policing. While, as will be demonstrated in the following chapter, in China also the balance between people, party and police is ambiguous and variable, in the USSR the importance of the public in policing and the influence of the public over police operations is markedly less.

SUMMARY

The Soviet version of communism leans heavily on a centralized, tightly controlled system, in which power is in the hands of the party elite. The legal system, based on the Roman-law tradition, was established relatively soon after the Bolsheviks attained control and followed this basic pattern. However, the secret police seem to have been largely absolved of any accountability to the law, and in practice the separation of the legal system from the political system appears more fiction than reality.

As is now openly recognized, neither communism, nor the complex apparatus of state control, nor severe sentencing, have eliminated crime in the USSR. Violence levels are relatively high, alcohol abuse rife, and crimes associated with state-owned firms and supply shortages common. Rather less is known of the current status of the police system. However, policing in the Soviet Union can be described on three levels. First, the notorious secret police attains both numerical and symbolic importance; in contrast, the militia, or regular force, provides an organized, centralizd and more formally accountable arm to conventional law enforcement; finally, citizen groups, ideologically a key feature of communist legal thinking, attained some significance, especially in the Krushchev era, but feature less in more recent reviews of the system.

In many respects, the Soviet police system bears the hallmarks of continental police systems and, as will become evident in the following chapters, is distinctly different to the Chinese and Cuban equivalents. How this will change in the future is a matter for discussion. The current Interior Minister, Vadim Bakatim, interviewed by Chernenko (1989), envisages a more professional and efficient force, more open to public scrutiny and with more open recruitment. We might also anticipate a more devolved structure. While it is difficult to predict the pace and direction of change, it is important to appreciate the extent to which current policing has its roots both in post-revolutionary Soviet socio-political structure and in the earlier structures from which it was moulded.

9

China: the People's Police?

INTRODUCTION

The case for including China in any comparative analysis is persuasive. With a population in excess of 1000 million and an area of over 3,705,000 square miles it poses questions for social control which are perhaps unique. The internal conflicts that have characterized Chinese society in the twentieth century, both before and since the introduction of communism, have been most recently highlighted in the ruthless carnage of Tiananmen Square in 1989. They also make outside analysis difficult, because the socio-political structure, and correspondingly the legal system, has been subject to quite marked shifts in emphasis at different times.

Additional problems however have been caused for non-Chinese academics by the relative inaccessibility of the country, and the extent to which commentaries have been coloured by the political slant of their authors. Brady (1982b, 5–11), for example, having attacked earlier Western academic 'collaborators' for their naive acceptance of the Kuomintang dictatorship, argues that critics of the new communist regime, first 'cold warriors' and later 'legalists', shared common assumptions that the only worthwhile model was the Western professional legal system. Yet as 'functionalists' later argued, not only did Chinese socialist legality operate according to quite different principles, but to dismiss it as inferior was simplistic (Li 1973; Pepinsky 1976). The portrayal by Brady (1981; 1982b; 1983), himself a Marxist sociologist, thus contrasts markedly with those by liberal or rightwing legal scholars on both disciplinary and political grounds.

In fact, many of the works on China have been written by legal experts, perhaps the most notable being Cohen (1966; 1968; 1971; 1977) and Lubman (1967; 1969), and more recently Leng (1981; Leng and Chiu 1985). Most of these writings are 'from without', based either on secondary sources or interviews with émigrés, whose accounts are scarcely representative or unbiased, although the anthropological work of Parish and Whyte (1978; Whyte and Parish 1984) is an excellent example of such an approach.

More recently, the new directions taken by the Chinese leadership in the post-Mao era have opened up the country to a much greater degree of outside scrutiny, reflected in brief accounts of the police by academics such as Johnson (1983) and Ward (1984c; Ward and Bracey 1985) and police officials like Alderson (1981a), Finch (1984) and Hirst (1989), although as the latter notes accessibility does not as yet imply that one gets a valid picture of the police system as it operates. Moreover, these more limited but more police-focused accounts are of the 1980s, while much of the more substantial research focused on the period up to the mid-1970s when rather different conditions applied. Indeed, as will become evident, compared with other countries considered in this section the Chinese system is characterized by constant change. To identify the police system of the late 1980s is thus hazardous, not merely because of the inadequacy of recent sources but because the situation could well change overnight.

THE SOCIAL AND POLITICAL STRUCTURE OF THE PEOPLE'S REPUBLIC OF CHINA

China was eventually accredited as a communist state in 1949 after years of bloody conflict. With its population and land-mass it is perhaps the only underdeveloped non-oil-exporting country with a significant presence on the world stage. Only 21 per cent of its population lives in urban areas, and 69 per cent are employed in agriculture. With an infant mortality rate of forty-nine per 1,000 live births and illiteracy at 31 per cent China endures problems well above those of the other countries included here (Tissier 1983), although its levels of public provision compare favourably with those elsewhere in the Third World (Deacon 1983; Whyte and Parish 1984).

While the impact of the communist regime, in its various forms, has been considerable, the influence of Chinese history, with Confucian ethics and a bureaucratic tradition, is still evident. Elements of its legal system, for example, are similar to those in capitalist Taiwan and pre-revolutionary China (Cohen 1977; Lubman 1967), and studies of individual perceptions – for example of the relationship of self to group – reveal similarities between different Asian Chinese compared with US Chinese, French and Americans, with the former more group-oriented and less self-assertive and individualistic (Bloom 1977; Wilson 1977). Emphasis upon group obligations and responsibilities, rather than individual rights (legal or moral) (Tsou 1973), is as much a feature of former dynastic rule and Confucian ideology as it is of current communist structures.

Group obligations are at the heart of most public provisions. State expenditure, for instance on welfare, is low. For example, although primary education is now near-universal, parents are required to pay basic fees. Since 1956 citizens have been given 'five guarantees' – adequate food, clothing, medicine, housing and burial expenses. However, it seems that these guarantees are only applied as a last resort: children are expected to provide for elderly parents, a point emphasized in the 1950 Marriage Law, and indeed it is an *offence* not to do so (Mok 1983; Parish and Whyte 1978; Zhu-Cheng 1983).

As already noted, the force which originally brought Mao to power was rurally based. It incorporated a perspective of urban life as threatening and potentially debilitating, which was partly derived from the experience of Western influence in the nineteenth century, when the coastal cities had become centres of vice and corruption. Additionally there was an ideological emphasis on capitalist cities as parasitic, centres of consumption rather than production. Consequently the new leadership sought to remould urban life according to the rural blueprint:

> In the 1950s the new Communist government set out not only to redistribute the population of cities and limit that growth but also to rid them of the social ills which had become so common in the century since initial western impact. In order to help eliminate crime, vagrancy, corruption, prostitution, and hunger and to help recreate the kind of political commitment known in Yanan, everyone was to be organised from the ground up. City residents were to live no longer in isolated families and alone but in cellular organisations, much as had been true in earlier times. Only this time the cells were not to be autonomous units operating on their own, like the guilds and neighbourhood associations of the past, but integral parts of the national bureaucracy extending all the way from Peking down to the local neighbourhood and work group. (Whyte and Paris 1984, 20).

This interlinkage of the local area with central government was not confined to city dwellers. In the countryside, for example, areas were organized into communes, of some 13,000 people, the main unit of rural government, below which were production teams at village or neighbourhood level. At each level party activists worked closely with other leaders (Parish and Whyte 1978). Although urban communes never achieved the same level of commitment, they characterized the priorities of the new leadership: to control the rate of urbanization, extend city services to new migrants, ovecome the 'estrangement and anomic' characteristics of urban lifestyles and increase social control (Salaff 1967).

Two key features of urban government were the residents' committees and household registers. The former fulfilled a variety of welfare and control tasks, interlinking upwards with municipal government, downwards with small residents' groups of perhaps a dozen families (Salaff 1967; Whyte and Paris 1984). They 'lightened the load of the official bureaux by forming volunteer auxiliaries to assist government census takers, health workers, teachers and police' (Brady 1982b, 77). They also incorporated responsibilities for updating household registers, whereby control was maintained over who lived in the cities. Based on nineteenth-century practices, later modified by the Japanese and Nationalists, registers were the passport to urban services. Only those who were registered as resident within the area were allowed access to state housing, schooling and employment, and the food rationing was also based on the household registration system (White 1977).

That said, the balance between central and local concern, between control at local level or accountability to central government, between professional and neighbourhood responsibilities, has shifted markedly on a number of occasions. Although the emphasis placed by different commentators has varied somewhat (see, for example, Brady 1982b; Brewer *et al.* 1988; Cohen 1966; Leng and Chiu 1985; Lubman 1967), we can perhaps distinguish seven periods since the end of civil war in 1949:

(1) The period 1949–53 when the new, rurally based government consolidated its position and emphasized policies and strategies, such as the 'mass line' and neighbourhood justice, which had proved successful in the rural south.

(2) The period 1953–7 when China became more influenced by the USSR, with a resulting emphasis upon bureaucracy, central control, industrialization, material incentives and a professional legal system, culminating in the phase of the Hundred Flowers Blooming.

(3) The period 1957–61 of the Great Leap Forward, characterized by a bid to cut inequalities, large-scale commune developments, the Red and Expert emphasis, and popular justice.

(4) The period 1961–4 when there was a descaling of the movement,

a shift towards professionalism, a central bureaucracy and material incentives.

(5) The period 1964–8 of the Cultural Revolution with Red Guard activity again emphasizing radical, locally based activity rather than conservative centralism, and a renewed attack on professional aspects of the legal system.

(6) The period 1969–75 when the radical movement continued but was toned down.

(7) The period since 1975 and the death of Mao, with a shift towards centralized bureaucratic control, industrialization, Westernization, material incentives and consumerism, and a re-establishment of a codified legal system.

Essentially, then, any critique of the socio-political and legal structure of China since 1949 needs to encompass two contrasting sets of priorities. On the one hand, there is that which emphasizes ideology, equality, community control, struggle and the rural agricultural base; on the other, there is that which emphasizes production, economic incentives, central bureaucratic control, professionalism and specialism, and urbanization. The first gained ascendancy in the periods 1949–53, 1957–61 and 1964–8, the second in the periods 1953–7, 1961–4 and since 1975. We can follow through these contrasts in subsequent sections on the criminal justice system and the police.

CRIME AND THE CRIMINAL JUSTICE SYSTEM

Any assessment of the level of crime in post-revolutionary China has to be balanced against conditions in the cities during the nineteenth century (Whyte and Paris 1984) and throughout the country during the civil war. In the context of the latter, for example:

> Today, life in the Chinese countryside is much more secure than it was in the immediate prerevolutionary period. Gone are the armed bandits who harassed villagers, and gone are the lineage and ethnic feuds which, in the absence of government control, sometimes escalated into brutal physical fights. Nevertheless some of the old disputes over water, land, and animals remain. (Parish and Whyte 1978, 308).

Equally, compared with its neighbours like Hong Kong, the crime problem in China appears negligible (Alderson 1981a; Starak 1988).

However, reliable statistics are difficult to extract and, as Ward (1984c) points out, a considerable amount of 'minor theft' is not legally defined as 'crime'. But crime has been of considerable public concern, and not just in recent years. As Cohen (1977) wryly observes, residents of a crime-free society would scarcely padlock bicycles and fit bars to the windows of ground-floor apartments to the extent that the Chinese do! Whatever the situation prior to 1975, more recently, as in capitalist societies, crime problems appear to have been on the increase (Chang 1989; Fenwick 1987; Leng and Chiu 1985; Xu 1983). On the one hand, a number of authors have noted a rise in juvenile delinquency (Brady 1983; Jian 1987). On the other, the problems of 'white-collar' crime, most notably official corruption, have been identified (Baogue 1988; Mirsky 1989).

What then of the official response to crime in China? How best can we characterize the criminal justice system? One initial problem in any discussion surrounds the terminology. As Brady (1983, 109) explains:

> It is quite significant that the Chinese have no equivalent to the term 'criminology' in their language. Instead they use the words '*chen fa*' which are best translated as 'political legal'. Police officers, judges, lawyers, justice planners, law professors, and research scientists are all described as political legal specialists or 'cadre'.

This confusion is well illustrated in an article by Yun (1983) in which officials we would consider to be prison officers are referred to as police. It is aggravated by the predominance of concerns over public order and the interlinking of crime with wider issues of political conflict described in one article, aptly entitled 'Campaigns and the manufacture of deviance in Chinese society' (Greenblatt 1977).

In many respects, the legal system has its roots in traditional Chinese society, when there was an inquisitorial judicial system closely affiliatd to the political elite, widespread use of torture, no concept of legal rights, and a priority accredited to informal mediation processes (Allen 1987; Cohen 1977; Lubman 1967). Lawyers, for example, were of low standing in the pre-communist period and have remained so, especially those representing the accused (Brady 1983; Leng and Chiu 1985). A codified system of law was, however, established (Pepinsky 1976) and in the 1950s it seemed that, influenced by the USSR, China would adopt a Soviet-style legal system. The 1954 constitution, for example, established people's courts and procuracy. However the Great Leap Forward saw a reversal of policy when legal principals were seen as emphasizing individualsim rather than collectivism, impeding the revolution and leading to the establishment of a bourgeois society (Pepinsky 1976). The Cultural Revolution similarly heralded a shift away from legal procedures towards community justice, with the slogan 'smashing *gong-jian-far*' (the police, procuracy and courts) (Leng 1981).

In comparison, the period since Mao's death is acknowledged as one in which legal principles have been re-established and codified. In terms of personnel, for example, Shanghai would appear to be awash with lawyers (Huanzhang 1986). The changes have been marked:

> In a series of measures undertaken from early 1978 to the present (1983), the PRC has twice revised the Constitution, codified a number of important laws, restructured the judicial system, and restored and expanded legal education and research. The jural model of law has more than regained the respectability it once enjoyed in the mid-1950s. (Leng and Chiu 1985, 35).

For example, the 1954 provision was restored making the courts and procuracy responsible to the law and independent of political or administrative authority, the conditions whereby a search is illegal are specified, and the Ministry of Justice re-established (Leng and Chiu 1985, 62–84). Referring to the 1982 constitution, Baum (1986, 93) concludes that 'The dominant theme expressed throughout the document was the overwhelming need to create orderly, accountable, legally-regulated political institutions and procedures'. However, as the events of Tiananmen Square illustrate, order may be established with scant reference to the rule of law, and even those sympathetic to the post-Mao changes have acknowledged the tighter controls introduced as part of the legal changes, with restrictions on wall posters introduced and the death penalty made easier to impose (Leng and Chiu 1985). Moreover:

> Viewed from the perspective of the Anglo-American adversary system of criminal justice, a number of flaws were evident in the new Chinese code of criminal procedure. These included the absence of a formal presumption of innocence, the absence of defendant's rights to refuse to give self-incriminating testimony, the stipulation of lawyer's primary obligation to assist the court in uncovering the facts of a case (rather than to defend his client), and the absence of any provision for defendants (or their lawyers) either to subpoena witnesses on their own behalf or to directly cross-examine prosecution witnesses. (Baum 1986, 89).

In this context, the finding that over 99 per cent of defendants are found guilty (Leng and Chiu 1985, 70) is scarcely surprising!

While the court system has retained essentially the same structure over the period since the 1950s, the balance between its various units has shifted. During periods of central bureaucratic control the formal people's courts were accredited with particular significance. At other times, locally based people's tribunals, run by community activists, were of central importance. Since 1975 community involvement in law enforcement, including mediation, has been maintained, but the role of the people's courts has been re-established as the core of the legal structure (Brady 1982b; Leng and Chiu 1985). People's courts are divided on three levels: higher courts within each province or region, intermediate courts within the prefectures and basic courts at county or district level.

Less formal structures are now most commonly used in cases of juvenile crime, i.e. offences committed by those aged 18 or under, although those under 15 are not considered criminally responsible:

> In minor cases of law infraction teenage offenders are turned over to neighbourhood organizations, parents, and teachers for help. Educational aid teams are organized by street committees, residential groups, schools, factories, enterprises, parents, and the police to re-educate the problem youth and make them improve their ways. (Leng and Chiu 1985, 143).

Indeed the whole emphasis of the juvenile justice system appears to be geared towards a conception of delinquency as the result of misguided, inadequately educated youth, and the ideology of reform is underpinned by a paternalism which sounds strange to Western ears. For example:

> The teachers who are teaching at reform schools treat the students as blossoms damaged by insect pests and they try to wash away the dirt on the blossoms and get rid of the insect pests. (Zhu-cheng 1983, 25).

And:

> In carrying out the strict measures of juvenile justice administration and education, delinquents should be treated as children are treated by their parents, as patients are treated by their doctors, or students are treated by their teachers. The object is always to educate and to rescue and rehabilitate juveniles who commit minor offences for which no criminal penalty is deemed necessary. (Jian 1987, 182).

For adults, re-education is also the primary function of sentencing. Prisons, for example, emphasize reform through work and education (Allen 1987), reiterating the policy of the communists prior to 1949 (Griffin 1974). At the extreme, the death penalty is both an acceptance that the offender is beyond re-education and, when carried out, is public, a means of further educating the masses (Hirst 1989) reminiscent of nineteenth-century England. At the other extreme, community-based sanctions, including 'supervised labour', emphasize re-education.

Mediation is an alternative for formal sanctioning which has a long history in China, although its use in the communist system has been shifted towards an emphasis on education in good socialist relationships (Cohen 1968; 1971; Lubman 1967). Mediation committees are also a feature of the local community networks, being located within the sphere of the neighbourhood committees in the cities and of the production brigades elsewhere. It seems that their role has been maintained in the post-Mao era (Zhu-cheng 1983).

At one extreme, then, criminal sanctions are imposed formally by the courts; at the other, more so in particular periods, extra-legal, community-based units have been responsible for sentencing. There is, however, a third alternative, in that the police have themselves been accredited with the authority to impose 'administrative' (as opposed to 'criminal') sanctions. Whilst these include cautions and small fines (as in the West), they also incorporate more severe sanctions such as supervised labour and 'rehabilitation through labour' which, while in theory distinct from imprisonment, are in practice virtually the same (Cohen 1966; Lubman 1969). Interestingly, police powers in this respect have been maintained by the post-Mao leadership (Leng and Chiu 1985, 152).

Clearly, in the Chinese context a review of the criminal justice system is confused by the interlinkage of a number of agencies which in the west fulfil quite separate functions. Equally, the role of community groups, admittedly more pronounced in some periods than others, is more notable than in capitalist or Soviet communist societies. A similar picture emerges when we focus on the police system itself.

THE HISTORY OF POLICING IN CHINA

Confucianism, the orthodox philosophy of the state from 210 BC, identified the aim of government as being to preserve natural harmony. Social order was maintained by a combination of *li*, ethical rules strongly bound to status and privilege, and *fa*, the more formal aspects of social control. *Li* was by far the more important. *Fa*, however, operated where the *li* had broken down and disputes threatened the natural harmony which linked individual, group and society (Lubman 1967).

Informal aspects of social control were vital in a society of such a size. The formal apparatus of government, centred on the emperor in Peking, operated through provincial and subdivisional levels to the counties, or *hsien*, each with between 100,000 and 250,000 inhabitants. At this level, justice came under the responsibility of magistrates, appointed centrally and moved regularly to prevent local factions forming, who were trained in the Chinese classics. These magistrates were responsible for policing and wider legal services as well as other administrative functions such as tax collection, supervision of public works, education and social welfare (Brady 1982b, 31–40; Lubman 1967).

Magistrates were aided by an early form of police, namely agents whom they themselves appointed to deal with complaints that were made by the population (Cohen 1968; Brady 1982b). However, the corruption of these minor officials, combined with the Confucian emphasis upon harmony – which implied that where disputes arose there were no innocent parties – encouraged the people to deal with conflicts on an informal basis. At local level, the medium for the settlement of disputes was kin, village, or guild, with mediation attaining particular significance. Ironically, at this local level responsibility for maintaining order was very similar to Anglo-Saxon England. Magistrates delegated responsibility to village headmen who themselves, under the *pao-chia* system, looked to smaller groups of ten household units to report crimes and identify offenders (Lubman 1967).

In other respects, though, the system was more akin to that of continental Europe in the seventeenth and eighteenth centuries, with a system headed by an emperor, authority delegated to bureaucratic officials, and an inquistorial system of justice. The basis for bureaucratic authority was however, markedly different, although it began to change towards the end of the nineteenth century with increasing Western influence (Brady 1982b; Cohen 1977).

The overthrow of the Ch'ing dynasty in 1911 was followed by a period of open conflict, with rural warlords competing for power. Formal government tended to be concentrated in the cities, and rural areas – controlled in theory by absentee landlords – formed rural associations and village militia. The eventual elevation of Chiang Kai

Shek to power in 1928, backed by those absentee landlords and the urban bourgeoisie, heralded a Nationalist government (the KMT) which attempted to override local traditions and impose a centralized police state from its urban power base. Legal training was prioritized and a modern police system created, characterized by state and individual corruption. Using the model derived from the Japanese invaders cities were organized into neighbourhood networks with elected representatives reporting directly to the local police (Brady 1982b, 41–56).

Until 1928 the Communist Party had worked with the KMT. Following the smashing of the unions, the communists retreated to their rural power bases, particularly in the south. With its emphasis on the 'mass line', the party prioritized community-based dispute settlement, with peasants' associations and mass organizations of women responsible, among other things, for dispute settlement, and workers' and peasants' courts reflecting more bureaucratized approaches to law enforcement. Police work was assigned to the revolutionary army (PLA) assisted by local militia units (Brady 1982b, 57–73). In sum:

> Justice was firmly established as a community affair, emphasising political education and social pressure rather than legislative procedures or punitive sanctions. The people of the countryside were effectively organized and became experienced in the new socialist version of mediation, investigation and volunteer peace-keeping. (Brady 1982b, 73).

Following the success of the communist forces in 1949 mass-line politics, demonstrably successful in the rural areas, was applied across the nation. Volunteer peasant militia were deployed in mop-up campaigns in the countryside. Urban branches of the peasant militia were established, and city dwellers used to participate in volunteer civil defence and street patrol work. Some KMT officials were retained in the police, but new recruits were drawn from the army and local activists (Brady 1982b, 74–112). However:

> The most important mass organizations were the urban militia and the security defence committees. These volunteer police units helped patrol the streets, guard factories and (along with the police) arrested suspected counter-revolutionaries. (Brady 1982b, 88).

Early campaigns in which the police were assisted by residents' committees concerned street crime, organizational corruption, and drug trafficking. By the mid-1950s neighbourhood police in the cities were working in conjunction with the street offices, the base for the local party, and residents' committees (Brady 1982b; Salaff 1967). This alliance has been maintained, although the balance of power between the three has shifted at various times. For example, during the Great Leap Forward the link between police and party was strengthened and the role of residents' committees expanded; but by the early 1960s the role of residents' committees became more passive and the police emerged as a more centrally controlled, conservative force. As a result, the police became one of the main targets of the Cultural Revolution:

> The radicals in justice demanded that the professional agencies (meaning primarily the police) work as agents of revolutionary social change, rather than stand behind legal codes as the flat-footed guardians of the status quo. (Brady 1982b, 189).

Conservative reaction, in which the police were instrumental, led to renewed attacks on the police in 1967, and many police stations were besieged and even overrun. In Canton, for example, more than 200 police were subjected to mass criticism and were paraded through the streets wearing dunces' hats (Brady 1982b, 180–221).

Clearly this represents an extreme. The Cultural Revolution epitomized police authority at its lowest point since 1949. At other times the power of the police has been considerable, both compared with local street organizations and also *vis-à-vis* other elements of the criminal justice system. It is important to stress this, since the following sections emphasize continuities, rather than change, in the police organization.

THE POLICE TODAY

In focusing on the police in China today we are reliant upon two kinds of source. On the one hand there are the recent, fairly restricted discussions of the police, mostly by Western visitors, both practitioners and academics. On the other hand there are the references to the police in fuller accounts of the criminal justice systems by academics, usually confined to the period prior to 1975. In citing the latter sources, it is therefore important to remind ourselves continually that the police system has been subject to considerable variations.

What then of the organization of the police? At national level the police came under the authority of the Ministry of Public Security. As well as the uniformed police, the ministry is also responsible for the plain-clothes secret police and the armed police who protect public buildings and were formerly attached to the military. Each of the twenty-nine provinces and the three major cities has its own public security bureau which is attached to the ministry (Ward and Bracey 1985). In rural areas it appears that further subdivision occurs at special district and county levels, with one officer assigned to each rural district (Cohen 1968). However, detail of the police outside the cities is sparse, possibly because their presence in rural areas is episodic (Parish and Whyte 1978).

Within cities there is a public security bureau, with a sub-bureau within each district of the city. At the neighbourhood level there are stations with an average of twelve patrol men (Cohen 1966; 1968). Li (1971) describes the Hui-yang *hsien* as comprising fourteen stations each with between four and twenty-four officers. Rather later, Ward (1984) describes Shanghai as divided into fourteen districts each with some ten stations, at each of which about thirty-five officers are stationed.

On a formal level, political/legal work is divided between the public security system, responsible for the prevention and detection of crime, and the procuracy, responsible for the supervision of investigations and the processing of cases, although the balance of power between the two organizations has varied over time. Li (1971), for example, describes the situation prior to 1964 as one in which the procuracy operated as a rubber stamp and the police maintained effective control. Within the city, the procuracy operates at city and district levels equivalent to the public security bureau and sub-bureau (Cohen 1968). In contrast the party street office is located at station level, and individual police officers cover a beat containing a number of residents' committees (Cohen 1968; Lubman 1967).

The police system of Chinese cities is closely integrated with both other arms of government and local neighbourhood networks: the *pao-chia* system, as designed by the communists, was based around groups of residental blocks (Salaff 1967). However, the local station is scarcely a *neighbourhood* one. In the Hui-Yang district in the 1950s, for example, each station covered a population of about 35,000 (Li 1971), and Vogel (1971) quotes similar figures for Canton. More recently Johnson (1984), describing the Keiko Road station in Jinan, notes that it serves an area of about sixty factories and 27,000 inhabitants, with eleven residents' committees. In the policing of neighbourhoods, then, individual officers, responsible for a beat of anything from 500 to 5,000 households (Finch 1984; Li 1971; Ward 1984c), are the key personnel.

However, the 'community police officer', while the best publicized of the public security personnel, is at one extreme of an organization which includes considerable specialization. The political arm of the police, centrally controlled, has already been noted. Other specialisms include traffic police, the criminal investigation section and police involved in census work. Indeed, at station level a *majority* of the officers are assigned to census work (Ward 1984c; Ward and Bracey 1985). Again, in contrast to most Western forces, the fire brigade is incorporated as a separate unit within the police (Li 1971; Ward and Bracey 1985).

Not surprisingly, the role of the police has, at least since 1949, been defined broadly to incorporate a wide range of public administrative and welfare tasks. Local officers keep a register of each family in the neighbourhood and all births, deaths and marriages must be reported to the police, as well as temporary residents (visitors). Part of this check on residence entails the police, in conjunction with residents' groups, in carrying out night-time raids on suspect addresses (Vogel 1971; Whyte and Parish 1984), although this practice is more restricted than in the past (Brewer *et al.* 1988).

The police are also involved in neighbourhood-based programmes aimed at rehabilitation (Leng and Chiu 1985; Ward 1984c). But their welfare role is much wider than this. As the public agency with most local contact, the police provide an administrative and welfare service within the community. Describing the 1950s, Li (1971, 61) notes:

> Each patrolman was responsible for virtually everything that occurred in the area under his control: he not only had to maintain order and enforce the law, but also had to look out for the general welfare of the inhabitants and see that government policies were implemented.

More recently, Chang (1984, 96) has likened the police station to 'a general management office for all the affairs of the community' and Johnson (1984, 9) describes how 'good deeds are done for the masses' (especially the old and sick) by the police. Ironically, the control element of household census enables the community police to identify those in need of support:

> The household registration police are familiar with the needs of widowers, widows and other elderly people in their vicinities. They often help them wash clothes, buy food grain, clean their houses, manage household affairs and get to hospitals when they fall ill. (Yun 1983, 22).

This somewhat idealized picture raises one final question of relevance here: namely, who are the police? Unfortunately the answer is by no means clear. Certainly during the civil war, policing in communist-held territory was an army (PLA) responsibility, and after 1949 former military personnel were drafted in to replace KMT police (Brady 1982b; Johnson 1984). Recruits were not necessarily party members (Cohen 1977) although there was a tendency for activists to join the police from 1957 onwards, and again in the early 1970s (Brady 1982b, 218–19; 1983, 123). Equally little is known of the extent of female officers, although it seems unlikely that there were many in the early period. Leng and Chiu (1985, 65), however, quoting local sources, suggest that by the 1980s there were some 50,000 policewomen and that women were by then playing a significant role as judges, procurators and police.

POLICE AND PUBLIC

The representativeness of the police is of course one aspect of police/public relations, and while there is little data available on the social characteristics of the police it is evident that at different times the police have been attacked as members of an elite organization, not representing the interests of the people. Equally clearly, though, when the early communist regime prioritized the 'need to close the gap between the law officials and local populace' (Salaff 1967, 84), promoting a role for the public in the law-enforcement process was the key plank to this platform.

In the countryside, local militia units had been formed during the civil-war period and these operated after 1949 in a public-order capacity (Brady 1982b). Parish and Whyte (1978, 40–1) describe the organization of these militia at both commune and village level. In the former, retired army men operated armed units. In contrast, village militia units, comprising younger males and some females, were unarmed, although one or two guns were kept in the brigade office. The village militia was deployed in night patrols in order to protect property and capture those attempting to escape to Hong Kong, but it also operated in a non-police capacity as a study unit for local activists.

The rural militia had established urban branches by 1950 and these volunteer police units were active in street patrols, especially against counter-revolutionaries and organized-crime syndicates (Brady 1982b, 75–90). During the 1950s militia units were placed under the control of the local police and given special responsibility for traffic incidents. However, during the Great Leap Forward they were reorganized under party control, renamed 'people's patrols', and given wider responsibilities, ranging from education to the maintenance of public order and exposure of child neglect. They subsequently played a central part in the public exposure and ridicule campaigns of the time (Cohen 1968).

Of even more significance were the residents' committees formed in the early 1950s. By 1951, over 80 per cent of Shanghai's population was organized into such committees which became involved in war-bond sales, fire-prevention work, education, and implementing the registration system (Brady 1982b). Their policing role expanded with the campaign against drug abuse, and residents' committees subsequently formed specialist security-defence committees. Each individual police officer within an urban neighbourhood would consequently find himself or herself dealing with a multitude of local groups. Representing the party there was the local branch, subdivided into small groups, a small group of the Young Communist League and a Women's Association group. There was also a mediation committee, a residents' committee with street-based small groups, a specialist security-defence committee and similar street-level small groups. At this level, the community was involved in crime prevention, the detection of crime and the reintegration of offenders, as well as a wider range of other local responsibilities (Alderson 1981; Lubman 1967; Vogel 1971). The role of the community police officer was thus closely integrated with such groups:

> The patrolman assigned to the area of the residents' committee works closely with the chairman and other responsible members of that committee, the secretary of the Communist Party unit within the residents' committee, and the secretary of the Communist Youth League unit. Together with the patrolman this group forms the local power elite and brings surveillance of the teeming urban masses down to the level of the individual household, a task the police alone could not perform. (Cohen 1966, 490).

In this context, the representativeness of this local elite becomes of crucial relevance. However, while Cohen (1968) provides a positive image of local leaders, Whyte and Parish (1984) argue that in the cities, unlike the countryside, they tended to be proposed by the party rather than elected by the community, a result of apathy as much as political manipulation. As Brady (1982b, 76–7) accepts,

> the organizations failed to bring urban shut-ins into the forefront of socialist politics and could not break the dark fatalism which lingered in the back streets. The long-silent housewives and the extremely poor only rarely served as

> officers or leaders in the committees, and usually did the legwork for the younger and more educated residents who ran the committees.

More recently, Johnson (1984) suggests that local leaders tend to be retired government officials with reputations for effective work styles and ideological correctness, but who are also respected representatives of the community.

How far, then, are the police influenced by local opinion? At different times, control over the police appears to have shifted between party, local community, procuracy and the police organization itself. During the immediate post-revolutionary priod, for example, the police achieved considerable autonomy: 'During the turbulent years following Communist takeover (1950–1953) the police dominated sanctioning processes, and the courts functioned either not at all or as police auxiliaries' (Lubman 1969, 562). Li (1971) similarly described police dominance of the procuracy and the court in the Hui-yang *hsien* in the 1950s, a period when police discretion over 'extra-court' sanctioning was considerable. As party street offices were set up, however, the residents' committees and local police tended to be controlled by the party (Brady 1982b, 127). Similarly, in the backlash against the Great Leap Forward:

> The public, represented by residents' committees, street offices and the rural communes, were largely restricted to a passive role as auxiliaries and information bearers . . . The conservatives effectively crushed the popular justice check and after 1961–62 the police and other government officials were answerable only to the Party apparatus. The police became increasingly a conservative force, committed to order and social discipline, but little concerned with social change, educational reform and mass line politics. (Brady 1982b, 177–9).

Control of the police by the party, whether at local or national level, is similarly identified by both Lubman (1969) and Cohen (1977).

But what of changes since 1975? Two trends can be identified. On the one hand, the shift towards a constitutional framework, the reintroduction of a Ministry of Justice, and the expanding role of the procuracy, are all directed at establishing legal controls over police practices. Thus legislation in 1980 introduced legal safeguards over a number of police procedures including the length of time suspects can be held in custody before arrest, acceptable methods of interrogation, and the need for search warrants, and legislation in 1979 established the role of the procuracy in supervising police operations. It is, however, notable that police 'extra-court' sentencing is maintained, and that party influence on the procuracy is still evident (Baum 1986; Leng 1981; Leng and Chiu 1985).

A second trend, again perhaps predictable, is towards greater levels of specialism and professionalism within the police. It did, of course, underpin much police work in earlier periods. Li (1971), for example, highlighted the dangers of police specialization leading to the emergence of an occupational culture which would protect its members from outside influence. However, policies since 1975 have tended to reinforce and accelerate such trends both in the military (Joffe 1983) and in the police. Ward and Bracey (1985), for example, describe recent moves towards specialization and professionalism apparent in the expanding training programme, some of which is highly centralized. Most recently, Chang (1989), employed by the Research Institute of Public Security in Beijing, emphasizes both the importance of professionalism within the police and the consequential role of internal (ministry) levels of accountability.

The 1980s have seen a continuance of public involvement in the policing of neighbourhoods (Alderson 1981a; Chang 1984; Johnson 1984; Leng and Chiu 1985; Ward 1984c). However, the balance of power between local party, residents and beat officers appears to have shifted in favour of the police. Although speculative, it seems that a more specialized and professional police force has become more subject to internal control and that neighbourhood groups will become more like those in capitalist Japan, rather than executing any degree of control over local policing.

SUMMARY

The police system of China is very complex. While on the one hand it has been moulded by the ideological priorities of the rural communist forces, equally its ancestry can be traced to Confucianism and directly to the influence of the Japanese invaders. That said, Mao explicitly set out to shape cities according to all that he saw as best in rural community life, and at the same time attempted to build a complex network of controls linking the local neighbourhood with the central state, with the role of the party crucial at all levels.

Crime has scarcely been eliminated. Equally, as in the Soviet Union, communist property structures provide opportunities and incentives for new versions of old crime involving bribery and corruption. Additionally, China has periodically been the battleground on which crusaders have fought to identify new forms of deviant activity: incorrect thoughts, inappropriate fertility patterns, or activities suggesting adherence to pre-revolutionary values. However, the organization of urban populations into residents' committees, security-defence committees, and similar street-level small groups, provides a structure in which privacy is more difficult to attain and consequently criminal acts – and even criminal thoughts – less easily hidden.

The positive side to this is that local community influence has been more pronounced, and especially during the Great Leap Forward and the Cultural Revolution the police were particularly vulnerable to criticism. The predictable finale to the Cultural Revolution in fact was that the process of accusation and counter-accusation got so out of hand that Mao was forced to withdraw his support from the Red Guards. Moreover, while the balance between police power and community influence has been subject to shift, the influence of the party on both has been evident.

As in the Soviet Union, 1989 saw considerable changes within China. However, while in the former there is a shift towards more openness and a reorganization of the economic and administrative structures, China's *perestroika* was not accompanied by *glasnost*, and when links with the West appeared to be bringing more benefits for the elite than for the general population, popular protest was squashed. We might therefore expect greater emphasis to be placed on the police as the upholders of public order at the same time as there is a pronounced move towards a more professionalized, trained and centralized police system. It thus seems unlikely that community influences on policing will receive any further official encouragement. Whether or not they ever were the people's police, policing in China in the immediate future will most certainly not 'belong' to the public.

10

Cuba: Between the USSR and China

INTRODUCTION

Since the 1959 revolution which brought Fidel Castro to power, Cuba has rarely been out of the news. Constantly in conflict with the United States, its troops evident in a number of Third World countries, and its larger-than-life president, it presents in high profile the threat posed by and the problems facing communism in South America.

With its social and political system influenced, at different stages, by the USSR and China, Cuba has also attracted considerable attention from social scientists. Among these, a number of legal specialists were drawn to Castro's emphasis on public participation in law (Berman and Whiting 1980). Of particular relevance to the criminal justice system as a whole is Salas's (1979a) account of social control in Cuba.

Other critiques of the legal system by criminologists or sociologists are, however, sparse. Perhaps the most notable exception is Brady's (1981; 1982a) work, useful not merely because he, like Salas (1979a) views policing in the wider context of Cuban society, but also because, with wide experience of the Chinese situation, Brady (1981) is well placed to draw comparisons between different communist societies. As he himself notes in the Chinese context, however (Brady 1982b), analyses of the system vary markedly according to the political perspective of the writer. In the case of Cuba, this is evident not merely in comparing the work of those in the American law tradition with more radical social scientists, but also in terms of arguments within the left, with some critics like Binns and Gonzalez (1980) denouncing Cuba's right to be considered socialist at all! Bearing this in mind, it is appropriate to begin with a consideration of Cuba's socio-political structure.

CUBAN SOCIETY

With a population of about 10 million, Cuba is the second smallest country to be considered in detail here. Being half the size of the United Kingdom, it has a relatively low density of population (85.6 per square km), slightly below that of France, and only 69 per cent of its population is classified as urban. Conversely, a comparatively high proportion of its employed population is engaged in agriculture (Vergara 1983).

Cuba was in fact a Spanish colony until the end of the nineteenth century when the Americans replaced the Spanish as the dominant influence (Leo Grande 1982). The United States was concerned both to maintain a suitable government in Cuba and to protect its own financial interests, with the result that 'the Cuban economy was completely subordinated to the US sugar barons' (Binns and Gonzalez 1980, 2).

The 1959 revolution was, indeed, more of a nationalist-inspired war of independence than a communist revolution, and socialist principles have to some extent been pragmatic responses to specific problems rather than dogma (Binns and Gonzalez 1980). As Leo Grande (1982, 33) subtly expresses the situation: 'Cuba was the first country to have a Marxist-Leninist revolution without a community party in the vanguard of the revolutionary struggle.' Indeed, the old style Cuban Communist Party has often been seen as a reactionary rather than a revolutionary force. Further indication of the ambiguous basis for the revolution is the fact that the Soviet Union was not intimately involved in Cuba until the United States cancelled Cuba's sugar quota in the mid-1960s (Leo Grande 1982). Binns and Gonzalez (1980, 6), indeed quote Fidel Castro as saying in 1959: 'Our revolution is neither capitalist nor communist! . . . Capitalism sacrifices the human being, communism with its totalitarian conceptions sacrifices human rights. We agree neither with the one nor the other.'

What then were the key changes introduced by the new regime? Essentially there were at least five major reforms (Binns and Gonzalez 1980). The first of these was the land-reform policy which abolished the very large estates, often owned by absentee landlords, and redistributed them among the poorest peasants. The second, nationalization of major assets owned by multinationals, particularly the oil refineries, was provoked by their refusal to refine oil imported from the USSR. Thirdly, Castro instigated a number of measures to improve social conditions through increasing wages, reducing rents and cutting the prices of services such as electricity. Fourthly, and related to this, was an emphasis on improved welfare services, especially regarding education and health. Finally, Castro aimed to pay for many of these reforms and limit the costs of others by diversifying the economy, improving the efficiency of both industry and agriculture, and expanding citizen participation in the provision of goods and services in a 'voluntary', or at least unpaid, capacity.

In order to finance many of its reforms and escape from economic dependence on the United States and other unsympathetic foreign governments, the Cuban government tried a number of alternative reform policies. In the early 1960s, for example, emphasis was placed on the expansion and diversification of industry; then in the 1963–5 period Castro attempted to increase sugar production by introducing material incentives in accord with practices in the USSR; following this, in the late 1960s, Cuba shifted towards closer relations with China and a re-emphasis upon moral incentives (Binns and Gonzalez 1980). For all these shifts in policy, Salas (1985) characterizes the period 1959–69 as the revolutionary phase, replaced in the 1970s by an institutional phase in which Cuban communism came more closely to resemble the East European model.

In fact, Cuba's increased dependency on the USSR, which led Binns and Gonzalez (1980) to argue that Cuba had changed its political master rather than its political system, is largely finance-led. Foreign debt, crippling and inequitable trade agreements with the Eastern bloc, and dependence on sugar exports, leave Cuba in a precarious financial position, exacerbated by the fall in sugar prices in the early 1980s (Vergara 1983).

In complete contrast to its financial situation, social and welfare conditions in Cuba compare favourably both with its pre-revolutionary situation and with the rest of Latin America (Eckstein 1982). Life expectancy is similar to the UK, and while infant mortality and illiteracy are higher than in industrialized Western societies they have improved dramatically since 1959 and are low by Latin American standards, reflecting Castro's commitment to improved welfare services (Eckstein 1982; Vergara 1983).

However, it is the principles behind the structure of welfare services as much as levels of expenditure which bring approval from radical social scientists such as Deacon (1983) and Brady (1982a). Partly spurred on by a need to improve services at low cost, partly through a rejection of the pre-revolutionary professional classes and corrupt bureaucracy, the Cuban government is committed to a series of grassroots movements which have increased lay participation in the planning and provision of a range of public services, as well as encouraging the public to volunteer their leisure time to increase production, for example by harvesting the sugar.

In the public-service context, these grassroots movements include the Federation of Cuban Women, youth associations, and most especially committees for the defence of the revolution (CDR) (Berman 1969; Binns and Gonzalez 1980; Brady 1982a; MacEwan 1975; Salas 1979a, 296–329). Initially formed to guard against counter-revolution and outside aggression, CDR provide a link between central government and local community and form the basis for a number of initiatives concerned with social control and public and individual welfare. Their crime-related role will be assessed later. Here it is important to stress their part in such initiatives as the census, the administration of the rationing system, mobilization of the labour force, health campaigns, the 1961 literacy campaign, neighbourhood cleaning and repairs and political education campaigns. Eight months after their formation they could boast over 100,000 units with 500,000 members; at their height they included 3 million people or some 70 per cent of the population aged over 14. It is generally acknowledged that the 1970s saw a move away from this degree of dependence on grassroots movements (Salas 1979a, 296–329; 1985) paralleling a shift towards welfare specialization and professionalism (Deacon 1983). Nevertheless, in 1986 CDR still allegedly boasted some 6.5 million members, or 84 per cent of those aged over 14 (Third Congress of the Communist Party of Cuba 1986, 68). Moreover, the level of community participation implied by such developments, engendering as it did a widespread and continuing commitment to the revolution and the regime, has had considerable implications for both levels of social order and the nature of the criminal justice system.

CRIME AND THE CRIMINAL JUSTICE SYSTEM

Any consideration of crime levels in post-revolutionary Cuba must take account of the pre-revolutionary period, especially the Batista regime, when Cuba served as 'vice island', a resort within easy distance of the USA where any services could be provided for those with money to pay. A corrupt political system co-existed with organized crime profiting from gambling, drugs and prostitution. The shanty towns and slums provided ample recruits for the mobs and nurtured 'a predatory culture of violence, thievery, impulsive crime, immorality and fear' (Brady 1982a, 253).

The new government, aware of the close association between state corruption and organized crime, prioritized crime control, focusing especially on official corruption and gang leaders. Prostitution was also targeted (Olmo 1979). While we should treat falls in official crime rates with scepticism, especially in a time of turbulent change, a decline in homicide rates from 38.2 per 100,000 population in 1959 to 6.1 in 1968 indicates a real shift (Dominguez 1979). This is not to say that Castro's government has solved the crime problem. Juvenile delinquency, for example, is seen as a continuing problem, and indeed is identified, as in the West, with lower-class, inner-city males with low educational achievements (Salas 1979b). Nevertheless:

> While juvenile delinquency, black marketeering, and domestic conflict remain as problems, virtually all available hard evidence supports travellers' subjective impressions: Cuba had, in the first decade of the revolution, broken the back of the crime problem. (Brady 1982a, 279).

To some extent this has been countered by the new regime's criminalization of acts not previously considered deviant. Loney (1973), for example, cites the repression of political dissidents, including intellectuals, and the imprisonment of homosexuals. Attempts to impose the work ethic by punishing the workshy (modelled on the Soviet anti-parasite laws) centred on the 'law on loafing', *Ley Contra La Vagrancia* (Kennedy 1973).

The need for a law to prohibit malingering illustrates the limits to attempts to create national solidarity, commitment to the revolution, and willingness to purge society of crime. Nevertheless, in exposing and dismantling the injustices of the old system and undermining the role of bureaucrats and professionals in supervising the system, the government induced new levels of participation in and commitment to law enforcement.

There was some gradual improvement in prison conditions and a greater emphasis on re-education, at least of the lower echelons of the criminal fraternity (Brady 1982a). Work camps, run by the army, were used for a variety of deviants, including homosexuals, vagrants and delinquents (Salas 1979a). But the most significant changes were to the prosecution processes. Dissatisfaction with a professional legal system led to the introduction, in 1964, of popular tribunals (Berman 1969; Cantor 1974; Salas 1979a, 211–15). First organized in rural areas, by the end of the 1960s there were estimated to be 500 tribunals dealing with civil disputes, petty crimes and juvenile delinquency. Local volunteers, many of them working-class, usually nominated by the party or the CDR, presided over cases which were tried in public within the neighbourhood or workplace. Indeed many took place in the open air, and participation from the audience was encouraged, even if in some cases it was prearranged. The advantages of popular tribunals were seen in terms of their control by those closest to the crime and defendant, able to take account of the environment which might have contributed to the crime being committed and assess culpability in the wider context of offenders' past behaviour. Sanctions imposed by the courts included public admonition and a series of requirements regarding, for example, further education and restrictions on freedom of movement, the main aims of the tribunals being conflict resolution and conformity through re-education and community moral pressure.

However, criticism of the inefficiency of the popular tribunals in dealing with a perceived increase in disorder, especially juvenile delinquency, led to a reorganization of the judicial structure in 1973. Municipal courts, presided over by one professional and two lay judges, replaced the tribunals. While this is to some extent indicative of a shift from a popular to a professional legal system, it must be noted that public involvement is maintained through the lay judges and the informal court setting, and that education is still seen as a primary goal of the legal system (Salas 1979a; 1985). The contrast between the pre-revolutionary system of corrupt 'justice', the post-revolutionary phase of the 1959–69 period, and later moves towards institutionalization and professionalism is, however, notable, and paralleled within the context of policing.

THE HISTORY OF THE POLICE IN CUBA

Little information is available on the police prior to the 1959 revolution. What is clear, however, is that they formed an integral part of the repressive system. The extent of the openness of organized crime is also indicative of levels of corruption within the police (Brady 1982a; Salas 1979a).

The police were organized on a national level into an urban force and a rural guard. There was also a secret police system with a network of informants. The police operated as a paramilitary force, armed, and notorious for both political repression and looting, rape and intimidation. The force was considered of lower status than the army, and while a means of upward mobility for the urban poor, offered little by way of training.

During the revolution the police played a big if ultimately unsuccessful role in supporting the Batista government, and after its fall many senior officers fled the country. Those who did not were tried and invariably executed. Many of the lower ranks changed their loyalties and continued their duties under the new regime.

Not surprisingly, Castro saw the old police as unreliable. A trusted rebel commander, Efigenio Amejeiras, was made chief of police and stations came under the direct command of the rebel forces. Gradually, police ranks were purged, replacements being drawn from the rebel army. To increase morale, rates of pay were raised, and a new uniform was introduced to distinguish the new police force from its discredited predecessor.

Nevertheless, replacement of the old police force was a convoluted process. Potential new recruits tended to be lacking in education and training, and Salas (1979a, 259) recounts the story of one policeman who felt so humiliated by his illiteracy that he offered his resignation.

Partly because of recruitment problems, partly to minimize the need to rely on the police, in the early stages of the new government Castro formed a national revolutionary militia and the CDR as civilian groups with responsibilities for maintaining order. By the beginning of the 1960s, then, the army, the police and local volunteer groups provided alternative, and sometimes conflicting, means of enforcing the law and preserving order while enabling the government to avoid over-reliance on any one faction.

THE POLICE IN POST-REVOLUTIONARY CUBA

The police faction comes under the remit of the Ministry of the Interior, which is directly accountable to the Central Committee of the Communist Party (Salas 1979a, 257–95). The ministry is divided into three vice-ministries, Security, Technical, and – the largest – Internal Order and Crime Prevention. The Vice-Ministry for Security, which includes border guards, is concerned with counter-revolutionary activity, whilst the Technical Vice-Ministry deals with foreign intelligence. The Vice-Ministry for Internal Order and Crime Prevention has three general directorates concerned with penal establishments, the fire service and the police.

The latter is the largest of these, with some 10,000 personnel, producing a comparatively low rate of one per 1,000 citizens. The police organization operates at central, provincial and local (municipal) levels. At national level there are specialist units concerned with such matters as traffic, juveniles, crime prevention and detection. These specialist sections are repeated in the 14 provinces. The municipal police operate on routine patrol activities and are armed. They are divided into mobile units and foot patrols, and do not have specialist responsibilities, for example *vis-à-vis* detection. Detectives, who work in technical investigation departments at central and provincial level, are further subdivided into specialist sections dealing with robbery, homicide, drugs etc.

Further than this, little detail is available concerning day-to-day policework. Certainly in the early 1960s the police prioritized the fight against counter-revolutionary activities rather than traditional crime, and were also involved in investigation of new crimes, such as inefficient or corrupt management practices, poor work practices, and homosexual activities. They also appear to have been accredited with considerable discretion.

> During this stage police roles went far beyond those of maintaining order or enforcing the law. They were in fact spearheading drives for radical social change, a role contradictary to traditional ideas about the role of police. An interesting feature of this process is that the police did not seem to favor the unbridled discretion enjoyed . . . In fact they were at the forefront of the forces advocating a return to legality, which was characterized by the abolition of popular courts and regulation of CDR power. (Salas 1979a, 284).

At local level, police involvement in the community has continued to be prioritized. Crime-prevention work, including work within the schools, is seen as important, with the police incorporated into social education programmes covering both uncontentious issues such as road safety and rather problematic areas like homosexuality and childrearing (Salas 1979a). Less contentious is the involvement of the police within the local community in a service capacity. In Santiago for example:

> The police move fluidly in and out from the rear offices, stopping to sit on benches alongside the citizens, sharing soft drinks and bits of (Orient) humour whilst listening to accounts of events or problems. Always civilians and police address one another simply as comrade, and conversations do not carry the stress one generally feels in the jails and police stations of other nations. Indeed, most of these conversations are not of formal accusations or complaints, but general discussions of social relations, potential problems and conditions in the neighbourhoods. Such discussions would most likely be dismissed as 'trivial' or too vague and unfocussed to warrant official action by hard-pressed police in North American cities; in Cuba they are considered essential to proper law enforcement. (Brady 1982a, 249).

Such quotes suggest a lack of distance between police and public which we might expect to be reflected in the representativeness of the police. What little information is available presents a rather mixed picture (Salas 1979a).

It is perhaps not surprising, especially in Latin America, to find the police to be male-dominated. As already noted, in the early post-revolutionary period they tended to be poorly educated, rural males drawn from the rebel forces. To improve overall quality, priority was given to education and training, added to which, as overall educational standards in Cuba rose, so did the qualifications of the typical recruit. Political commitment is, however, still an important criterion for selection and from the late 1970s emphasis has been placed on attracting applicants from political organizations like the Union of Young Communists. As elsewhere, then, we see a move to recruit the police from factions seen as sympathetic to the status quo, producing, like China, a markedly different profile from the police of capitalist societies.

POLICE AND PUBLIC

The police may not, strictly speaking, be representative of the population, but the image conjured up by authors like Brady (1982a) is of a congruence between police and public. The comparatively low levels of police personnel also imply a degree of public commitment. It is, moreover, ideologically important that policing should not become the responsibility of an occupational elite:

> The meaning of the police–community relations in Cuba goes far beyond that in capitalist society. While a close nexus between police and the public is a desired goal of most societies, it acquires much greater significance in a nation so dominated by concepts of egalitarianism and mass participation. Should either the Ministry of the Interior or the army become an elite force, the ideological underpinnings of the regime would be undermined seriously. (Salas 1979a, 281).

Equally, since crime is seen as an anti-state activity, its control is the responsibility of the total population:

> The control and prevention of crime does involve most of the population in some direct or indirect role; since to be a 'revolutionary' means to take an active role in community problem-solving through local volunteer associations. (Brady 1982a, 249).

In a society in which levels of public participation are extraordinarily high, citizen involvement in the policing process takes two basic forms – police auxiliary units and CDRs.

Police auxiliary units were first formed in rural areas in 1962 with their primary function being the protection of vital installations from counter-revolutionary factions (Berman 1969). Their use was subsequently extended to urban areas where they are formally attached to the police. Applications are closely vetted, at least partly because auxiliaries are armed and have the same powers of arrest as do regular officers. In other respects, however, they appear very similar to volunteer reserve units in Western capitalist societies (Salas 1979a).

In comparison with these *police* volunteers, CDRs incorporate a far greater proportion of the population and are involved in a variety of projects of which crime-related work is only one aspect (Salas 1979a, 296–329). Nevertheless, the primary role of the CDRs has always been one of vigilance, first against the threat of counter-revolution, then crime. They are responsible for regular censuses and keep up-to-date records of local residents, as well as more specific social-control functions.

Membership of CDRs is open to all those aged over 14, with few restrictions, upon payment of membership fees. Members then receive an identification card. About half the members are women, but younger people and professionals are underrepresented. Units are based within local neighbourhoods and integrated through a series of zonal, municipal and provincial structures with a national executive.

The main crime-related activity of CDRs involves neighbourhood patrols. At first these were organized independently by each unit, but by the early 1970s zones were given responsibility for co-ordinating about 20 local units, with perhaps 12–24 volunteers on duty each night. Patrol members wear armbands for identification but – unlike police auxiliaries – are not officially armed. Patrols act as a crime deterrent and are also instrumental in the detention of suspects. Anyone seen committing an offence can be subject to a citizen's arrest. In other cases, patrols have the authority to demand to see the identification documents of any member of the public and to detain suspects while the police are called.

In addition to these pro-active initiatives, CDRs are also responsible for gathering data at the local level which allows for further involvement in the criminal justice process. Local information, for example, is used by CDR units to prepare pre-sentence investigations on local offenders and contribute advice on bail decisions.

CDRs also set up meetings to consider what lessons might be

learned from specific crimes which have taken place. A repudiation meeting is called within twenty-four hours of the crime, at which the police, CDR patrol, victims and other local residents or businesses consider what might be done to prevent similar crimes occurring in the future. Where the crime is solved a further meeting is called at which the police explain their actions. At this point, interestingly, the offender might be called to give advice on target hardening and patrol activities.

This account suggests a considerable openness to the police organization and a close involvement of the community, not merely as aides to the police but as participants in the policing process. However, a few cautionary words need to be added here. First, it is arguable that, rather than facilitating public involvement in policing, the CDRs were a primary means by which the political elite policed the people. As already noted, they were centrally co-ordinated, centrally initiated and, indeed, centrally controlled:

> at no point were the CDRs controlled by their mass base. On the contrary their leadership was universally *appointed* by the Communist Party. They were never permitted to formulate policy, only to implement the policy given to them from above. (Binns and Gonzalez 1980, 27).

Allied to this, it is clear that the periods when CDRs were most evident coincided with those times when they fulfilled important functions for the government – in providing a reserve labour force or in countering the power of the army or police. None the less, while most significant in the 1960s, they were revitalized in the mid-1970s when Castro criticized the police for losing touch with the people (Salas 1979a), and still feature prominently, at least on an official level (Third Congress of the Communist Party of Cuba 1986).

In fact, the relationship between police and CDRs appears to have been characterized by conflict, and disputes over responsibilities and duties. Such issues are at the heart of questions concerning police accountability.

Salas (1979a, 273–9) argues that the Cuban police in the post-revolutionary phase are characterized by a number of military features, and like the army have been least affected by the philosophy of community control and anti-elitism. In particular he notes the hierarchical chain of command, paralleling that of the army, an emphasis on military discipline, the origins of the police in the rebel army and involvement in political activities. These militaristic tendencies have been accelerated in the period since 1970 with a renewed emphasis upon an elite, professional bureaucracy. The extent to which this bureaucracy can be insulated from political control is limited given the close association between police personnel and party membership, and the influence of the party within the Ministry of the Interior since 1965. Equally the procuracy has considerable latitude in reviewing the operation of the Ministry of the Interior, including police practices (Salas 1979a, 284–7). Nevertheless, there is some evidence of a shift away from political or legislative accountability towards internal accountability, consistent with the East European model.

Clearly the relationship between police and public, while considerably closer than in many capitalist societies, is both ambiguous and subject to change. While the power of party-based bureaucracies, dominated by cadres, is less evident, as in China there is a tendency towards such elitism and away from grassroots involvement. Given the closer ties with the Soviet Union which a precarious economy has forced upon Cuba, it seems likely that such tendencies will increase.

SUMMARY

Although the Cuban revolution was not based around Marxist-Leninist ideals, hostile reaction from the US pushed Cuba into closer and closer co-operation with the Soviet Union. However, while economically it has become highly dependent upon the USSR, many features of the Cuban social and criminal justice systems show greater affinity with Chinese communism. Thus popular involvement in health programmes and literacy campaigns were matched by the creation of popular tribunals and street patrols.

CDRs formed the basis for a number of welfare and crime-related initiatives. While varying in the official support they received, they provided a balance between military and police and have been maintained as a key element of Cuban life. At neighbourhood level, they operate as the equivalent of the residents' committees in China, but as in China evidence a coherence and structure which links them with central government.

While police operations are to some extent influenced by CDRs, the police organization is more centralized, militaristic and autonomous than in China, due at least partly to the fact that Cuba's size makes a centralized force feasible. As in other areas of public life, the composition of the post-revolutionary force was determined by the unreliability (or absence) of its previous incumbents. In restructuring the police, then, the rebel army provided a number of recruits, many from the lower classes, and in this sense at least the police have been fairly representative of the people. Nevertheless, with increased Soviet influence and a corresponding shift towards professionalism in the public sector, it may well be that the police system is gradually becoming a more traditional force. Nevertheless, in the immediate post-revolutionary period, Cuba like China provides us with a police system that is in marked contrast to those of Western capitalist societies.

11

Community Involvement in Policing: a Comparative Analysis

INTRODUCTION

The preceding chapters have been focused on specific countries; in each case a similar set of issues has been addressed so as to allow ready comparisons to be drawn. In this and the following chapter the approach is varied. In Chapter 12 the eight countries covered in Chapters 3–10, plus England and Wales and the US, will be reviewed in terms of the range of criteria introduced in Chapters 1–2 as applicable to a definition of the police and the assessment of variations between different policing systems. First, however, this chapter provides a more detailed analysis of one specific area of interest, namely the relationship between police and public in the policing of communities.

Historically, as noted in Chapter 2, the extent to which the local community or the state was involved in maintaining order and responding to deviance has varied. In France, in particular, following the Roman model, specialists were employed from an early period. However, in many of the other countries considered, responsibility for law enforcement was delegated to the local community. In Japan and China, for example, while there was some degree of state-imposed control through the samurai and the magistracy respectively, ultimate responsibility still rested on the small group at village or kin level. A similar picture is evident in a range of countries prior to colonial rule (Griffiths 1971; Jeffries 1952).

The extent to which modern police systems, especially in the UK and North America, built on this community base is more problematic. True, mythology accords nineteenth-century policing systems a community base (Manning 1984), and Jackson (1985) in his interviews with senior British police officers describes their faith in a tradition of policing by consent, which they interestingly contrasted with the US position. However, as Miller (1977) stresses, while

London Metropolitan police officers were deliberately recruited from outside the area, in New York local officers were sought. Reppetto (1978) indeed suggests that this over-reliance on the community both as a source of recruits and as the base for accountability engendered corruption and inefficiency. Undoubtedly, reformers such as Fosdick and Vollmer saw the road to improvement marked by a bureaucratic, public-service professionalism, based on scientific administrative and management practices (Manning 1982; Reppetto 1978).

Such concerns were never as prevalent in the UK. However, while US reforms stopped short of providing larger, more centralized police forces, with overall responsibility for police services within a state or county, for example, in England and Wales there has been a move towards a smaller number of larger forces, and more recently government initiatives have strengthened central co-ordination and control of individual forces (Reiner 1985), vividly illustrated during the miners' strike (Fine and Millar 1985). Common to both countries and indeed other industrialized societies, however, was the impact of technology: the widespread introduction of patrol cars and improvements in communication shifting the emphasis from police proximity to speedy response to an emergency. In Britain such shifts were characterized by the natural history of police television series: 'Dixon of Dock Green' gave way to 'Z Cars' which was replaced by 'Softly Softly Task Force'. A similar shift occurred in the US (Kelling 1987) and Canada (Murphy 1988). Japan, scarcely immune to technological innovations, was only temporarily delayed by the complexity of its urban road networks (Ames 1981; National Police Agency 1984).

There was, however, an almost immediate reaction against what came to be termed 'reactive' or 'fire-brigade' policing (Alderson 1979). In the US, for example, the President's Crime Commission of the 1960s, concerned a public reluctance to play a part in crime control, stimulated a variety of initiatives. By the early 1970s, 'community policing', 'team policing' and 'problem-oriented approaches' were being advocated as means of re-establishing a significant policing presence at neighbourhood level (Goldstein 1979; Kuykendall 1974; Sherman, Milton and Kelly 1973). By the 1980s, definitions of community policing had been widened to incorporate policing *by* the community, through initiatives such as block watch and neighbourhood watch (Figgie Report 1983; Rosenbaum 1988).

In England and Wales, similar concerns found expression in 1966 in the 'Accrington experiment' into unit beat policing, whereby resident beat officers (possibly) living in local areas were backed up by patrol cars, detectives and centralized collation facilities. The aims of the experiment included attempts to increase efficiency and the better use of resources, improve contacts with the public, and 'create a new challenge in the method of beat working particularly for the younger constables' (Home Office 1966, 139). These concerns to 'put the bobby back on the beat' were reiterated in the work of John Alderson (1979; 1981b), then Chief Constable of Devon and Cornwall, and further provoked by the Scarman (1981) Report on the Brixton riots of 1981. Neighbourhood watch was later imported to Britain from the US, first in Cheshire and then in London and south Wales (Bennett 1987); by 1987 some 14 per cent of citizens defined themselves as members of a scheme (Mayhew, Elliott and Dowds 1989).

Overall, the development of community-related policing initiatives in the UK can be associated with a number of traditions. As well as a general appreciation of the important part played by the public in the policing process and a commitment to public involvement as a commendable goal, the current Conservative government, like the US and Canadian governments, has pursued a policy of minimal government with an expanding role for the private, voluntary and informal sectors in the provision of a variety of public services (Ericson, McMahon and Evans 1987; Gill and Mawby 1990b). Additionally, community initiatives have been encouraged by Home Office interest in crime prevention policies (see, for example, Hope and Shaw 1988) and on a rather different level by Scarman's (1981) concerns over police *accountability* to the areas being policed. Thus community consultative groups and lay-visitor initiatives have become elements of strategies aimed at providing some, albeit restricted and limited, role for the public in monitoring police work (Burney 1985; Kemp and Morgan 1989; Morgan 1987; Morgan and Maggs 1985; Walklate 1987).

PROBLEMS OF DEFINITION

This raises the problem of *definition*. As various authors have noted, terms such as community policing have been adopted and accepted despite the fact that the terms 'community', 'police' and 'community policing' are open to numerous alternative definitions (Cohen 1985; Fielding 1986; Gill and Thrasher 1985; Manning 1984). The term 'community', for example, encapsulates considerable emotive appeal. However, it may be defined in a variety of ways, based on territory, shared history, a common culture, or an established set of relationships. In practice this means both that there is no guarantee that people will have any idea of, much less agree on, the boundaries to 'their' area (Bottoms, Mawby and Xanthos 1981; Murphy 1988), and that within a neighbourhood conflicting interests make any assumptions of a shared community viewpoint problematic. As Alderson (1979, 46) conceded:

> The cultural diversity of some neighbourhoods makes the concept of the common good difficult to envisage, let alone achieve. Furthermore, communities are divided by politics, religion and class as well as by economic disparities.

This point has been reaffirmed more recently by Stubbs (1987) in a critique of the Gifford (1986) inquiry into the Broadwater Farm riots.

Discussions of the precise nature of community policing are equally diverse, and it is perhaps worth looking at a few in some detail. In one early review, Kuykendall (1974, 229) described four 'styles of community policing', that is, 'policing methods in relation to their impact upon the general community', based on the extent to which policing followed a counselling or an enforcement style. That in which neither counselling nor enforcement was emphasized was described as passive policing, similar to Wilson's (1968) watchman style; an emphasis on enforcement only was described as punitive policing; an emphasis on counselling only was termed social policing; and finally an emphasis on an integration of counselling and enforcement was defined as integrated policing. Both social policing and integrated policing styles are, implicitly, equated with community policing defined more narrowly than in the title to Kuykendall's article.

This emphasis upon *policing styles* is also evident in both Alderson's (1979) and Schaffer's (1980) books. Indeed, while the latter does stress the role of the public, as well as that of the police and crime-prevention work, she focuses on police relationships with other agencies such as social work, and police work in schools, which, from the perspective of the individual officer, may well take him or her out of the community and into a specialist post covering a wider geographical area.

Both Alderson (1979) and Schaffer (1980) also make it clear that if community policing is to be successfully implemented it depends on the personnel involved, reflecting the abilities and interests of police recruits and the importance of the training programmes. These points are also stressed in much of the North American literature. Goldstein (1987), for example, referring to *community-oriented policing*, describes it in terms of police recruitment and deployment, as well as the role of the public in helping the police and having some impact on policing policies and practices. Essentially, though, community policing is defined in terms of a numbr of key elements:

> Most common among these are the involvement of the community in getting the police job done; the permanent assignment of police officers to a neighbourhood in order to cultivate better relationships; the setting of police priorities based on the specific needs or desires of the community; and the meeting of these needs by the allocation of police resources and personnel otherwise assigned to responding to calls for police assistance. (Goldstein 1987, 7).

Eck and Spelman (1987), building on Goldstein's (1979) earlier work, also envisage the police responding to widely defined community problems and consider a decentralized police structure in which generalist roles are accredited with additional importance as the most effective means of so responding. They also stress, along with Alderson (1979), the importance of the police taking the initiative within the neighbourhood and building bridges with other agencies active in the area. Similar ingredients are proposed by Murphy (1988) in his evaluation of a Toronto initiative and by Manning (1984) in a review of the literature. Nevertheless, what seems like an agreed set of criteria in fact contains a variable element in so far as community perspectives are to inform police practices. Thus where Scarman (1981) made the same point, and barely resisted defining community policing as the type of policing the community desires, one could argue that *any* form of policing is community policing so long as it gains the approval of the community.

If we wish to assess the various dimensions of police/community relations, then, it is necessary to accept that there are, firstly, a number of dimensions on which such relations might be measured, not all of which are necessarily compatible, and that specific police systems might rate differently on these different dimensions. Here police/ community relations will therefore be assessed on four dimensions: namely, police involvement in the community, police role in the community, community involvement in policing, and the location of power with regard to policing. Each of these, equally, may be further subdivided.

By police involvement in the community is meant, firstly, the physical location of the police. Whether policing is organized and controlled centrally or locally is one aspect of this, but principally here the issue is whether or not police officers are assigned to work in small areas, and whether police units, substations or stations are located at neighbourhood level; or alternatively whether the police are 'housed' in a station or barracks serving a large area of a city or a wider region. A second aspect of police involvement refers to the affinity the police have with the area being policed. Thus we might consider whether they are recruited locally, or, if not, in some other way representative of local residents, and whether they are assigned to a specific area for a considerable time period, or alternate, or are posted regularly from one area to another. Part of this is whether the police 'commute' to the area where they work (Mawby 1986) or live in the area, the latter an ideal scarcely achieved under the British system of unit beat policing (Home Office 1966). Finally, and slightly differently, we might consider how far on a local level the police are involved in liaising with, and perhaps co-ordinating, other agencies with similar area responsibilities, a key feature of Alderson's (1979) Exeter initiative (see also Blaber 1979; Moore and Brown 1981).

The police role within the community is the second dimension to be distinguished. Essentially this is derived from an appreciation that much police work is only marginally related to crime and that communities may value the work of the police in a wider problem- or conflict-oriented context, rather than as a law-enforcement agency (Kelling 1987; Wilson and Kelling 1987). Thus Goldstein (1979; 1987) in particular has argued that community-oriented policing should encompass the police taking the initiative in involving the community in tackling the problems which precipitate crime. Tackling the symptoms is insufficient. This argument is taken further by Eck and Spelman (1987), who suggest that a shift of emphasis has far-reaching implications for the police organization, necessitating a re-emphasis on locally based generalists rather than centrally organized specialists. This is not, however, merely a distinction between a crime-specific and a wider police role. It is a focus on a community welfare priority for the police which is distanced both from an emphasis on law-enforcement work and those administrative tasks on behalf of central government associated with continental police forces.

It is, moreover, important to include one further aspect of the police role within the community, namely the extent to which this wider role is valued by management. As a number of authors have noted, even where the public value a service role for the police, management measurements of performance, reflected in higher status police jobs, is in many cases crime-specific (Jones 1980; Jones and Winkler 1982; Goldstein 1987; Manning 1984). Thus the extent to which police management values a community-welfare role for the police is an important criterion.

The third dimension relates to the involvement of the public in the policing of their communities. Of course, the importance of citizens in the reporting and detection of crime has long been recognized. Here however is meant a more organized and systematic public role. Two aspects of this can be distinguished. The first of these refers to the use of the public as police auxiliaries, normally on an unpaid basis but where expenses will be met and selection and training procedures are significant (Gill and Mawby 1990a). The second refers to community-based groups, separate from but possibly associated with the police, that play a role in crime-prevention activities. Neighbourhood watch, or block watch, is the example that comes to mind in the context of North America and Britain, but clearly the dimension is wider than this and incorporates community patrolling and perhaps community involvement in deciding how to deal with offenders.

The final dimension refers to the location of power. Most authors acknowledge that community involvement in policing has tended to be as aides to the police rather than involving any real transfer of power. Indeed, as Goldstein (1987) notes, community influence raises problems of corruption at the extreme and, on a lesser level, poses questions about the areas of policing which should be subject to local influence. For example, should neighbourhoods have some say in assigning individual officers, in drawing up policing priorities, in formulating police strategies, or what? Equally, where post-Scarman initiatives in Britain have led to increased community consultation, questions arise both concerning the real extent of community influence and regarding the representativeness of the community figures drawn in to the consultation process (Fyfe 1987; Morgan 1987). We might therefore distinguish as two aspects of community power: the *mechanisms* by which citizens can evaluate police policies and practices and the extent to which such mechanisms actually *influence* policies and practices.

These four dimensions are specified in Table 11.1. In the following four sections each is considered in more detail. In each case, evidence will be drawn from the UK and the USA and the eight countries considered in earlier chapters. Additionally, though, where examples from elsewhere are of particular relevance, wider comparisons will be drawn.

POLICE INVOLVEMENT IN THE COMMUNITY

Both England and Wales and the United States differ from most of the other countries considered here in having a relatively localized police structure. However whereas in the US the size of individual

Table 11.1 *Dimensions of police/community relations*

Police involvement in community	Physical location of police within neighbourhoods
	Police officers have some affinity with neighbourhood
	Police involvement with other agencies at local level
Police role within community	Problem-solving prioritised over law-enforcement
	Emphasis on local generalists not central specialists
	Community-oriented role valued by officers and management
Community involvement in policing	As police auxiliaries
	In organized groups liaising with police re crime control
Location of power	Structured mechanisms for making police accountable
	Evidence that police policies and practices are influenced

forces varies enormously (Shane 1980; Sweatman and Cross 1989), in England and Wales the forty-three separate forces, normally based on a city or county structure, are all too large to be considered truly 'local' by most citizens. In 1987, Gwent, the smallest force (excluding the unique City of London force) served a population of 442,000 while the largest, the Metropolitan Police, covered an area of over 7 million inhabitants (Home Office 1988). Moreover, the tendency in recent years has been towards increasing central-government control (Reiner 1985).

As already noted, community-policing initiatives have emerged as a means of countering such tendencies by improving the level of contact between police and local people. As far as police involvement in the community is concerned, this has meant some reallocation of resources to neighbourhood police substations or units, although in England and Wales at least this has been minimal. Rather the emphasis has been placed more on the reallocation of individual officers to generalist duties within residential areas. A further key feature of police work within local areas has been a greater involvement in some forces on inter-agency links. In many cases this is stressed more on a divisional level than at local level, but the experiment initiated by John Alderson in Exeter is but one early example of attempts to tackle local community problems by organizing inter-agency consultations (Blaber 1979; Moore and Brown 1981). More recently the Gifford (1986) Report on the Broadwater Farm disturbances has revived interest in such initiatives.

Similar recent developments can be identified in Canada and the Netherlands, possibly influenced by the US and UK. In Canada, such moves are probably less evident with regard to the RCMP. However, the federal government has, apparently, been effective in a number of initiatives, including a move towards more substations and area foot patrols (Nuttall 1988). Murphy's (1988) account of initiatives in Toronto reflects the influence of slightly earlier developments in the US.

The Netherlands government was also influenced by research in the USA and UK (Steenhuis 1979), although early discussions revealed a typically Dutch attempt to reorganize police practices starting from the first principles. Attempts to decentralize the police organization are well documented (Broer and Vijver 1983; Fijnaut 1983), and while in many respects the difficulties have been recognized, approaches such as that in Amsterdam and particularly in the Staatsliedenbuurt demonstate considerable commitment at senior-management level (Visser and Wierda 1987). There are, of course, marked variations between different Dutch forces, where the size of the force varies considerably, and neighbourhood policing may be more a feature of smaller cities (Ijzerman 1987). On the other hand, the national police, responsible for policing rural areas, provide minimal local cover, especially at night; like the rural policing strategy of the French *gendarmerie* the force appears to operate a reactive strategy to a greater extent than in urban areas where a more constant police presence is required.

What is, however, a notable feature of the Dutch approach is the emphasis upon inter-agency co-operation, most especially in the context of crime-prevention initiatives. This is a particular feature of Dijk's (1989) discussions of current policies, evident at local level in Haarlem. In Enschede, also, Ijzeiman (1987) describes 'multi-disciplinary coordination' as occurring on three levels: at municipal level between town clerk and heads of services; in the buildings, housing and the environment policy group *vis-à-vis* environmental planning; and on the precedence policy group concerned with vulnerable groups at neighbourhood level. The importance of inter-agency consultation is then translated to local level in the context of debates over the quality of life in neighbourhoods with relatively high crime rates (Junger-Tas 1987).

Despite such initiatives, these four countries appear to share two other features regarding police involvement in the community. First the focus is on the physical location of the police during working hours; there is no suggestion that police are drawn from the areas that they police, live in the same areas, or are in many ways representative of those they police. Second, in the context of the wider police organization, police involvement within the community appears relatively marginalized; it is not the focus, nor the ideal, for policing in general and the central features of police work remain untouched by community-oriented philosophies. This appears true even in the Netherlands, where despite national initiatives the police themselves appear to have acted in such ways as to prevent community programmes from expanding further.

Nevertheless, these countries evidence considerably more by way of community-based police initiatives than either France or the Soviet Union. Notably, while their political and economic systems differ markedly, in both France and the Soviet Union policing is derived from the early continental policing model.

In France, both the major police forces are centralized as national institutions. Little of the available material on the *police nationale* mentions policing at local level, a perhaps significant omission. In most respects, the *gendarmerie*, with its militaristic features, including barracks as the living and working bases for its officers, appears totally divorced from a community orientation although, as Emsley (1983) notes, traditionally its members were recruited, and presumably deployed permanently, at local level. While the recent community crime-prevention initiatives in France have clearly drawn the police into more involvement at local level, and indeed increased inter-agency co-operation (King 1987; 1988; Liege 1988), there is little evidence that this has had any effects on everyday policing practices.

In some respects, literature on the Soviet Union is similar in avoiding the same issues. The centralized militia is rarely described in terms of its neighbourhood policing operations and what evidence there is suggests that its staff is drawn from the military or those loyal to the party rather than being in any way representative of the population being policed (Conquest 1968). While some emphasis is placed on police co-operation with other agencies at local level in dealing with the crime problem, such agencies appear to be informal and dominated by the police; the equivalent formal agency structures operating within the criminal justice system in the West appear either non-existent, powerless, or subsumed within the police organization itself.

At the other extreme, China and Cuba, and to a lesser extent Japan and Hong Kong, evidence considerably greater levels of police involvement in the local community. In many respects, Japan appears distinctive, and indeed it may be considered somewhat controversial to include any reservations on this count. American academics such as Bayley (1976) and British practitioners like John Alderson (1981a) have emphasized the place of Japanese officers within local neighbourhoods. In rural areas, Japanese police live and work in relative isolation from their colleagues and are accorded esteem within the local community (Ames 1981). In urban areas, the *koban* features as the neighbourhood substation and clearly provides a community policing presence unrivalled in other societies; and with sleeping facilities provided the police may spend considerable periods of time in the area over the period of a shift (Bayley 1976). Nevertheless, the highly centralized nature of police organization militates against any more comprehensive immersion of the police within their neighbourhoods. As has been noted, the policy is to move officers at regular intervals to prevent them forming too close relations with locals, reflecting a concern to minimize corruption and uphold occupational loyalty. Indeed, if occupational solidarity itself limits community involvement (Bennett and Corrigan 1980) then the role of the Japanese police is likely to be limited. Concern over conflicting loyalties also affects police representativeness. As Westney (1982, 325) notes, this was evident from the early days of the Tokyo force, when Satsuma recruits were preferred, being 'outsiders to the social environment in which they functioned' which 'enhanced their commitment to the organization and their responsiveness to organizational directives'.

Information on the Hong Kong police is less detailed. However, there is considerable evidence of a plethora of local police substations and an emphasis upon the police working within residential communities (Royal Hong Kong Police 1988; Sinclair 1983). While such developments are of recent origin, and reflect Japanese wartime influences, attempts to make the police more representative of the local community, at least by employing Chinese in junior and intermediate ranks, have a longer history. Nevertheless, there is no indication of police working for long periods in the same area, or living on their 'patch', and little evidence of inter-agency co-operation at the area level.

In China, equally, it is apparently uncommon for the police to be drawn from the local area, and they are more likely to have army or party pedigrees (Brady 1982b; Cohen 1977; Johnson 1984). There is scant detail about where they live. However, in other respects, the police are firmly located within the urban neighbourhood. As already noted, the low proportion of police to population means that so-called neighboourhood stations cover very wide areas of perhaps 30,000 or so population (Johnson 1984; Li 1971; Vogel 1971). The physical location of the police at a more local level therefore depends on the individual officer responsible for a beat which may vary from 500 to 5,000 households (Finch 1984; Li 1971; Ward 1984c). At this level the sole police representative works alongside the local mediation committee, the local branch of the party, street associations of the Women's Association and a residents' committee (Cohen 1968). As Salaff (1967) noted, the location of the police within clearly defined, relatively small urban areas was a priority of the early administration: the *pao-chia* policing system was introduced based on groups of residential blocks and deliberately interlinked with the *p'aich'uso*, which was responsible for dealing with urban administration, population registration and public safety.

Although more clearly militarized than in China, the Cuban police organization evidences many features of the Chinese model (Brady 1981). Again with low rates of police per head of population, policing is dependent upon public co-operation, and the police appear to spend much of their time on duty working within the local neighbourhoods. Again as in China, this local focus is facilitated by the close working relationships the police have with community groups such as the CDR. Thus, although details are sparse, according to Brady (1982a) police/community relations are characterized by informality and regular contacts. Moreover, although police recruits have tended to be drawn from the party or the military, there has been a conscious attempt to recruit from the poorer classes and ensure that the police remain representative of the people rather than become an elite (Salas 1979a).

In terms of police involvement at local level, then, there are marked variations between the countries considered here. At one extreme, France and the Soviet Union appear to have placed little priority on such initiatives. In contrast, in the US, UK, Canada and the Netherlands decentralization of police work has received considerable attention in recent years. Nevertheless, local policing initiatives have been taken further in countries such as Cuba, Japan and Hong Kong, the latter drawing on the Japanese example as a model. At the extreme, the Chinese police appear to have been most fully integrated into small areas within the city, although, as noted in Chapter 9, this could possibly change as China follows the West in an emphasis on specialization and professionalism.

Conclusion

This brings us to the second dimension of police/community relations, the police role within the community.

THE POLICE ROLE WITHIN THE COMMUNITY

Community-policing initiatives in the USA and UK frequently involve an assumption that the police role within the neighbourhood will be wider, and more atuned to the problems faced by residents, than simply crime-specific and legalistic. Such a view is commonly associated with the work of John Alderson (1979) in Devon and Cornwall, although it has sometimes been criticized by those on the left who see police responsibilities extending into areas more properly the mandate of other, welfare agencies. Kinsey (1984), for example, cites some public criticism of these trends. An emphasis upon the importance of generalist local officers, rather than headquarters specialists, is a secondary feature of the police role.

A similar emphasis can be discerned in Canada (Murphy 1988) and in the changes proposed by the POS report in the Netherlands (Nordholt and Straver 1983), distinguishing these countries from the USSR and France, where despite recent community initiatives the role of the police appears to be more closely identified with control and administration than local community problem-solving. Similarly, in Hong Kong, the police role, while evident in the local community, is largely control-oriented. However, while there are some degrees of difference between these countries, in each the community-welfare orientation of the police role appears to receive little encouragement either from the police subculture or in management terms. In each country police work is defined by officers primarily in terms of action, excitement, work on the streets, and with the goal of making an arrest. Similarly, despite management emphasis upon community relations, police work is evaluated in terms of crime clearance rather than neighbourhood service. Moreover, while in some countries detective work is formally recognized as superior, with detectives being engaged at higher ranks, in all these countries detective work is highly prized among the police, and local policing associated with 'dead-end', routine, dull or safe options.

The contrast with Japan, China and Cuba is marked. In Japan, admittedly, officers prefer traffic, detective or administrative work to police posts in the *koban* (Ames 1981), but considerably more emphasis is placed on the problem-solving qualities of individual officers. *Koban* officers are expected to deal with a whole range of local community issues, acting as an advice centre, a mediation forum and a first line of help for local residents as well as completing the household census. This expectation that community welfare is a core feature of police work is expressed throughout the police organization and is clearly valued by the hierarchy in a way not found in the West (Ames 1981; Bayley 1976; National Police Agency 1984). The latter report, for example, refers to 'police activities to deepen the friendly ties with the residents' (National Police Agency 1984, 7), and details worries brought to the police including noise, the lonely elderly, and domestic conflicts, suggesting both that such concerns are a central part of police work and that policing skills extend much further than crime detection.

In China, as in Japan, the community-based officer must be contrasted with specialists involved with traffic, detection, and public security. Nevertheless, the role of the local officer has, since 1949, been defined as a generalist one to include a variety of administrative and welfare responsibilities, including household registration, care of the elderly and rehabilitation initiatives (Li 1971; Chang 1984; Yun 1983). What is also evident from these texts, moreover, is the value accredited to the local officer as someone who cares about local residents; the folk hero approximates to a community worker rather than an urban guerrilla!

A similar image of the police role appears in the Cuban literature (Brady 1982a; Salas 1979a), although there is little detail on police involvement in community-welfare activities, other than in liaison with CDR. The police are, however, heavily involved in crime-prevention work, most notably in schools. Thus, while there is undoubtedly an emphasis on specialism at national or provincial level, the municipal police appear to spend much of their time on foot, working in residential areas as one arm of government support for community participation on a variety of welfare fronts. Clearly, though, in countries such as Japan, China and Cuba where the police are expected to take on these generalist roles, the key to their success lies in the ties which are made within the neighbourhoods and the integration of police with local community groups.

COMMUNITY INVOLVEMENT IN POLICING

Initiatives with regard to increasing the role of the community in the policing process have been particularly prevalent in the UK and North America in recent years. In the United States, the vigilante tradition (Brown 1969b) has been sustained, with renewed emphasis on citizen partols in the 1960s (Washnis 1976). While some neighbourhood organizations, such as the Guardian Angels (Boothroyd 1989; Ostrowe and DiBiase 1983; Pennell, Curtis and Henderson 1986), may operate independently of the police, most are run in conjunction with the police. Neighbourhood watch, or block watch, for example, emphasize crime prevention and the immediate reporting of crime or other suspicious incidents to the police, and by and large citizens' groups are not encouraged to take direct action. Involvement in neighbourhood watch has grown rapidly in the United States (Figgie Report 1983; Rosenbaum 1988) and has been exported to Canada (Nuttall 1988), the UK (Bennett 1987) and Hong Kong, although the latter may also have been influenced by Japan.

The other aspect of community involvement featured here, the police auxiliary, has a much more established history in the UK, where police special constables were deployed on a part-time, temporary basis both before and after the formation of public police forces, largely in a public-aides capacity (Gill and Mawby 1990a). In the postwar period the role of specials has been widened and transformed, and they now play a long-term role as police aides, an established volunteer unit regularly deployed on a variety of police duties. In some areas of Canada and the United States, police auxiliaries play a similar role. However, they are of much more recent origin, in some cases provoked by a desire to save money on regular officers, are less well established, and have a lower community-oriented profile than in the UK (Gill and Mawby 1990a, 57–76, 98–101). Interestingly, in Hong Kong the Special Constabulary emerged and was utilized in similar conditions to the UK but has continued to play a major role in public-order policing. The reserve is, essentially, a part-time paid force which, while it has some community features, has a rather different emphasis (Gill and Mawby 1990a, 105–8).

In comparison, community involvement in policing figures marginally in France and the Netherlands. In France, a standing army and the availability of the *gendarmerie* meant in the past that public-order problems were handled rather differently to the UK, and postwar developments in both France and the Netherlands have confirmed the use of national police units as reserve forces. There is no volunteer auxiliary force in either country, although the Netherlands is currently proposing to modify its relatively small, paid part-time reserve. Equally, neighbourhood watch-type initiatives do not feature prominently in literature on French policing while in the Netherlands initiatives have not proved successful and there are currently only a handful of such schemes in existence.

At the other extreme, community involvement appears considerably greater in the USSR, China, Cuba and Japan. In the Soviet Union, public involvement was encouraged soon after the revolution despite the parallel growth in highly centralized secret and regular police, and the role of the public as police auxiliaries and in community-based patrol units has received considerable attention in the literature (Bakhanstaia 1974; O'Connor 1964; Timoshenko 1977).

A much greater emphasis upon the mass line in Communist China, however, resulted in far greater prioritization of citizen involvement in the policing process. One aspect of this is police auxiliary units, necessary in rural areas in the post-revolutionary period and also introduced into the cities (Brady 1982b; Cohen 1968). Of considerably more importance, however, were the security defence small groups, integrated with the security defence committees, residents' committees and street offices and providing a network of local area controls which, while working with individual police patrol men and women, were also largely independent of them. The extent of this independence, of course, varied at different times, and local community organizations were more successful in some areas than others; in China, as in the West, urban dwellers are not immune to apathy. Local groups are, however, involved in a much wider range of policing tasks than are commonly associated with neighbourhood watch, and indeed have considerably greater powers. They include, for example, mediation work, house searches to check for illegal residents, work with offenders and crime-prevention patrols (Alderson 1981a; Brady 1982b; Vogel 1971).

Cuba, while politically allied to – and economically dependent on – the Soviet Union, has been considerably influenced by Chinese initiatives in the provision of public and welfare services (Brady 1981). On the other hand, its volunteer police units also emerged in response to counter-revolutionary activities (Berman 1969), and have taken on many of the features of their Western equivalents. They are armed and have similar powers of arrest to the regular police (Salas 1979). As in China, though, community involvement in Cuba is dominated by local community groups fulfilling a range of policing activities which again mark them off as 'neighbourhood watch-plus'. Grassroots involvement, a key feature of the post-revolutionary period, led to the establishment of CDRs which took over specific law-and-order responsibilities *vis-à-vis* population checks, administering the rationing system and identity cards, and patrol and guard duties. While they are given only restricted powers of arrest they can detain a suspect until the police or auxiliary police arrive. They are also involved in rehabilitation work (Salas 1979a). While popular justice is less evident today, CDRs continue to figure prominently (Third Congress of the Communist Party of Cuba 1986).

Although the political structure of Japan contrasts with that of China and Cuba, its ethos of community obligation is remarkably similar. With high levels of voluntary activity, involvement of the public as volunteers in specialist areas such as traffic duty or youth work is considerable. Again, though, the most notable aspect of community involvement is at neighbourhood level through crime-prevention associations. These act as contact points for the police, publicize crime-prevention material, and also organize street patrols (Ames 1981; Bayley 1976). The location of the police at neighbourhood level in the *koban*, moreover, facilitates such developments in a way not found in the other countries considered here. In fact, the influence of the Japanese system is to be found elsewhere, most notably in countries occupied by the Japanese during the Second World War. It seems likely that initiatives in Hong Kong are to some extent modelled on Japan, and indeed the same has been suggested of China (Brady 1982b). Both Singapore and Malaysia, for example, appear to have modelled their Special Constabularies on the British model but borrowed neighbourhood initiatives – including *koban*-style police posts, residents' committees, local mediation groups and neighbourhood watch – from the Japanese (Austin 1987; Ismail 1987; Sharma 1982). As in Japan, one notable feature of these developments is their success in high-density and especially high-rise communities.

Undoubtedly the most complete involvement of the community in policing within the formal structure of government, however, is to be found much closer to home, on the Channel Island of Jersey (Gill and Mawby 1990a, 78–83). With only some 80,000 residents, Jersey has maintained a voluntary police force (called the Honorary Police) which comprises 284 citizens, compared with 194 regular, paid police. In fact, the paid police force has only had island-wide responsibilities since 1951 and its work is to some extent constrained by the honorary system. Police volunteers are organized as separate, autonomous units, on a parish level, with their own patrol cars, parish headquarters, and uniforms, and their senior officers play a significant role in the prosecution process. There is a separate rank structure that is integrated with the parish (and ultimately island-wide) political structure. Police units within each parish carry out duties for one week each in rotation.

As a small island, Jersey is a useful illustration of the extent of community involvement which would be impractical in other settings, and indeed even there the dual police structure is the subject of considerable controversy. Nevertheless, given its Norman roots, it is notable that if France epitomizes a police system with minimal community involvement, Jersey is to be found at the other extreme, with community involvement well established and the paid police sometimes feeling insecure and under threat. This raises the question of community power and the accountability of the police to their communities.

THE LOCATION OF POWER

Miller (1977) has argued that when the New York police rejected the Metropolitan model and appointed local people as police, they also gave less priority to the need for accountability. Thus, while in London the commissioners themselves dealt with public complaints, signalling the emergence of intra-agency accountability, in New York direct, informal accountability was considered sufficient. The unintended consequence was that American urban forces became dominated by corrupt political machines, leading reformers to advocate a move towards more professional accountability (Reppetto 1978). The fact that more direct community control of the police is no panacea is thus well appreciated by North American academics. Goldstein (1987), for example, notes that increased local accountability and greater discretion for individual officers brings with it the possibility of corruption.

Control of the police in the US, and investigation of alleged misconduct, varies considerably between different forces (McKenzie and Gallagher 1989; Loveday 1988). In general, however, the role of the public is a minimal one. The same applies in Canada (Hogarth 1982), most notably in the case of the RCMP, but in other municipal and provincial forces it appears both that civilian review is more evident in theory than in practice and that since the nineteenth century the emphasis has been upon provincial accountability at the expense of more localized interests (Sewell 1985; Stenning 1981; Weller 1981). Thus while in both the US and Canada structures exist for some public involvement in evaluating policing, in practice there is little evidence of the wider public having any significant impact on police policies and practices.

Not surprisingly, the location of power is further removed from the public in countries influenced by continental or colonial styles of policing. In France, accountability is clearly specified as intra-agency (Fogel 1987; Regan 1984); in the Soviet Union, despite the dual accountability of the militia, it seems unlikely that community involvement exists in practice. The Netherlands provides some element of contrast. However, local police forces, and the importance in the tripartite structure of the burgomaster, do not appear to result in any appreciable degree of local accountability, and in general public services seem insulated from popular opinion. Moreover, while in Amsterdam the police have demonstrated an awareness of the sensitivity of certain issues, most notably *vis-à-vis* urban renewal and the opposition from squatters' groups, the bottom line appears to be public relations rather than public accountability (Reenen 1981; Visser and Wierda 1987). In Hong Kong, despite the physical location of the police in local neighbourhoods and community involvement in policing, the location of power resides most clearly with the Governor and, ultimately, the British government.

Indeed, in comparison with other Western societies, the formal mechanisms for public involvement in the policing structure in England and Wales are impressive. Outside London, the tripartite structure allows for some level of input by political and magisterial representatives on the Police Authority, and at national level the Police Complaints Board has a degree of independence from the police. Truly *local* mechanisms, in the post-Scarman era, are reflected in community consultation groups and lay visitors to police stations. Even here, though, it seems that the 'public' involved is scarcely representative of the community being policed, and that the major effects of such initiatives are with regard to public relations (Morgan 1987; Morgan and Maggs 1985; Walklate 1987). There is no evidence, moreover, that these mechanisms have significantly increased public influence over local policing arrangements.

What, then, of those countries which have scored highest on the first three dimensions of police/community relations, namely Japan, China and Cuba? The example of Japan is striking because, from the first, a central, professional police force, controlled and accountable internally, was devised (Westney 1982), and resurrected when the Americans withdrew in the postwar period. True, public safety commissions at prefecture level include lay representatives, but the overall philosophy of the police organization is that public influence on police work should be minimized. For this reason, it is viewed as important that officers should be transferred regularly between areas (Ames 1981).

The situation in China and Cuba is more ambiguous, partly because it has been subject to a number of changes over the years, partly because of the intermeshing of local and national structure, and partly because of the confusion between local control and local *party* control. Thus Binns and Gonzalez (1980) argue that in Cuba the CDRs are controlled by party appointees and in China activists have been most evident in the plethora of local small groups, at least in the cities (Brady 1982b; Salaff 1967). Nevertheless, in both Cuba and China these small neighbourhood groups have been able to influence local policing arrangements and indeed the wider sentencing structure through their role in presenting reports on local offenders. In Cuba, where the potential influence of the CDRs has caused friction in the past, Salas (1979a) notes Castro's use of them to ensure that the police do not become isolated from the people. In China, most notably during different purges, the police have indeed been particularly vulnerable to local pressure (Brady 1982b).

The extent to which local influences can be maintained is, however, open to question. In Cuba, police/public relations have always been more ambiguous than relations between citizens and other welfare or public agencies, partly because the police organization has maintained some degree of military structure (Salas 1979a). There are also indications from China that Western influence is likely to accelerate moves towards a more specialist, professional and autonomous force (Ward 1984c; Ward and Bracey 1985).

This suggests that community control of policing, albeit local party control of policing, is most evident in Third World communist societies, and is likely to weaken as these societies stabilize and become more industrialized. However, Jersey does provide an example of a capitalist society – even though a very small one – in which local community influence is considerable. As already noted, community involvement in policing is most fully expressed through the Honorary Police, who volunteer, or are elected, in their local parishes. While the system was originally one which allowed for control of policing by prestigious local families, the opportunity now exists for any parishioner[1] to become involved in the volunteer force. Moreover, the influence of this unit over the regular force is evident on three levels. First, Honorary Police have some policing powers (for example, regarding searching premises) that are greater than those of the paid police. Second, because of the intertwining of the voluntary police organization and local and island politics, senior members of the Honorary Police have considerable political influence. Third, and more directly, the States of Jersey Police Force is accountable to a police committee on which the parish constables figure prominently (Gill and Mawby 1990a). Consequently, while the states force might wish to compare itself with the larger forces of mainland Britain, the small size of the island and its political autonomy mean that the local community has a far greater impact on police policies and practices than might have been anticipated.

SUMMARY

There are clearly considerable differences between the eight countries described in earlier chapters and the UK and US in police/community relationships. Overall, relationships appear most distant in France, the USSR and the Netherlands and closest in China, Cuba and Japan. The picture is summarized in Figure 11.1. As is also evident in Figure 11.1, there is less evidence of public influence over the police than in terms of the other three criteria used.

There are, moreover, some marked differences in the key features of police/community relations in these different societies. Japan, for example, while similar to China and Cuba in many respects, shows slightly less evidence of police involvement in the community and differs significantly in terms of the location of power. At the other extreme, while France rates poorly on all four criteria, Dutch police have some degree of involvement in local communities and the Soviet public have considerable involvement in policing. Hong Kong, following the Japanese example, also evidences high levels of police involvement in the community and fairly high levels of public involvement in policing.

How then do we account for these differences? At one extreme, both France and the Soviet Union are examples of countries where the emphasis was placed, following the continental model, on the police as a force separate from society, responsible for public control

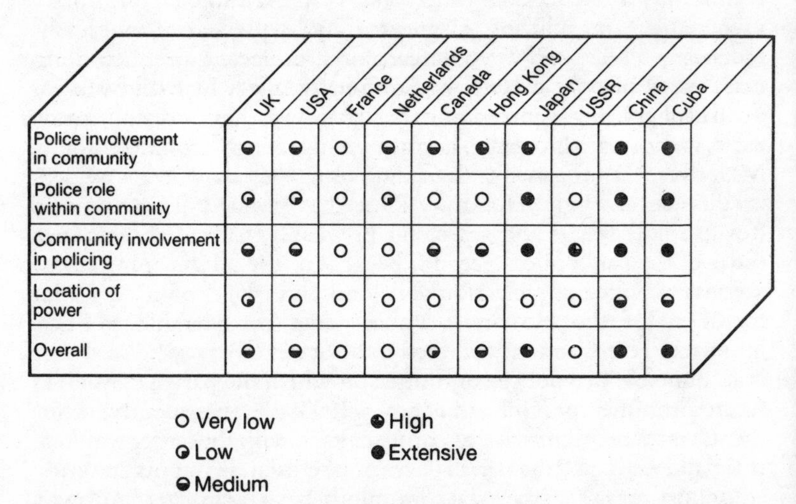

Figure 11.1 ***Police/community relations in different societies***

on a level far wider than crime control. In neither case, despite Soviet attempts at community involvement, has the gap between police and public been significantly closed. However, although the same might have been expected in Hong Kong, early assumptions that the Chinese should accept responsibility for policing the Chinese community, Japanese wartime influence, and Asian culture with its emphasis on community responsibilities, combine to produce rather different sets of police/community relations.

The importance of culture and tradition is also crucial in the context of Japan and China. Indeed, the major impact of political ideology on earlier cultural traditions appears to be that there is a greater involvement of the public in police decision-making in China. The same seems to be the case in Cuba, although here the importance of community or national responsibilities are a more recent development as a feature of the Castro regime.

On the one hand, the difference between police/community relations in Eastern Europe, illustrated by the USSR, and Third World communist societies like China and Cuba, is stark and parallels the marked differences in political priorities of the different systems. On the other hand, the close participation of the public in the policing process in Japan, and rather differently in Jersey, illustrates that close police/community relations are not the sole property of communist societies.

Nevertheless, we should not assume that improved police/community relations are necessarily beneficial. For example, there is little hard evidence that in themselves they influence crime rates. Moreover, while in Japan public involvement has been maintained without any increase of power over the police by the public, in Jersey, China and Cuba public accountability brings both advantages and disadvantages. Thus although it may provide a better basis for full public involvement and participation, police morale may suffer and accountability may become the property, not of the public in general, but of quite distinct groups within the public, based on class, party affiliation etc.

The point is that police accountability is a means rather than an end in itself. It is a means towards a police system within which the police are better integrated with and less divorced from the public; in which police priorities are the subject of public debate and are influenced by local public concerns, and where the police are not expected to accept total responsibility for crime control. It is, consequently, important that the location of power is not promoted as the key issue in police/community relations. Equally, discussion of police/community relations needs to consider all aspects of such relations, where the location of power is one element alongside police involvement, police roles and community involvement.

12

Policing Systems: a Retrospective Analysis

SUMMARY

International comparative analysis is not the only form of comparative work, but it does allow us the opportunity to compare a wide range of structures and practices. It has been a common technique of inquiry throughout the social sciences, but has only recently aroused interest among criminologists and police-studies academics. However, there are at least three approaches to comparative analysis in police studies: that in which two or more countries are compared *vis-à-vis* their police systems; a focus on one specific country, but with implicit or explicit reference to other countries; and an interest in a specific issue whereby policing can be compared across a variety of societies.

There are various difficulties involved in such comparisons. Some are avoidable, but others relate to the difficulty of becoming an 'expert' on such a range of material. From a personal perspective, each chapter written in this text has added to my feelings of inadequacy! At the same time, there are considerable advantages, both theoretical and practical, in the endeavour. Essentially, any analysis which allows us to see beyond our own direct experiences, challenging the 'taken for granted', and enabling us to see how our own systems are moulded by other facets of our society, is beneficial.

In fact, much of the history of police development is a story of learning from the experiences of police systems elsewhere. Emigrants to the US and Canada, for example, took with them an awareness of policing in Europe, which then shaped early developments in North America. Conquerors attempted to impose police systems of their own on subjugated populations, in the colonies for example, but we also see US influence on postwar Japan, and Japanese influences in China and Hong Kong. Borrowing has become a favoured pastime of the present, with ideas on community involvement, for example neighbourhood watch, exported across the Atlantic to Britain and also the Netherlands and Australia, a voyage that earlier Asian community initiatives somehow failed to make. In the future, comparative analysis will become of particular relevance with closer links throughout the European community and the return of Hong Kong to China. Current shifts in Eastern Europe may, in addition, mean that countries like Poland and Romania look elsewhere for models on which to base modified police structures.

In focusing on police systems in other countries it is crucial to begin with a structure within which 'the police' can be defined and compared, and in Chapter 1 three criteria, 'legitimacy, structure and function', were identified. Then in Chapter 2 the emergence of modern police systems was considered using these criteria and incorporating Bayley's (1985) notion of modern police as characterized by their public, professional and specialist features. However, there are considerable differences in the ways in which modern police systems have been constructed in different societies. In the literature, British and US models are often contrasted with continental and colonial systems. This attempt at categorization, however, raises two further questions. First, are these models still appropriate for comparing different police forces today? Second, are there alternative models that need to be added?

While there is insufficient space in this text, or indeed data available, to allow analysis of all the possible combinations, in Chapters 3–10 eight countries have been selected for more detailed consideration. Two of these, France and the Netherlands, might be anticipated to fit a continental model of policing; Hong Kong is an example of a colonial force. Of the rest, Canada was chosen as a country dominated by settlers, with US, French and British colonial influences. Japan, as an Asian example, provides a further contrast. The USSR is then considered as an example of an East European communist system, compared with Third World communist examples from China and Cuba.

In each case, a similar structure has been adopted to facilitate comparisons. Chapters start with a short introduction to the country and the available material. This is followed by brief reviews of social and political structure and culture and the criminal justice system. Policing is then assessed in terms of its development, the current situation, and the relationship between police and public.

An alternative way to draw international comparisons is to focus on specific issues and consider relevant material from a range of countries. One problem here is that the extent of available material, especially on the countries already discussed, varies considerably.

Any attempt to take an issues such as, say, the place of policewomen, firearms and the police, or police militancy, would have been patchy, with data readily available in some countries and relatively sparse in others. For this reason, only one issue has been included here, namely the relationship between police and community, which is the subject of Chapter 11. While other countries are cited where they illustrate particular features of police/community relations, the emphasis in Chapter 11 is on the eight countries discussed previously, so as to relate particular aspects of police/community relations to wider aspects of policing. Following a similar approach, the remainder of this chapter is an attempt to draw together the various strands in the analysis, first by reconsidering the criteria of legitimacy, structure and function.

LEGITIMACY

In Chapter 1, legitimacy was described in terms of the police being granted some degree of monopoly with regard to certain tasks on behalf of 'society'. It must however be noted from the outset that in most developed societies some degree of competition is allowed. While the public police are considered the pivot of the law-enforcement system, private alternatives are tolerated (or even welcomed) and prescribed within law. Thus although this text has focused on the *public* police, some level of private policing can be identified in all five capitalist societies included, and even in Cuba there are some private security guards. Although private police are historically better established in the US than in most other countries (Bowden 1978; Reppetto 1978), they now outnumber the public police in countries such as Canada (Shearing and Stenning 1983) and have found particular favour in the current political climate of the UK (Matthews 1989; South 1988). Moreover, as already noted, early incorporation of private security into the public police in England and Wales finds parallels in other countries like Japan.

In none of the countries included here, however, are the private police – regardless of any numerical superiority – granted the same level of public legitimacy as the public police. But from where is public legitimacy derived? Essentially we may distinguish at least five bases: the law, the organization, the state, the party and the community. In distinguishing between continental, colonial and Anglo-Saxon police systems, a number of authors have identified the latter as legitimized through the law: the police are accountable to the courts in the same way as are other systems.

Whilst on some levels this is currently true of all the police systems described here, the extent of legal control over the police organization varies between countries and indeed between forces within a country. In the Soviet Union, for example, the KGB operates outside the law to a greater extent than the militia; in France the *gendarmerie nationale* has traditionally been better 'protected' from the law than the *police nationale*; in Canada the RCMP appears to have avoided legal restraints more 'successfully' than other forces. In Hong Kong, and to a lesser extent France, the police are in fact directly accountable to the state, evidence respectively of the colonial and continental police structures. In Japan, although the French model was adopted, a greater emphasis upon professionalism plus traditional occupational loyalty have resulted in a considerable degree of autonomy for the police organization.

In the three communist countries detailed, there is evidence of various 'mixes' between the influence of law, party and community. In the Soviet Union, early emphasis upon a written constitution placed the police, in theory, under the law, although the security forces clearly operated outside the law from the first. In practice it appears that the party exerts considerable influence on police practices, and that public involvement is restricted to that of police aides. In China and Cuba the role of the public has been more positive and active. In China, an unwillingness to rely on formal law has not left the police in control, but rather subject to the influence of party and local community. In Cuba, Castro's concern to operate a balance of power between police, army and CDRs, with the party influential within each, has also opened up police to local community influence. Thus we might say that in the recent past both China and Cuba have experienced periods when the police were genuinely open to public pressure in a way not evident in Western capitalist systems. At other times, however, the party has had a more direct influence, with the main difference between China and the USSR being that in the latter the party's influence has been imposed more directly from the centre, rather than permeated through local community groups. More recently, moreover, in both China and Cuba emphasis has been placed on increasing the professionalism of the police. We should therefore expect the influence of local community groups to weaken, with the police accredited with legitimacy by the organization itself and by the formal law.

STRUCTURE

All modern police forces are structured to a large extent. However the form of that structure varies considerably. Thus organizations vary according to degrees of centralization, specialization, and rank-structure and authority, expressed for example through laws or codes defining what is an acceptable level of force, or what requirements regulate the use of deadly force. While concepts such as 'militaristic features' are somewhat difficult to define, others have been more widely discussed. Bayley (1985, 53–60), for example, focuses on degrees of centralization in a review of police structures.

Of course, most countries, including those examples discussed here, will have some degree of centralization, where specialist units, most notably covering very serious crimes or political offences, are concerned. The key distinctions would appear to concern specialism and balance. Thus where everyday police work is organized on a decentralized basis and where centralized, specialist units comprise only a small portion of police personnel, police structure may be described as decentralized. Bayley (1985), however, makes two further distinctions. First he notes that in some countries both centralized and decentralized forces co-exist. Thus there are four alternatives: a single centralized force; multiple centralized forces; multiple decentralized forces; and multiple forces comprising both centralized and decentralized forces. Second, he makes a distinction according to whether the jurisdictions of multiple forces overlap, distinguishing between co-ordinated and unco-ordinated forces.

By these criteria, four of the countries discussed in detail here have centralized, singular forces; China, Cuba, Hong Kong and Japan, although Bayley (1985), in line with his earlier emphasis upon the community basis of Japanese policing (1976), describes its police structure as decentralized. The Netherlands is clearly an example of a country with multiple forces, one of which is centralized. Canada, like the US and England and Wales, has multiple decentralized forces. The USSR and France have multiple centralized forces. However, given the wide-ranging and flexible authority invested in the KGB and the *gendarmerie*, in neither case can one describe relationships between different centralized forces as co-ordinated, although Italy's national police are evidently even less co-ordinated (Collin 1985).

Specialization is a feature of all the modern police systems described here, although the basis for specialization varies considerably. Thus in Hong Kong, the USSR and China a specialist political force is particularly prominent. In France the range of tasks assigned to the *gendarmerie* has necessitated considerable internal specialism.

The structure and authority of the police are other features of police structure which are worthy of note, especially given their association with rather vague descriptions of the 'militaristic' features of various forces. In fact, in all the countries included *except* China the police are routinely armed, and it is thus difficult to justify an armed police as such as evidence of militarization. Rather, it seems more appropriate to ask why some forces, like the British, are unarmed, rather than why the majority are armed. What is perhaps more relevant is the use of arms by the police, and control over their use. Thus, compared with the US, in Japan (Bayley 1976) and the Netherlands (Colijn, Lester and Slothouwer 1985) arms are rarely deployed. Information from elsewhere is rather vague. Stead (1983), for example, notes the strict controls over the use of weapons imposed on the *police nationale* and, to a lesser extent, on the *gendarmerie nationale*, but suggests that rates of police fatalities in France are high. Confrontational policing, through the deployment of riot squads, has features in media coverage of events in Japan and Hong Kong, but in the former the riot police do not carry weapons, while in Hong Kong firearms are infrequently used in crimes. In China, recent street protests appear to have been dealt with by the army rather than the police, and while the police have been featured in public-order policing in the USSR the extent of police use of arms *vis-à-vis* everyday criminal incidents nowhere appears to reach US levels. Here the relationship between police and public use of arms is significant (Tonso 1982).

What then of other militaristic features? All modern police systems to some extent appear to evidence a military-type command structure. One aspect of this, internal accountability, has already been considered. Another, the notion of dual (or multiple) entry, with senior officers recruited separately, occurs in a number of the countries included here: for example in France, the Netherlands and Hong Kong. However, while this may have implications for the development of an occupational culture or cultures and for the 'working personality' of the individual police officer, its precise link with militarization is questionable. In other respects, for example, the police of France and Hong Kong are noticeably distinct from those of the Netherlands.

FUNCTION

Police functions vary considerably between different countries. Bayley (1985, 125), for example, suggests that in England and Wales non-crime 'welfare' work takes up a relatively high proportion of police time, and argues that with the exception of the US the police in most developed societies spend proportionally more time on non-crime work compared with underdeveloped societies (Bayley 1985, 149). In contrast, he identifies American police as particularly concerned with crime. On the other hand Monkkonen (1981) describes nineteenth-century American police as devoting considerable attention to welfare issues.

In general, it appears that the police in some countries, like France and the USSR, place little emphasis on welfare work. At the other extreme, it is quite evident that welfare is considered an appropriate police function in Japan, China and Cuba. Moreover, while in both Japan and China state emphasis upon public-welfare services is minimal, the same cannot be said for Cuba. Rather, it appears that where welfare is seen as principally the responsibility of the local community, rather than large-scale state bureaucracies, and the police are organized on a local level, then the police may be given a mandate for overseeing local initiatives, ensuring that informal care exists and filling in the gaps where is does not.

However, the distinction between crime and welfare work is only part of the issue *vis-à-vis* the function of the police; political and administrative roles must also be taken into account. It is, obviously, tautological to describe the police as having a role in maintaining political order and stability. Nevertheless, the extent to which this is accorded priority by the state is an important means of distinguishing between different police systems. In the three communist countries, for example, the political function of the police is explicit. In Hong Kong and France this is also evident. In Japan it is true to a lesser extent, but was a crucial feature of the Japanese police until the postwar period, and indeed was one of the reasons why the French-style police system was adopted (Westney 1982). In Canada also the political role of the RCMP was of particular importance in the past (Horrell 1980; Morrison 1985), but is arguably (Taylor 1986; Weller 1981) less so today. In the Netherlands, as in the US and England and Wales, the political function of the police has been less important, although it is clearly not absent and has been emphasized in times of political instability, such as the 1984 miners' strike in Britain (Fine and Millar 1985), and where the police have acted as public censors to protect the government from political embarrassment (Reiner 1984).

Again there are marked differences between forces in the extent to which the police provide administrative services. Communist countries once more stand out in this respect, partly because of the degrees of control imposed on the population with residential registration requirements and some forms of rationing. In Hong

Kong the internal passport system similarly falls within the orbit of the police. In Japan the household register also provides the police with a major administrative task. In the Netherlands and especially in France the police are also responsible for a range of administrative services, the *gendarmerie* in particular having taken on a range of public-service duties over the years. Similarly in Canada the RCMP were originally burdened with a number of such tasks, including customs and postal duties, although this is less evident today.

Generally speaking, then, the US and UK stand out from all the examples included here in traditionally relying less on the police to provide a wide variety of public services and general administrative duties. However, while some countries expect their police to be responsible for a wide range of welfare, administrative and political tasks, others may stress welfare, administrative or political responsibilities to the exclusion of the other two.

ALTERNATIVE MODELS

The literature described in Chapter 2 identifies three broadly distinctive modern policing traditions: the Anglo-Saxon, continental and colonial alternatives. Thus while distinct from one another, the police systems in the US and England and Wales which emerged in the nineteenth century were quite different from those of continental Europe, and the system adopted in the British Empire was different again from that on mainland Britain, sharing many characteristics with the continental system. However, police patterns change – indeed the colonial model suggested by Jeffries (1952) is a dynamic one – and it is pertinent to ask how far these models are still appropriate. Equally, as policing patterns shift in one particular country it becomes pertinent to consider whether changes are such as to mark a transformation from one form of policing to another.

Take England and Wales, for example. Asking whether Britain is 'turning into a police state' Reiner (1984) starts by suggesting that 'police states' might be defined according to five criteria. Two of these, the power accredited to the police and police accountability, refer to matters of legitimacy; two, centralization and military structure refer to structure; and the final one, pervasiveness, refers to function. In fact, Reiner (1984) dismisses the two structural criteria and suggests that in the British case evidence of increased police powers following the 1984 Criminal Justice Act is ambiguous. He thus focuses on pervasiveness and accountability: pervasiveness being where the police dominate other social agencies, particularly in the context of protecting the government; accountability being measured in terms of close police/public relations. In contrast, Bayley's (1985) US perspective leads him to play down the significance of accountability, arguing that external accountability is a product of the extent of problems arising under internal control. Thus in the US social heterogeneity and an individualistic ideology combine with weak internal supervision of the police to produce an emphasis on external accountability. At the other extreme, in Japan social homogeneity and a community-oriented culture combine with high levels of internal supervision to obviate the necessity for external supervision. Thus: 'External intervention is more likely to be used when internal regulation is thought to be ineffective. If police can be counted on to keep their own house in order, then civilian oversight can afford to relax' (Bayley 1985, 181). The problems here, of course, are that the public may not be aware of how disordered the police 'house' is, and the police may have the power to block moves to greater public accountability. Thus to see France, as Bayley does, as nearer to Japan is scarcely explicable in terms of public faith in the police or indeed in internal accountability!

Let us therefore return to the criteria of legitimacy, structure and function and consider whether the eight societies considered differ sufficiently from one another to be identified as having different policing systems according to the models defined in Chapter 2. In three cases this appears to be the case.

The Hong Kong police still evidences many of the characteristics of a colonial force. Its legitimacy is derived from the colonial authority vested in the governor, with minimal public accountability and considerable power. Its structure is militaristic, and centralized; it is an armed force, with dual entry, in which British senior officers still play a significant part. In terms of its functions, the political situation, exacerbated by the immigration problem, means that crime is still subsumed within a wider concern for administration and especially political order.

Similarly, France and the USSR can still be identified with the continental model. In France, the police forces are internally accountable and, especially with regard to the *gendarmerie nationale*, answerable to the government rather than the public. Forces are centralized and armed, with dual or multiple entry systems, and the *gendarmerie* is clearly militaristic. With regard to functions, political and administrative roles are still central to police activities. A similar pattern exists in the Soviet Union. The police wield considerable power with little evidence of external accountability; both KGB and militia are centralized, armed and structured along military lines;

and political and administrative concerns feature prominently in police work.

In contrast, the situation in the Netherlands and Canada is more ambiguous. In terms of structure and function the Dutch police evidence some features of the continental model. For example there is a dual-entry system, officers are armed, and police work incorporates many administrative functions. However, there is more evidence of public (or at least political) accountability, forces are more localized, and functions are more welfare-oriented than in France and the USSR. If policing in the Netherlands appears comparable to the US and UK in some respects, the same can be said of Canada. However, the RCMP, in terms of legitimacy and structure, if no longer function, retains affinity with some aspects of the colonial system. In the Netherlands and Canada, then, Anglo-Saxon policing traditions intermingle with influences from continental and colonial systems respectively.

What then of Japan, China and Cuba? In China and Cuba, the police's wide powers are counterbalanced by a greater degree of public involvement in the policing process, ultimately making the police more publicly accountable. Forces are centralized, and in the case of Cuba armed, but in each case the most notable structural feature is the continuity between central and local organization. The police have a local presence and operate closely with local groups which are themselves structured into a more centralized network. Finally, the functions of the police are wideranging, including not just crime, political and administrative responsibilities but also a crucial welfare function largely absent from the continental and colonial systems. In Japan, a markedly different political system has produced a similar police system, except that, in line with its French model, accountability is largely internal. These three countries can therefore be categorized together as having police systems that might best be described as comprehensive or pervasive, distinguished from the colonial or continental models by their greater emphasis on welfare and by the fact that policing is more evidently a responsibility of the public than an autonomous group using the public only as informers.

In comparison, British and US forces are distinct on all three criteria. In terms of legitimacy, the police are more accountable to the law and local government than under the continental and colonial systems, but are less directly accountable to the public than under the pervasive system. Structures are more decentralized and civilianized than under the other three models, although in terms of use of arms and its sanctioning by the courts there are marked differences between Britain and the US. Finally, the functions of the police receive different emphasis. There is less of a focus upon the administrative and political roles of the police than in the colonial, continental or pervasive models. However, while crime is prioritized, a welfare role for the police is also accepted, more so than in colonial or continental systems but to nowhere near the extent of Japan, China and Cuba. If colonial, continental and pervasive policing systems are then identified as alternative versions of 'police states', in Reiner's (1984) terms, then the police of England and Wales and the US are quite clearly different from each.

OUTCOMES

In Chapter 1 the advantages of international studies were described ultimately in terms of outcomes. One outcome relates to policing changes: could police practices from one society be translated into another? Another outcome relates to police systems: how do societies end up with the police systems they have?

Each question is clearly tied up with the interrelationship of police and society. Many writers on the countries considered here have noted at some point that the police are characteristic of the society. Thus to transplant practices from one society to another requires careful planning. Attempts by the US, British and French to restructure the police of postwar Germany, and by the US to decentralize the Japanese police, failed. Prospects for a Japanese community-based police system in Britain – or indeed a Japanese welfare system here – would equally seem doomed. However, the translation of neighbourhood watch from the USA to Britain, and of Japanese community initiatives to Hong Kong and Singapore, have been relatively successful, because either the police systems or the societies themselves share certain characteristics.

What then are these characteristics that affect policing? Four have received particular attention in this text. Political factors are especially crucial. The importance placed by pre- and post-revolutionary French and Soviet governments on central control is evident. Similarly in Hong Kong the police force was fashioned to maintain British colonial administration and many of its features preserved in the face of rather different political pressures since 1945. The political functions of the RCMP, while less evident now, have certainly influenced the current structure of Canadian policing. Finally, it is notable that the Meiji dynasty in Japan modelled its new police on the French system since its emphasis upon a centralized, public order force was compatible with Japanese political structure.

However, cultural and wider social structural aspects are also important if we are, for example, to explain many of the similarities between the Japanese and Chinese police. In each country, cultural expectations of duties, minimal emphasis upon rights, and a prioritization of community over individual, have combined to produce a social structure in which the local community plays a significant role. Police systems consequently have been shaped at the community levels. Again in Hong Kong, with a very different political structure, the police role within the community has tapped into local structures. In Cuba, in contrast, emphasis upon community, or national concerns taking priority over individual interests, is of more recent origin; the plethora of local neighbourhood activities that have developed, however, provide a background to many police practices. Finally, and rather differently, cultural and structural conditions in the Netherlands, with public services run relatively autonomously of the public, have meant that the police and other aspects of the criminal justice system have remained relatively free from public influence or involvement; one result is that neighbourhood watch has not been successfully adopted.

If political, cultural and structural features are internal influences on policing, external influences must also be considered. The impact of US models on Canada, UK and US influences on the Netherlands, and the French police system as a basis for Japanese policing have already been noted. Improvements in communication, and a greater awareness of examples from abroad, mean that it is more and more likely that changes will be introduced against the backcloth of international experiences. On the one hand, this highlights the need for comparative analysis. On the other, it makes it even more important that such analyses should be careful and comprehensive rather than superficial. A text such as this is only a beginning. The hope is that it will provide an early staging post *en route* to using experiences from other countries both to improve our understanding of policing and to improve our own police.

Notes

CHAPTER 1

1 Further details of Fosdick's involvement in police administration is contained in Reppetto (1978).
2 Thus in the UK victim surveys indicate a 100 per cent or more reporting of car thefts: 100 per cent because of insurance; more because drivers involved in minor incidents after consuming alcohol may, if able, abandon their vehicles and subsequently report them stolen. Clearly in societies where different laws apply, we should not expect victims, or pseudo-victims, to necessarily act in the same way, and crime rates for car thefts will 'mean' something different.
3 Methodological problems arise when cultural factors influence respondents' answers to particular questions. For example, we should not assume that males in different societies will be equally willing (or unwilling) to admit that they have been the victim (i.e. loser) of an assault!

CHAPTER 2

1 This is, of course, likely to change given the political upheavals of 1989–90. For the Soviet Union more details are provided in Chapter 8. Volgyes's (1978) reader provides a mixture of contributions on crime and deviance in various East European countries. Los (1988), a Polish emigrant, and Walczak (1976) provide academic discussions of crime and the criminal justice system in Poland. Further detail of the Hungarian police system can be found in the writing of visiting academic Richard Ward (1984a; 1984b) and Rudas (1977), an official at the Ministry of the Interior.

CHAPTER 3

1 I am grateful here for information provided by Pat Mayhew on the basis of preliminary analysis of the results. Subsequent to the completion of this chapter further details have been published in Dijk, Mayhew and Killias (1990).
2 Council of Europe figures for 1988, cited in *Guardian*, 31 October 1989.

3 However, in a recent discussion, Kania (1989) argues that the decentralization policies of the Mitterrand government have allowed right wing local governments to increase police personnel by employing more municipal police.

CHAPTER 4

1 For example Doornebal (1987) and *The Kingdom of the Netherlands: Facts and Figures*. I am also particularly grateful for the advice of Jan van Dijk, Cas Wiebrens, Jaap de Waard and Andre Rook of the Ministry of Justice.
2 A twelfth province was established in 1986.
3 Block (1983) accounts for this in terms of lifestyle factors. For example, since fewer Dutch women are employed outside the home, residences are less likely to be empty during the day.
4 Police unions, some Christian, some secular, are affiliated to the trade union movement, although as with other public-service officials strikes are prohibited.
5 I am grateful here for information provided by W. Toet, J. K. Pietersma, and my colleague Martin Gill.

CHAPTER 5

1 Discussions on the introduction of electronic monitoring took place at the Fourth Annual Canadian Law Conference, 'The Electronic Monitoring of Offenders – Canadian Initiatives', Canada House, London, 30 October 1987.
2 Renamed this in 1904.
3 Figures here abstracted from Statistics Canada (1986).
4 Interestingly Morrison (1985, 178) describes how the RCMP was given responsibility for distributing welfare payments in remote areas in the immediate postwar period.
5 See also Commissioner Inkster's address to the Conference on Multiculturalism and Policing, Richmond, British Columbia, 5 January 1988.

CHAPTER 6

1 In addition to those in the reference section, I have for example drawn on Hong Kong in Figures; 1989 edn; Police Public Relations Branch material; *Hong Kong: the Facts, the Police*, March 1988.

CHAPTER 8

1 On crime see for example Ministry of Interior Affairs briefings: 15 February 1989, 'Criminal statistics disclosed' (*Izvestia*, 14 February); 11 October 1989, 'Briefing at the Soviet Ministry of Internal Affairs' (*Izvestia*, 10 October); January 1990, 'Crime statistics 1989' (*Izvestia*, 10 January). These show a marked increase in crime, but whether this is 'real' or due to a change in recording practices is open to question. On more open discussion of the police see Chernenko's (1989) interview with the new Minister of the Interior, Vadim Bakatin.
2 According to Shelley's (1980, 120) sources, the USSR offender rate at 1,045 per 100,000 population is about 40 per cent that of the USA. However, rates for the very largest cities (442) and smaller cities (500), derived from different sources, are well below this average.
3 My estimates here are derived from the English-language press release of 15 February 1989 (from *Izvestia*, 14 February); according to this there were 16,710 homicides in 1988 and 14,651 in 1987.
4 Reported in First Tuesday documentary, 'Murder in Ostankino Precinct', 1989.
5 More serious cases are presided over by panels of professional judges. Even where lay assessors are involved, however, experts tend to see them as largely influenced by the professionals.
6 Based on press release figures of 14 February 1989 following briefing at Ministry of the Interior by Major General Anatoly Smirnov.
7 See note 4.
8 See note 4.

CHAPTER 11

1 Although one parish at least still refuses to accept women as members of the honorary force.

References

Alderson, J. C. (1979), *Policing Freedom* (Plymouth: McDonald & Evans).

Alderson, J. C. (1981a), 'Hong Kong, Tokyo, Peking: three police systems observed', *Police Studies*, vol. 3, no. 4, pp. 3–12.

Alderson, J. C. (1981b), 'The case for community policing', submission to Scarman Inquiry.

Allen, G. F. (1987), 'Reforming criminals in China: implications for corrections in the West', *International Journal of Comparative and Applied Criminal Justice*, vol. 11, no. 1, pp. 77–86.

Ames, W. L. (1979), 'Police in the community', *Police Journal*, vol. 52, pp. 252–9.

Ames, W. L. (1981), *Police and Community in Japan* (Berkeley, Calif.: University of California Press).

Ardagh, J. (1977), *The New France: A Society in Transition 1945–1977* (Harmondsworth: Penguin).

Armstrong, M. (1967), 'The campaign against parasites', in P. H. Juviler and H. W. Morton (eds), *Soviet Policy-Making* (New York: Praeger), pp. 163–82.

Arnold, D. (1986), *Police Power and Colonial Rule: Madras 1859–1947* (Oxford: Oxford University Press).

Ashford, D. E. (ed.) (1978), *Comparing Public Policies: New Concepts and Methods* (Beverly Hill, Calif.: Sage).

Ashford, D. E. (1982), *British Dogmatism and French Pragmatism: Central–Local Policymaking in the Welfare State* (London: Allen & Unwin).

Ashford, D. E. (1986), *The Emergence of Welfare States* (Oxford: Basil Blackwell).

Austin, W. T. (1987), 'Crime and custom in an orderly society: the Singapore prototype', *Criminology*, vol. 25, no. 2, pp. 279–94.

Ayrton, P. (ed.) (1983), *World View 1984* (London: Pluto).

Babin, M. (1986), 'The making of the Mounties', *Police Review*, 22 August, pp. [illegible]7–9.

Bagley, C. (1973), *The Dutch Plural Society: A Comparative Study in Race Relations* (Oxford: Oxford University Press).

Bakhanskaia, N. (1975), 'New legislation on the volunteer auxiliary police', *Soviet Law and Government*, vol. 14, no. 2, pp. 3–11.

Balvig, F. (1988), *The Snow-White Image: The Hidden Reality of Crime in Switzerland* (Oslo: Norwegian University Press).

Banton, M. (1964), *The Policeman in the Community* (London: Tavistock).

Baogue, X. (1988), 'The function of the Chinese procuratorial organ in combat against corruption', *Police Studies*, vol. 11, pp. 38–43.

Barron, J. (1985), *KGB Today: The Hidden Hand* (New York: Berkley).
Baum, R. (1986), 'Modernization and legal reform in post-Mao China: the rebirth of socialist legality', *Studies in Comparative Communism*, vol. 19, no. 2, pp. 69–103.
Bayley, D. H. (1969), *The Police and Political Development in India* (Princeton, NJ: Princeton University Press).
Bayley, D. H. (1976), *Forces of Order: Police Behaviour in Japan and the United States* (Berkeley, Calif.: University of California Press).
Bayley, D. H. (ed.) (1977), *Police and Society* (Beverly Hill, Calif.: Sage).
Bayley, D. H. (1983), 'Accountability and control of police: lessons for Britain', in T. Bennett (ed.), *The Future of Policing* (Cambridge: Cropwood Papers, Institute of Criminology), pp. 146–58.
Bayley, D. H. (1985), *Patterns of Policing: A Comparative International Analysis* (New Brunswick: Rutgers University Press).
Beames, T. ([1852] 1970), *The Rookeries of London* (London: Cass).
Bennett, R. R. and Corrigan, R. S. (1980), 'Police occupational solidarity: probing a determinant in the deterioration of police/citizen relations', *Journal of Criminal Justice*, vol. 8, no. 2, pp. 111–22.
Bennett, T. (1987), 'Neighbourhood watch: principles and practices', in R. I. Mawby (ed.), *Policing Britain* (Plymouth: Plymouth Polytechnic), pp. 31–51.
Bennett, T. (1988), 'An assessment of the design, implementation and effectiveness of neighbourhood watch in London', *British Journal of Criminology*, vol. 27, pp. 241–55.
Benton, G. (1983), *The Hong Kong Crisis* (London: Pluto).
Berg, G. P. van den (1983), 'The Soviet Union and the death penalty', *Soviet Studies*, vol. 35, no. 2, pp. 154–74.
Berman, H. J. and Spindler, J. W. (1963), 'Soviet comrades' courts', *Washington Law Review*, vol. 38, pp. 842–910.
Berman, H. J. and Whiting, V. R. (1980), 'Impressions of Cuban law', *American Journal of Comparative Law*, vol. 28, pp. 475–86.
Berman, J. (1969), 'The Cuban popular tribunals', *Columbian Law Review*, vol. 69, pp. 1317–54.
Bianchi, H. (1975), 'Social control and deviance in the Netherlands', in H. Bianchi, M. Simondi and I. Taylor (eds), *Deviance and Control in Europe* (New York and London: Wiley), pp. 51–7.
Binns, P. and Gonzalez, M. (1980), 'Cuba, Castro and socialism', *International Socialism*, ser. 2, no. 8, pp. 1–36.
Birks, C. (1987), 'Social welfare provision in France', in R. Ford and M. Chakrabarti (eds), *Welfare Abroad* (Edinburgh: Scottish Academic Press), pp. 66–98.
Blaas, H. and Dostal, P. (1989), 'The Netherlands: changing administrative structures', in R. Bennett (ed.), *Territory and Administration in Europe* (London: Frances Pinter), pp. 230–41.
Blaber, A. (1979), *The Exeter Community Policing Consultative Group* (London: NACRO).

Blazicek, D. L. and Janeksela, G. M. (1978), 'Some comments on comparative methodologies in criminal justice', *International Journal of Criminology and Penology*, vol. 6, pp. 233–45.

Block, R. (1983), 'A comparison of national crime surveys', paper to World Congress of Criminology Conference, Vienna.

Block, R. (1987), 'A comparison of victimization, crime assessment and fear of crime in England/Wales, the Netherlands, Scotland, and the United States', paper to American Society of Criminology Annual Conference, Montreal.

Bloom, A. H. (1977), 'A cognitive dimension of social control: Hong Kong Chinese in cross cultural perspective', in A. A. Wilson, S. L. Greenblatt and R. W. Wilson (eds), *Deviance and Social Control in Chinese Society* (New York: Praeger), pp. 67–81.

Boothroyd, J. (1989), 'Angels with dirty faces?', *Police Review*, 6 January, pp. 16–17.

Bopp, W. J. (ed.) (1972), *Police–Community Relationships* (Springfield, Illinois: Charles C. Thomas).

Bottomley, A. K. (1986), 'Blue-prints for criminal justice: reflections on a policy plan for the Netherlands', *Howard Journal*, vol. 25, no. 3, pp. 199–215.

Bottoms, A. E., Mawby, R. I. and Xanthos, P. D. (1981), *Sheffield Study on Urban Social Structure and Crime Part 3* (Sheffield: Report to Home Office).

Bowden, T. (1978), *Beyond the Limits of the Law* (Harmondsworth: Penguin).

Boyer, J.-C. (1983), 'Benelux', in Ayrton (ed.), op. cit., pp. 416–19.

Brady, J. P. (1981), 'The transformation of justice under socialism: the contrasting experiences of Cuba and China', *The Insurgent Sociologist*, vol. 10, pp. 5–24.

Brady, J. P. (1982a), 'The revolution comes of age: justice and social change in contemporary Cuba', in C. Sumner (ed.), *Crime, Justice and Underdevelopment* (London: Heinemann), pp. 248–300.

Brady, J. P. (1982b), *Justice and Politics in People's China: Legal Order or Continuing Revolution* (New York: Academic).

Brady, J. P. (1983), 'People's Republic of China', in E. H. Johnson (ed.), *International Handbook of Contemporary Developments in Criminology: Europe, Africa, the Middle East and Asia* (Westport, Conn.: Greenwood), pp. 107–41.

Brenton, M. (1980), 'Getting a grip on the Dutch voluntary sector', *Voluntary Action*, spring, pp. 14–16.

Brenton, M. (1982), 'Changing relationships in Dutch social services', *Journal of Social Policy*, vol. 11, no. 1, pp. 59–80.

Brewer, J. D., Guelke, A., Hume, J., Moxon-Browne, E. and Wilford, R. (1988), *The Police, Public Order and the State* (London: Macmillan).

Brink, F. and Bulthuis, J. J. (1979), 'The Dutch police in evolution', *Police Studies*, vol. 2, no. 3, pp. 13–23.

Broer, W. and Vijver, K. van der (1983), 'Research and organizational control', in M. Punch (ed.), *Control in the Police Organization* (Cambridge, Mass.: MIT Press), pp. 60–74.

Brogden, M. (1987), 'The emergence of the police – the colonial dimension', *British Journal of Criminology*, vol. 27, no. 1, pp. 4–14.
Brogden, M., Jefferson, T. and Walklate, S. (1988), *Introducing Policework* (London: Unwin Hyman).
Brown, R. M. (1969a), 'Historical patterns of violence in America', in H. D. Graham and T. R. Gurr (eds), *The History of Violence in America* (New York: Praeger), pp. 45–84.
Brown, R. M. (1969b), 'The American vigilante tradition', in Graham and Gurr, op. cit., pp. 154–225.
Bryant, C. G. A. (1981), 'Depillarisation in the Netherlands', *British Journal of Sociology*, Vol. 32, No. 1, pp. 56–73.
Burney, E. (1985), 'Checking the nick', *New Society*, 8 November, pp. 239–40.
Cain, M. (1973), *Society and the Policeman's Role* (London: Routledge & Kegan Paul).
Cain, M. (1979), 'Trends in the sociology of policework', *International Journal of the Sociology of Law*, vol. 7, pp. 143–67.
Calderwood, A. (1974), *In Service of the Community, 1949–1974* (Hong Kong: Liang Yu Printing Factory).
Canadian Sentencing Commission (1987), *Sentencing Reform: A Canadian Approach: Summary* (Ottawa: Department of Justice, Canada).
Cantor, R. (1974), 'New laws for a new society', *Crime and Justice*, Vol. 2, pp. 12–23.
Carr-Hill, R. A. (1989), 'Police waves in Europe', paper to British Sociological Association Conference, Plymouth.
Chang, Y. (1989), 'The state of public security and social order in the People's Republic of China', *Police Studies*, vol. 12, no. 1, pp. 6–9.
Chapman, B. (1970), *Police State* (London: Pall Mall Press).
Chapman, B. (1978), 'The Canadian police: a survey', *Police Studies*, vol. 1, no. 1, pp. 62–72.
Chernenko, A. (1989), 'Bringing the militia under the public eye', *Soviet Weekly*, 1 April, p. 2458.
Clifford, W. (1976), *Crime Control in Japan* (Lexington, Mass.: Lexington).
Clinard, M. B. (1978), *Cities with Little Crime: The Case of Switzerland* (Cambridge: Cambridge University Press).
Cohen, J. A. (1966), 'The criminal process in the People's Republic of China: an introduction', *Harvard Law Review*, vol. 79, pp. 469–533.
Cohen, J. A. (1968), *The Criminal Process in the People's Republic of China: 1949–1963* (Cambridge, Mass.: Harvard University Press).
Cohen, J. A. (1971), 'Drafting people's mediation rules', in J. W. Lewis (ed.), *The City in Communist China* (Stanford, Calif.: Stanford University Press), pp. 29–50.
Cohen, J. A. (1979), 'Reflections on the criminal process in China', *Journal of Criminal Law and Criminology*, vol. 68, pp. 323–55.
Cohen, S. (1985), *Visions of Social Control* (Cambridge: Polity).
Cole, G. F., Frankowski, S. J. and Gertz, M. G. (eds) (1987), *Major Criminal Justice Systems: A Comparative Study* (Beverly Hills, Calif.: Sage).

Cole, G. F., Frankowski, S. J. and Gertz, M. G. (1987), 'Comparative criminal justice: an introduction', in Cole, Frankowski and Gertz (eds), op. cit., pp. 15–26.

Colijn, G. J., Lester, D. and Slothouwer, A. (1985), 'Firearms and crime in the Netherlands: a comparison with the United States of America', *International Journal of Comparative and Applied Criminal Justice*, vol. 9, no. 1, pp. 49–55.

Collin, R. O. (1985), 'The blunt instruments: Italy and the police', in J. Roach and J. Thomaneck (eds), *Police and Public Order in Europe* (London: Croom Helm), pp. 185–213.

Commissioner of Correctional Services (1988), *Annual Review 1987* (Hong Kong: Correctional Services).

Connor, W. D. (1970), 'Juvenile delinquency in the USSR: some quantitative and qualitative indicators', *American Sociological Review*, vol. 35, no. 2, pp. 283–97.

Connor, W. D. (1972), *Deviance in Soviet Society: Crime, Delinquency and Alcoholism* (New York: Columbia University Press).

Connor, W. D. (1973), 'Criminal homicide, USSR/USA: reflections on Soviet data in a comparative framework', *Journal of Criminal Law and Criminology*, vol. 64, no. 1, pp. 111–17.

Conquest, R. (1968), *The Soviet Police System* (London: Bodley Head).

Crisswell, C. and Watson, M. (1982), *The Royal Hong Kong Police (1841–1945)* (Hong Kong: Macmillan).

Critchley, T. A. (1978), *The History of Police in England and Wales* (London: Constable).

Crump, L. (1987), 'The economic sector of Japanese society: an exploration for social welfare activities', *International Social Work*, vol. 30, pp. 343–51.

Dando, S. (1970), 'System of discretionary prosecution in Japan', *American Journal of Comparative Law*, Vol. 18, No. 3, pp. 518–31.

Davies, R. W. (1968), 'Police work in Roman times', *History Today*, vol. 18, pp. 700–7.

Davis, J. A. (1988), *Conflict and Control: Law and Order in Nineteenth-Century Italy* (Basingstoke: Macmillan).

Day, P. and Klein, R. (1987), *Accountabilities: Five Public Services* (London: Tavistock).

Deacon, B. (1983), *Social Policy and Socialism* (London: Pluto).

Department of Justice, Canada (1986), *Annual Report 1985–1986* (Ottawa: Department of Justice, Canada).

D'Hautville, A. and Bruno, B. (1989), 'A better position for victims of crime-legislation and guidelines', in report of the First European Conference of Victim Support Workers, *Guidelines for Victim Support in Europe* (Utrecht: VLOS).

Dicey, A. V. ([1885] 1950), *Introduction to the Study of the Law of the Constitution* (London: Macmillan).

Diederiks, H. (1980), 'Patterns of criminality and law enforcement during the *ancien régime*: the Dutch case', *Criminal Justice History: an International Annual*, vol. 1, pp. 157–74.

Dijk, J. van (1985), 'Research and the victim movement in Europe', in Council of Europe, *Research on Victimisation* (Strasbourg: Council of Europe), pp. 5–16.
Dijk, J. van (1988), 'Ideological trends within the victims movement: an international perspective', in M. Maguire and J. Pointing (eds), *Victims of Crime* (Milton Keynes: Open University Press), pp. 115–26.
Dijk, J. van (1989), 'Confronting crime: the Dutch experience', paper to Crime Prevention Strategy Seminar, Adelaide.
Dijk, J. van and Junger-Tas, J. (1988), 'Trends in crime prevention in the Netherlands', in T. Hope and M. Shaw (eds), *Communities and Crime Prevention* (London: HMSO), pp. 260–77.
Dijk, J. van, Mayhew, P. and Killias, M. (1990), *Experiences of Crime across the World* (Deventer, Netherlands: Kluwer).
Dion, R. (1982), *Crimes of the Secret Police* (Montreal: Black Rose Books).
Domingo, V. A. (1982), 'Is there group development after migration? The case of Surinamers in the Netherlands', *New Community*, vol. 10, no. 1, pp. 95–114.
Dominguez, J. (1979), *Cuba* (Cambridge, Mass.: Belknap).
Doornebal, R. (1987), *The Police Service in the Netherlands* (The Hague: Police Affairs Department, Ministry of Home Affairs).
Dore, R. (1973), *British Factory, Japanese Factory* (London: Allen & Unwin).
Douthwaite, L. C. (1939), *The Royal Canadian Mounted Police* (London: Blackie).
Downes, D. (1988), *Contrasts in Tolerance* (Oxford: Clarendon).
Durkheim, E. ([1893] 1947), *The Division of Labour in Society* (New York: Macmillan).
Durkheim, E. ([1912] 1948), *The Elementary Forms of Religious Life* (Glencoe: Free Press of Glencoe).
Durkheim, E. ([1897] 1951), *Suicide: A Study in Sociology* (Glencoe: Free Press of Glencoe).
Echols, J. M. (1986), 'Does socialism mean greater equality? a comparison of East and West along several major dimensions', in S. White and D. Nelson (eds), *Communist Politics: a Reader* (London: Macmillan), pp. 361–79.
Eck, J. E. and Spelman, W. (1987), 'Who ya gonna call? The police as problem-busters', *Crime and Delinquency*, vol. 33, no. 1, pp. 31–52.
Eckstein, S. (1982), 'The impact of revolution on social welfare in Latin America', *Theory and Society*, vol. 11, pp. 17–42.
Eliasoph, E. R. and Grueneberg, S. (1981), 'Law on display in China', *China Quarterly*, vol. 88, pp. 669–85.
Emsley, C. (1983), *Policing and its Context, 1750–1870* (London: Macmillan).
Ericson, R. V. (1981), *Making Crime: A Study of Detective Work* (Toronto: Butterworth).
Ericson, R. V. (1982), *Reproducing Order: A Study of Police Patrol Work* (Toronto: University of Toronto Press).
Ericson, R. V., McMahon, M. W. and Evans, D. G. (1987), 'Punishing for profit: reflections on the revival of privatization in corrections', *Canadian Journal of Criminology*, vol. 29, pp. 355–88.
Farish, R. (1990), 'Rethinking Russia', *Guardian*, 6 February.

Fenwick, C. R. (1983), 'The juvenile delinquency problem in Japan: application of a role relationship model', *International Journal of Comparative and Applied Criminal Justice*, vol. 7, pp. 119–28.

Fenwick, C. R. (1987), 'Crime in post-Mao China: towards the construction of an integrated social systems theory', *International Journal of Comparative and Applied Criminal Justice*, vol. 11, no. 2, pp. 177–92.

Feofanov, Y. (1988), 'Mafia in our midst', *Moscow News*, August, p. 6.

Fielding, N. (1986), 'Social control and the community', *Howard Journal*, vol. 25, no. 3, pp. 172–89.

Fielding, N. G. (1988), *Joining Forces: Police Training and Occupational Competence* (London: Routledge).

Figgie Report (1983), *Reducing Crime in America: Part IV: Successful Community Efforts*.

Finch, R. J. (1984), 'An inscrutable force', *Police Review*, 10 February, pp. 274–5.

Fine, B. and Millar, R. (eds) (1985), *Policing the Miners' Strike* (London: Lawrence & Wishart).

Fogel, D. (1987), 'The investigation and disciplining of police misconduct: a comparative view – London, Paris, Chicago', *Police Studies*, vol. 10, no. 1, pp. 1–15.

Fosdick, R. B. ([1920] 1969a), *American Police Systems* (New York: Century).

Fosdick, R. B. ([1915] 1969b), *European Police Systems* (Montelair, NJ: Patterson Smith).

Fulcher, J. (1988), 'The bureaucratization of the state and the rise of Japan', *British Journal of Sociology*, vol. 39, pp. 228–54.

Fyfe, N. (1987), 'Contesting consultation', paper to British Criminology Conference, Sheffield.

Gabrichidze, B. N. (1987), 'Interrelations between local Soviets and law enforcement agencies', *Soviet Law and Government*, vol. 25, pp. 82–94.

Gerth, H. H. and Wright Mills, C. (eds) (1958), *From Max Weber, Essays in Sociology* (New York: Galaxy).

Gifford, Lord (1986), *The Broadwater Farm Inquiry* (London: Borough of Haringey).

Gilbert, G. and Guengant, A. (1989), 'France: shifts in local authority finance', in Bennett (ed.), op. cit., pp. 243–54.

Gill, M. L. and Mawby, R. I. (1990a), *A Special Constable: A Study of the Police Reserve* (Aldershot: Avebury).

Gill, M. L. and Mawby, R. I. (1990b), *Volunteers in the Criminal Justice System: A Comparative Study of Probation, Police and Victim Support* (Milton Keynes: Open University Press).

Gill, M. and Thrasher, M. (1985), 'Problems in administering community policing: some lessons from implementation analysis', *Policy and Politics*, vol. 13, no. 1, pp. 37–52.

Gittler, J. (1984), 'Expanding the role of the victim in a criminal action: an overview of issues and problems', *Pepperdine Law Review*, vol. 1, pp. 117–82.

Goldstein, H. (1979), 'Improving policing: a problem-oriented approach', *Crime and Delinquency*, vol. 25, no. 2, pp. 236–58.

Goldstein, H. (1987), 'Towards community-oriented policing: potential, basic requirements, and threshold questions', *Crime and Delinquency*, vol. 33, no. 1, pp. 6–30.
Greenblatt, S. L. (1977), 'Campaigns and the manufacture of deviance in Chinese society', in Wilson *et al.* (eds), op. cit., pp. 82–120.
Griffin, P. (1974), 'Prison management in the Kiangsi and Yenan periods', *China Quarterly*, vol. 58, pp. 310–31.
Griffiths, Sir P. (1971), *To Guard My People: The History of the Indian Police* (London: Benn).
Guest, D. (1984), 'Social policy in Canada', *Social Policy and Administration*, vol. 18, no. 2, pp. 130–47.
Gupta, A. (1979), *The Police in British India* (New Delhi: Naurang Rai).
Hackler, J. C. (1988), 'Practicing in France what Americans have preached: The response of French judges to juveniles', *Crime and Delinquency*, vol. 34, no. 2, pp. 467–85.
Hageman, M. J. (1985), *Police–Community Relations* (Beverly Hills, Calif.: Sage).
Hann, R. G., McGinnis, J. H., Stenning, P. C. and Farson, A. S. (1985), 'Municipal police governance and accountability in Canada: an empirical study', *Canadian Police College Journal*, vol. 9, no. 1, pp. 1–85.
Harasymiv, B. (1988), 'Gorbachev's reorganization and the Gorkom', *Studies in Comparative Communism*, vol. 21, no. 1, pp. 61–70.
Hauber, A. R. and Wemmers, J. (1988), 'An experiment of victim assistance in police stations in the Hague, the Netherlands', unpublished paper, State University of Leiden.
Hayes, B. (1986), 'The new Spanish police', unpublished paper, Police College Library, Bramshill.
Hayward, J. (1983), *Governing France: The One and Indivisible Republic* (London: Weidenfeld & Nicolson).
Hazard, J. N., Shapiro, I. and Maggs, P. B. (1969), *The Soviet Legal System* (New York: Oceana).
Hazard, J. N., Butler, W. E. and Maggs, P. B. (1984), *The Soviet Legal System: The Law in the 1980s* (New York: Oceana).
Heidenheimer, A. J., Heclo, H. and Adams, C. T. (1983), *Comparative Public Policy: The Politics of Social Choice in Europe and America* (London: Macmillan).
Heijder, A. (1973), 'Some aspects of the Dutch probation system: a search for identity', *International Journal of Offender Therapy and Comparative Criminology*, vol. 17, no. 1, pp. 106–10.
Hess, A. G. (1970), 'The volunteer probation officers of Japan', *International Journal of Offender Therapy*, vol. 14, pp. 8–14.
Higgins, J. (1981), *States of Welfare* (Oxford: Basil Blackwell/Martin Robertson).
Hirst, M. (1989), 'Policing China's millions', *Police Review*, 3 February, pp. 236–7.
Hoebel, E. A. (1961), *The Law of Primitive Man* (Cambridge, Mass.: Harvard University Press).

Hoeven, E. van der (1988), 'The juvenile investigation unit', in J. Junger-Tass and R. L. Block (eds), *Juvenile Delinquency in the Netherlands* (Amstelveen: Kugler), pp. 139–76.
Hoffmann, C. (1977), 'Work incentives and social control', in Wilson *et al.* (eds), op. cit., pp. 173–206.
Hogarth, J. (1982), 'Police accountability', in R. Donelan (ed.), *The Maintenance of Order in Society* (Ottawa: Canadian Police College), pp. 111–25.
Holdaway, S. (1983), *Inside the British Police: A Force at Work* (Oxford: Basil Blackwell).
Home Office (1966), *Report of the Working Party on Operational Efficiency and Management* (London: HMSO).
Home Office (1988), *Report of Her Majesty's Chief Inspector of Constabulary, 1987* (London: HMSO).
Home Office (1989), *Report of Her Majesty's Chief Inspector of Constabulary, 1988* (London: HMSO).
Hong Kong Link (1985), *H.K. Towards the Future: British Responsibilities* (London: CIIR).
Hooper, B. (1985), *Youth in China* (Harmondsworth: Penguin).
Hope, T. and Shaw, M. (eds) (1988), *Communities and Crime Reduction* (London: HMSO).
Horrall, S. W. (1980), 'The Royal North-West Mounted Police and labour unrest in Western Canada, 1919', *Canadian Historical Review*, vol. 61, no. 2, pp. 169–90.
Hudson, R. C. (1988), 'A matter of confidence: police, government and society in France since 1981', *Police Journal*, vol. 61, no. 2, pp. 169–74.
Hui, Y. F. (1989), 'Ideal models for social policies during the transition period', *International Social Work*, vol. 32, pp. 251–9.
Huonzhang, S. (1986), 'An introduction to Shanghai's legal system', *Police Studies*, vol. 9, no. 3, pp. 151–2.
Huskey, E. (1988), 'Specialism in the Soviet Communist Party apparatus: legal professionals as party functionaries', *Soviet Studies*, vol. 40, no. 4, pp. 538–55.
Ijzerman, P. D. (1987), 'Public safety policy in Enschede: a snapshop', in J. Junger-Tas, A. Rutting and J. Wilzing (eds), *Crime Control in Local Communities in Europe* (Lochen: Vanden Brink), pp. 40–50.
Ishimura, Z. (1985), 'Legal systems and social systems in Japan', in A. Podgorecki, C. J. Whelan and D. Khosla (eds), *Legal Systems and Social Systems* (London: Croom Helm), pp. 116–25.
Ismail, A. (ed.) (1989), *Hong Kong 1989* (Hong Kong: Government Information Services).
Ismail, K. M. (1987), 'The development, functions and organization of the Royal Malaysia Police (RMP)', *Police Studies*, vol. 10, pp. 23–9.
Jackson, D. W. (1985), 'Public police thyselves: deadly force and public disorder, two crises in British community policing', *Police Studies*, vol. 8, no. 3, pp. 132–47.
Jackson, R. (1979), 'Police labour relations in Canada: a current perspective', *Canadian Police College Journal*, vol. 3, no. 1, pp. 6–43.

Jammes, J. R. J. (1982), *The French Gendarmerie* (Bradford: MCB Publications).
Jeffries, S. C. (1952), *The Colonial Police* (London: Max Parrish).
Jian, X. (1987), 'The principles and development of juvenile justice administration in the People's Republic of China', *Police Studies*, vol. 10, no. 4, pp. 181–4.
Joffe, E. (1983), 'Party and military in China: professionalism in command?', *Problems of Communism*, vol. 32, no. 5, pp. 48–63.
Johnson, E. H. (1983), 'Neighbourhood police in the People's Republic of China', *Police Studies*, vol. 6, no. 4, pp. 8–12.
Johnson, E. H. (1984), 'Night patrol in Amsterdam's Warmoesstraat district', *Police Studies*, vol. 7, no. 3, pp. 131–5.
Johnson, R. J. (1975), 'Zagranichnaia Agentura: the tsarist political police in Europe', in G. L. Mosse (ed.), *Police Forces in History* (London: Sage), pp. 17–38.
Jones, C. (1985), *Patterns of Social Policy: An Introduction to Comparative Analysis* (London: Tavistock).
Jones, J. M. (1980), *Organisational Aspects of Police Behaviour* (Aldershot: Gower).
Jones, J. M. and Winkler, J. (1982), 'Beyond the beat: the facts about policing in a riotous city', *Journal of Law and Society*, vol. 9, no. 1, pp. 103–14.
Jones, S. J. (1983), 'The human factor and policing', *Home Office Research Bulletin*, no. 16, pp. 9–12.
Jones, S. J. and Levi, M. (1983), *Police–Public Relationships – a Study of Public and Police Perceptions of Each Other* (Cardiff: Department of Social Administration, University College Cardiff).
Junger-Tas, J. (1987), 'Crime prevention in practice', in Junger-Tas *et al.* (eds), op. cit., pp. 12–23.
Junger-Tas, J. (1988), 'Effects of intervention by the police and the prosecutor', in Junger-Tas and Block (eds), op. cit., pp. 177–201.
Juviler, P. H. (1976), *Revolutionary Law and Order* (New York: Free Press).
Kalish, C. B. (1988), *International Crime Rates,* US Department of Justice, Bureau of Justice Statistics, Special Report.
Kania, R. R. E. (1989), 'The French municipal police experiment', *Police Studies*, vol. 12, pp. 125–31.
Karpets, I. (1977), 'Principal directions and types of activity of the militia in the Soviet Union', *International Review of Criminal Policy*, vol. 33, pp. 34–8.
Kazuhiko, T. (1981), 'Change in traditional society and "delinquencization" ', *Japan Quarterly*, vol. 28, pp. 362–9.
Kelk, C. (1983), 'The humanity of the Dutch prison system and the prisoners' consciousness of their legal rights', *Contemporary Crises*, vol. 7, pp. 155–70.
Kelling, G. L. (1987), 'Acquiring a taste for order: the community and the police', *Crime and Delinquency*, vol. 33, no. 1, pp. 90–102.
Kelly, M. A. (1987), 'Western civilization's first detectives', *Police Studies*, vol. 10, pp. 36–41.
Kelly, W. and Kelly, N. (1976), *Policing in Canada* (Toronto: Macmillan).

Kemp, C. and Morgan, R. (1989), 'David and Goliath: using private citizens to monitor a public service: lay visitors to police stations', paper to British Criminology Conference, Bristol.

Kennedy, I. M. (1973), 'Cuba's *Ley Contra la Vagrancia* – the law on loafing', *University College of Los Angelese Law Review*, vol. 20, no. 6, pp. 1177–268.

Killias, M. (1989), Review of *The Snow-White Image: The Hidden Reality of Crime in Swizerland, British Journal of Criminology*, vol. 29, no. 3, pp. 300–3.

King, M. (1987), 'A counsel of prevention', *New Statesman*, 23 October, pp. 15–16.

King, M. (1988), *How to Make Social Crime Prevention Work: The French Experience* (London: NACRO).

Kinsey, R. (1984), *Merseyside Crime Survey: First Report* (Liverpool: Merseyside County Council).

Kinsey, R., Lea, J. and Young, J. (1986), *Losing the Fight Against Crime* (Oxford: Basil Blackwell).

Kowalewski, D. (1981), 'China and the Soviet Union: a comparative model for analysis', *Studies in Comparative Communism*, vol. 14, no. 4, pp. 279–306.

Kramer, R. M. (1979), 'Government–voluntary agency relationships in the Netherlands', *Netherlands Journal of Sociology*, vol. 25, pp. 155–73.

Kuykendall, J. L. (1974), 'Styles of community policing', *Criminology*, vol. 12, no. 2, pp. 229–40.

Laan, P. H. van der (1988), 'The Dutch juvenile justice system: an introduction', in Junger-Tas and Block (eds), op. cit., pp. 3–12.

Lacoste, Y. (1983), 'South East Asia' in Ayrton (ed.), op. cit., pp. 369–73.

Lamb, H. K. (1985), *A Date with Fate* (Hong Kong: Lincoln Green).

Lampert, N. (1984), 'Law and order in the USSR: the case of economic and official crime', *Soviet Studies*, vol. 36, no. 3, pp. 366–85.

Lane, R. (1967), *Policing the City: Boston 1822–1885* (Cambridge, Mass.: Harvard University Press).

Latouche, D. (1983), 'Canada: an aimless drift', in Ayrton (ed.), op. cit., pp. 164–8.

Lee, H. K. (1987), 'The Japanese welfare state in transition', in R. R. Friedmann, N. Gilbert and M. Sherer (eds), *Modern Welfare States: A Comparative View of Trends and Prospects* (Brighton: Wheatsheaf), pp. 243–63.

Lee, J. A. (1981), 'Some structural aspects of police deviance in relations with minority groups', in C. D. Shearing (ed.), *Organizational Police Deviance* (Toronto: Butterworth), pp. 49–82.

Lee, S.-M. (1973), 'The probation service in Hong Kong', *International Journal of Offender Therapy and Comparative Criminology*, vol. 17, no. 1, pp. 90–4.

Leeson, G. and Snyder, A. (1981), 'Specialized police response to the juvenile: the Ottawa Youth Liaison Section', in W. T. McGrath and M. P. Mitchell (eds), *The Police Function in Canada* (Toronto: Methuen), pp. 187–210.

Leng, S.-C. (1981), 'Criminal justice in post-Mao China: some preliminary observations', *China Quarterly*, vol. 87, pp. 440–69.

Leng, S.-C. and Chiu, H. (1985), *Criminal Justice in Post-Mao China: Analysis and Documents* (Albany, NY: State University of New York Press).
Leo Grande, W. M. (1982), 'Cuba', in R. Wesson (ed.), *Communism in Central American and the Caribbean* (Stanford, Calif.: Hoover Press), pp. 31–51.
Li, V. H. (1973), 'Law and penology: systems of reform and correction', in M. Oksenberg (ed.), *China's Developmental Experience* (New York: Academy of Political Services), pp. 144–56.
Liege, M.-P. de (1988), 'The fight against crime and fear: a new initiative in France', in Hope and Shaw (eds), op. cit., pp. 254–9.
Linden, R. (1983), 'Women in policing: a study of lower mainland RCMP detachments', *Canadian Police College Journal*, vol. 7, no. 3, pp. 217–29.
Lipietz, A. (1983), 'France: a certain sourness', in Ayrton (ed.), op. cit., pp. 186–90.
Lloyds Bank (1986), *Hong Kong Economic Report 1986* (London: Lloyds Bank).
Loney, M. (1973), 'Social control in Cuba', in I. Taylor and L. Taylor (eds), *Politics and Deviance* (Harmondsworth: Penguin), pp. 42–60.
Loree, D. J. (1985), 'Police in a plural society', *Canadian Police College Journal*, vol. 9, no. 4, pp. 391–412.
Los, M. (1988), *Communist Ideology, Law and Crime: A Comparative View of the USSR and Poland* (London: Macmillan).
Loshak, V. and Dyomin, V. (1988), 'Minister spills beans in billion rouble scandal', *Moscow News*, July, p. 2.
Loveday, B. (1988), 'Police complaints in the USA', *Policing*, vol. 4, no. 3, pp. 172–93.
Lowman, J. and Menzies, R. J. (1986), 'Out of the fiscal shadow: carceral trends in Canada and the United States', *Crime and Social Justice*, vol. 26, pp. 95–115.
Lubman, S. (1967), 'Mao and mediation: politics and dispute resolution in Communist China', *California Law Review*, vol. 55, pp. 1284–359.
Lubman, S. (1969), 'Form and function in the Chinese criminal process', *Columbia Law Review*, vol. 69, pp. 535–75.
Lunden, W. A. (1976), 'Violent crimes in Japan in war and peace, 1933–74', *International Journal of Criminology and Penology*, vol. 4, pp. 349–63.
Maanen, J. van (1975), 'Police socialization: a longitudinal examination of job attitudes in an urban police department', *Administration Science Quarterly*, vol. 20, pp. 207–28.
McClenahan, C. A. (1987), 'Victim/witness services: Vancouver, British Columbia, Canada', paper to American Criminological Association Annual Conference, Montreal.
MacEwan, A. (1975), 'Ideology, socialist development, and power in Cuba', *Politics and Society*, vol. 5, pp. 67–82.
McKenzie, I. K. and Gallagher, G. P. (1989), *Behind the Uniform: Policing in Britain and America* (Hemel Hempstead: Harvester Wheatsheaf).
McKenzie, I. (1984), 'Policing in Japan', *Police Review*, 14 December, pp. 2417–19.
Macleod, R. (1976), *The NWMP and Law Enforcement 1873–1905* (Toronto: University of Toronto Press).

Malinowski, B. (1926), *Crime and Customs in Savage Society* (London: Paul, Trench & Trubner).
Mangold, T. (1975), 'Tigers and flies', *Listener*, 16 January, pp. 66–8.
Manning, P. K. (1982), 'Modern police administration, the rise of crime focused policing, and critical incident analysis', in Donelan (ed.), op. cit., pp. 56–74.
Manning, P. K. (1984), 'Community policing', *American Journal of Police*, vol. 3, no. 2, pp. 205–27.
Manning, P. K. (1987), 'The police occupational culture in Anglo-American societies', in Strecher, V. *et al.* (eds), *Enclyclopedia of Police Science* (New York: Garland).
Marsov, V. (1988), 'Exposed . . . Kazan's outlaw street groups', *Moscow News*, September, pp. 8–9.
Maruo, N. (1982), 'The development of the welfare state in Japan – an alternative model', *Journal of Economics* (Society of Economics in the Chuo University), vol. 23, pp. 1–25.
Mather, F. C. (1959), *Public Order in the Age of the Chartists* (Manchester: Manchester University Press).
Matsumoto, I. (1986), 'Offenders and victims in the process of fraudulent borrowing', in K. Miyazawa and M. Ohya (eds), *Victimology in Comparative Perspective* (Tokyo: Seibundo).
Matthews, R. (ed.) (1989), *Privatizing Criminal Justice* (London: Sage).
Mawby, R. I. (1986), 'The geography of crime and the criminal justice system: gatekeepers as commuters', in D. T. Herbert *et al.* (eds), *The Geography of Crime*, Occasional Papers in Geography No. 7 (Stoke: North Staffordshire Polytechnic), pp. 54–75.
Mawby, R. I. and Gill, M. L. (1987), *Crime Victims: Needs, Services and the Voluntary Sector* (London: Tavistock).
May, D. (1981), 'Community relations in Hong Kong', *Police Review*, 9 January, pp. 68–70.
Mayhew, P. (1987), *How Are We Faring on the Burglary Front? A Comparison with the US and Canada*, Home Office Research Bulletin No. 23 (London: HMSO), pp. 42–7.
Mayhew, P., Clarke, R. V. G., Burrows, J. N., Hough, J. M. and Winchester, S. W. C. (1979), *Crime in Public View*, Home Office Research Bulletin No. 49 (London: HMSO).
Mayhew, P., Elliott, D. and Dowds, L. (1989), *The 1988 British Crime Survey*, Home Office Research Bulletin No. 111 (London: HMSO).
Menzies, K. (1986), 'The rapid spread of community service orders in Ontario', *Canadian Journal of Criminology*, vol. 28, no. 2, pp. 157–69.
Meyer, J. C. (1972), 'Methodological issues in comparative criminal justice research', *Criminology*, vol. 10, no. 3, pp. 295–313.
Meyer, J. C. (1985), 'Police strikes: a model to study underlying factors', *Australia and New Zealand Journal of Criminology*, September–December, pp. 191–208.
Miller, J. H. (1986), 'The Soviet Communist Party: trends and problems', in White and Nelson (eds), op. cit., pp. 135–56.

Miller, J. H. (1988), 'Planning party membership: how successful can it be?', *Studies in Comparative Communism*, vol. 21, no. 1, pp. 61–70.
Miller, W. R. (1977), *Cops and Bobbies: Police Authority in New York and London, 1830–1870* (Chicago: University of Chicago Press).
Mirsky, J. (1989), 'Chinese executioners take on crime wave', *Observer*, 5 February, p. 23.
Mishkin, B. D. (1976), 'Police of Hong Kong', *Garda Review*, March, pp. 23–31.
Mok, B. (1983), 'Social welfare in China', *Social Work*, vol. 28, pp. 269–72.
Mok, B. (1987), 'Social welfare in China in an era of economic reform', *International Social Work*, vol. 30, pp. 237–50.
Monkkonen, E. (1981), *Police in Urban America, 1860–1920* (Cambridge, Mass.: Cambridge University Press).
Moore, C. and Brown, J. (1981), *Community Versus Crime* (London: Bedford Square Press).
Morgan, R. (1987), 'Consultation and police accoutability', in Mawby (ed.), op. cit., pp. 5–30.
Morgan, R. and Maggs, C. (1985), *Setting the PACE: Police Community Consultation Arrangements in England and Wales* (Bath: University of Bath).
Morrison, W. R. (1985), *Showing the Flat: the Mounted Police and Canadian Sovereignty in the North, 1894–1925* (Vancouver: University of British Columbia Press).
Morton, J. (1986), 'The Canadian beat', *Police Review*, 22 August, p. 1735.
Mosse, G. L. (ed.) (1975), *Police Forces in History* (London: Sage).
Mulschlegel, F. and Stolwerk, M. (1989), *Facts, Figures and General Information for the International Conference for Policewomen* (Warnsveld: Politiestudiecentrum).
Murphy, C. (1988), 'Community problems, problem communities, and community policing in Toronto', *Journal of Research in Crime and Delinquency*, vol. 25, no. 4, pp. 392–410.
Myagkov, A. (1976), *Inside the KGB* (London: New Goswell).
Nakane, C. (1981), *Japanese Society* (Harmondsworth: Penguin).
Nakayama, K. (1987), 'Japan', in Cole, Frankowski and Gertz (eds), op. cit., pp. 168–87.
National Police Agency, Government of Japan (1984), *White Paper on Police* (Tokyo: Police Association).
Nelson, C. (1978), 'Third force', report on International Police Association Study Tour.
Nomura, Y. (1987), 'Recent trends in the Japanese prison service', *Prison Service Journal*, July, pp. 6–12.
Nordholt, E. and Straver, R. (1983), 'The changing police', in Punch (ed.), op. cit., pp. 36–46.
Nuttall, C. P. (1988), 'Crime prevention in Canada', in Hope and Shaw (eds), op. cit., pp. 246–53.
Nuyten-Edelbrock, E. and Tigges, L. (1980), 'Early intervention by a probation agency: a Netherlands experiment', *Howard Journal*, vol. 19, no. 1, pp. 42–51.

Oben, T. (1974), 'Victorian London: specialisation, segregation and privacy', *Victorian Studies*, vol. 17, no. 3, pp. 265–78.
O'Connor, D. M. (1964), 'Soviet people's guards: an experiment with civic police', *New York University Law Review*, vol. 39, pp. 579–614.
Olmo, R. del (1979), 'The Cuban revolution and the struggle against prostitution', *Crime and Social Justice*, vol. 12, pp. 34–40.
Ostrowe, B. B. and DiBiase, R. (1983), 'Citizen involvement as a crime deterrent: a study of public attitudes toward an unsanctioned civilian patrol group', *Journal of Police Science and Administration*, vol. 11, no. 2, pp. 185–93.
Outrive, L. van and Rizkalla, S. (eds) (1976), *Final Report on the International Seminar on Police Research* (Leuven: Centre for Interdisciplinary Studies of the Administration of Criminal Justice, Katholecke Universiteit).
Outrive, L. van and Fijnaut, C. (1983), 'Police and the organization of prevention', in Punch (ed.), op. cit., pp. 47–59.
Over, J. E. (1982), 'Independent element – yes or no', *Police Journal*, vol. 55, no. 3, pp. 238–43.
Owings, C. ([1925] 1969), *Women Police: a Study of the Development and Status of the Women Police Movement* (Montclair, NJ: Patterson Smith).
Parish, W. L. and Whyte, M. K. (1978), *Village and Family in Contemporary China* (Chicago: University of Chicago Press).
Parker, L. C. (1984), *The Japanese Police Today: An American Perspective* (Tokyo: Kodansha International).
Parker, L. C. (1986), 'The changing Dutch response to crime', *Police Studies*, vol. 9, no. 2, pp. 78–85.
Pennell, S., Curtis, C. and Henderson, J. (1986), *Guardian Angels: An Assessment of Citizen Response to Crime* (Washington DC: US Department of Justice, National Institute of Justice, Executive Summary).
Pepinsky, H. E. (1976), *Crime and Conflict: A Study of Law and Society* (Oxford: Martin Robertson).
Perger, E. (1989), 'An overview of East European developments', in Bennet (ed.), op. cit., pp. 93–110.
Perry, M. (1976), 'Recruiting and conditions of service in the police forces of France and Belgium'. Report on International Police Association Study Tour.
Pfeffer, R. M. (1973), 'Leaders and masses', in Oksenberg (ed.), op. cit., pp. 157–74.
Piffaut, G. (1989), 'Concrete achievements toward the implementation of the fundamental principles of justice for victims', in Heuni (ed.), *Changing victim policy. The United Nations Victim Declaration and recent developments in Europe* (Helsinki: United Nations), pp. 113–36.
Pinker, R. (1986), 'Social welfare in Japan and Britain: a comparative view. Formal and informal aspects of welfare', in E. Oyen (ed.), *Comparing Welfare States and their Futures* (Aldershot: Gower), pp. 114–28.
Pisani-Ferry, J. (1983), 'The EEC: facing a trade war', in Ayrton (ed.), op. cit., pp. 39–45.
Poel, S. van der and Punch, M. (1981), 'Everybody's watching: policewomen in Amsterdam', *Police Review*, 12 June, pp. 1142–4, 1173–5.

Pope, D. W. (1982), 'France and the *police nationale*', *Police Review*, 27 August, pp. 1664–5.
Pope, D. W. (1984), 'The Royal Hong Kong Police, preventive policing and young people', *Police Journal*, vol. 57, pp. 26–31.
Potts, L. W. (1982), 'The limits of police–community relations progress: a cross-national perspective', *Police Studies*, vol. 5, no. 2, pp. 10–20.
Pravda, A. (1986), 'Elections in Communist Party states', in White and Nelson (eds), op. cit., pp. 27–54.
Price, B. R. and Sokoloff, N. J. (eds) (1982), *The Criminal Justice System and Women* (New York: Clark Boardman).
Punch, M. (1979), *Policing the Inner City: A Study of Amsterdam's Warmoesstraat* (London: Macmillan).
Punch, M. (ed.) (1983a), *Control in the Police Organization* (Cambridge, Mass.: MIT Press).
Punch, M. (1983b), 'The comparative perspective', in Punch (ed.), op. cit., pp. 14–17.
Punch, M. (1983c), 'Officers and men: occupational culture, inter-rank antagonism, and the investigation of corruption', in Punch (ed.), op. cit., pp. 227–50.
Punch, M. (1985), *Conduct Unbecoming: The Social Construction of Police Deviance and Control* (London: Tavistock).
Punch, M. (1987), 'Institutional and political obstacles to planned change in the Dutch police: a comparative analysis of the dilemmas of implementing team policing', paper to American Society of Criminology Annual Conference, Montreal.
Punch, M. (1989), 'Researching police deviance: a personal encounter with the limitations and liabilities of field-work', *British Journal of Sociology*, vol. 40, no. 2, pp. 177–204.
Radcliffe-Brown, A. R. (1952), *Structure and Function in Primitive Society* (London: Cohen & West).
Radzinowicz, L. (1948), *A History of English Criminal Law and its Administration from 1750, Volume 1: The Movement for Reform* (London: Stevens).
Radzinowicz. L. (1956a), *A History of English Criminal Law and its Administration from 1750, Volume 2: The Clash Between Private Initiatives and Public Interest in the Enforcement of Law* (London: Stevens).
Radzinowicz, L. (1956b), *A History of English Criminal Law and its Administration from 1750, Volume 3: Cross Currents in the Movement for the Reform of the Police* (London: Stevens).
Radzinowicz, L. and King, J. (1977), *The Growth of Crime: The International Experience* (London: Hamish Hamilton).
Raef, M. (1975), 'The well-ordered police state', *American Historical Review*, vol. 80, no. 5, pp. 1221–43.
Ratner, R. S. (1986), 'Introduction to the conjunctural analysis of social control in Canada', *Crime and Social Justice*, vol. 26, pp. 1–10.
Reaves, B. A. (1989), *Police Departments in Large Cities, 1987*, Bureau of Justice Statistics, Special Report.
Reenen, P. van (1981), 'Urban crisis management and the police force: the case of Amsterdam', *Netherlands Journal of Sociology*, vol. 17, pp. 151–78.

Reenen, P. van (1985), 'Liberal policing in the interventionist state', *Police Studies*, vol. 8, no. 2, pp. 93–6.
Regan, D. (1984), 'Police status and accountability: a comparison of the British, French and West German models', paper to European Consortium for Political Research, Salzburg.
Reichel, P. L. (1988), 'Southern slave patrols as a transitional police type', *American Journal of Police*, vol. 7, no. 2, pp. 51–77.
Reiner, R. (1984), 'Is Britain turning into a police state?', *New Society*, 2 August, pp. 51–6.
Reiner, R. (1985), *The Politics of the Police* (Brighton: Wheatsheaf).
Reppetto, T. A. (1978), *The Blue Parade* (New York: Free Press).
Research Committee on Female Crime (1986), 'A study on the victims of homicide committed by females', in Miyazawa and Ohya, op. cit.
Roach, J. (1985), 'The French police', in Roach and Thomaneck (eds), op. cit., pp. 107–41.
Roach, J. and Thomaneck (eds) (1985), op. cit.
Robinson, C. D. (1978), 'The deradicalisation of the policeman', *Crime and Delinquency*, vol. 24, no. 2, pp. 129–51.
Rock, P. (1988), 'Government, victims and police in two countries', *British Journal of Criminology*, vol. 28, no. 1, pp. 44–66.
Rodgers, B. N. (1979), 'France', in B. N. Rodgers, A. Doron and M. Jones (1979), *The Study of Social Policy: A Comparative Approach* (London: Allen & Unwin), pp. 76–109.
Rose, R. (1985), 'Welfare: the lesson from Japan', *New Society*, 28 June, pp. 473–5.
Rose, R. and Shiratori, R. (eds) (1986), *The Welfare State East and West* (Oxford: Oxford University Press).
Rosenbaum, D. P. (1988), 'A critical eye on neighbourhood watch: does it reduce crime and fear?', in Hope and Shaw (eds), op. cit., pp. 126–45.
Rosenthal, U. (1984), 'The bureaupolitics of policing: the Dutch case', paper to European Consortium for Political Research, Salzburg.
Royal Hong Kong Police (1988), *Annual Review* (Hong Kong: Royal Hong Kong Police).
Rudas, G. (1977), 'The changing role, responsibilities and activities of the police in a developed society', *International Review of Criminal Policy* vol. 33, pp. 11–16.
Ruel, P. (1983), 'Japan: the danger of isolation', in Ayrton (ed.), op. cit., pp. 218–23.
Rutherford, A. (1984), *Prisons and the Process of Justice* (London: Heinemann).
Salaff, J. (1967), 'The urban communes and anti-city experiment in Communist China', *China Quarterly*, vol. 29, pp. 82–109.
Salas, L. (1979a), *Social Control and Deviance in Cuba* (New York: Praeger).
Salas, L. (1979b), 'Juvenile deliquency in post-revolutionary Cuba: characteristics and Cuban explanations', *Cuban Studies*, vol. 9, no. 1, pp. 43–61.
Salas, L. (1985), 'The judicial system of post-revolutionary Cuba', in Podgorecki *et al.* (eds), op. cit., pp. 229–54.
Sapir, J. (1983), 'USSR from Brezhnev to Andropov', in Ayrton (ed.), op. cit., pp. 276–82.

Savitsky, V. M. and Kogan, V. M. (1987), 'The Union of Soviet Socialist Republics', in Cole, Frankowski and Gertz (eds), op. cit., pp. 191–220.

Scarman, Lord (1981), *The Brixton Disorders: 10–12 April 1981*, Cmnd 8427 (London: HMSO).

Schaffer, E. B. (1980), *Community Policing* (London: Croom Helm).

Schwartz, B. (1973), 'China's developmental experience, 1949–72', in Oksenberg (ed.), op. cit., pp. 17–26.

Schwartz, R. D. and Miller, J. C. (1964), 'Legal evolution and societal complexity', *American Journal of Sociology*, vol. 70, pp. 159–69.

Sewell, J. (1985), *Police: Policing Urban Canada* (Toronto: Lorrimer).

Shane, P. G. (1980), *Police and Public: A Comparison of Five Countries* (St Louis, Miss.: Mosby).

Sharma, O. (1982), 'The Special Constabulary: a special tribute', *Police Life Annual*, pp. 92–9.

Shearing, C. D. (1981), 'Deviance and conformity in the reproduction of order', in Shearing (ed.), op. cit., pp. 29–47.

Shearing, C. D. and Leon, J. S. (1976), 'Reconsidering the police role: a challenge to a challenge of a popular conception', *Canadian Journal of Criminology and Corrections*, vol. 19, pp. 331–45.

Shearing, C. D. and Stenning, P. C. (1983), 'Private security: implications for social control', *Social Problems*, vol. 30, no. 5, pp. 493–506.

Shelley, L. (1980), 'The geography of Soviet criminality', *American Sociological Review*, vol. 45, pp. 111–22.

Sherman, L. (1977), 'Policewomen around the world', *International Review of Criminal Policy*, vol. 33, pp. 25–33.

Sherman, L. W., Milton, C. H. and Kelly, T. V. (1973), *Team Policing: Seven Case Studies* (Washington DC: Police Foundation).

Shoup, P. (1989), 'Leadership drift in the Soviet Union and Yugoslavia', *Studies in Comparative Communism*, vol. 22, no. 1, pp. 43–55.

Sidel, V. W. (1973), 'Medicine and public health', in Oksenberg (ed.), op. cit., pp. 110–20.

Sinclair, K. (1983), *Asia's Finest: An Illustrated Account of the Royal Hong Kong Police* (Hong Kong: Unicorn).

Smith, B. ([1940] 1960), *Police Systems in the United States* (New York: Harper).

Smith, G. B. (1980), 'Socialist legality and legal policy in the Soviet Union', in G. B. Smith (ed.), *Public Policy and Administration in the Soviet Union* (New York: Praeger), pp. 109–41.

Solomon, P. H. (1987), 'The case of the vanishing acquittal: informal norms and the practice of Soviet criminal justice', *Soviet Studies*, vol. 39, no. 4, pp. 531–55.

South, N. (1988), *Policing for Profit: The Private Security Sector* (London: Sage).

Spencer, H. (1874), *The Study of Sociology* (London: Appleton).

Starak, Y. (1988), 'Hong Kong: a model of "social happiness" for the new China', *International Social Work*, vol. 31, pp. 211–17.

Statistics Canada (1986), *Policing in Canada* (Ottawa: Canadian Centre for Justice Statistics).

Stead, P. J. (1957), *The Police of Paris* (London: Staples).
Stead, P. J. (1983), *The Police of France* (London: Macmillan).
Stead, P. J. (1984), 'The Roman police', *Police Studies*, vol. 6, no. 4, pp. 3–7.
Stead, P. J. (1985), *The Police of Britain* (London: Macmillan).
Stedman-Jones, G. (1971), *Outcast London* (Oxford: Clarendon).
Steedman, C. (1984), *Policing the Victorian Community: The Formation of English Provincial Police Forces, 1856–80* (London: Routledge & Kegan Paul).
Steenhuis, D. W. (1979), 'Experiments on police effectiveness – the Dutch experience', paper to Cambridge Criminology Conference, Cambridge.
Steenhuis, D. W., Tigges, A. C. M. and Essers, J. J. H. (1981), 'The penal climate in the Netherlands: sunny or cloudy?', *British Journal of Criminology*, vol. 23, pp. 1–16.
Stenning, P. C. (1981), 'The role of police boards and commissions as institutions of municipal police governance', in Shearing (ed.), op. cit., pp. 162–207.
Stubbs, P. (1987), 'Crime, community and the multi-agency approach: a critical reading of the Broadwater Farm Inquiry Report', *Critical Social Policy*, vol. 20, pp. 30–45.
Sweatman, B. and Cross, A. (1989), 'The police in the United States', *C. J. International*, vol. 5, no. 1, pp. 11–18.
Takahashi, T. and Someya, Y. (1985), 'Japan', in J. Dixon and H. S. Kim (eds), *Social Welfare in Asia* (London: Croom Helm), pp. 133–75.
Tancred, E. (1931), 'Women police abroad', *Police Journal*, vol. 4, pp. 175–87.
Taylor, I. (1986), 'Martyrdom and surveillance: ideological and social practices of police in Canada in the 1980s', *Crime and Social Justice*, vol. 26, pp. 60–78.
Terrill, R. J. (1989), 'Organization of law enforcement in the Soviet Union', *Police Studies*, vol. 12, no. 1, pp. 18–24.
Third Congress of the Communist Party of Cuba (1986), *Main Report* (La Habana: Editora Politica).
Thornton, R. Y. (1972), 'The Kidotai', in W. J. Bopp (ed.), *Police–Community Relationships* (Springfield, Mass.: Thomas), pp. 312–35.
Timoshenko, I. O. (1977), 'Collaboration of the militia and the community in crime prevention in the Byelorussian Soviet Socialist Republic', *International Review of Criminal Policy*, vol. 33, pp. 39–44.
Tissier, P. (1983), 'China: the end of Maoism', in Ayrton (ed.), op. cit., pp. 169–74.
Tjepkema, J. R. (1984), 'The police of the Netherlands – at the crossroads', *Police Studies*, vol. 7, no. 2, pp. 61–3.
Tobias, J. J. (1977), 'The British colonial police: an alternative police style', in P. J. Stead (ed.), *Pioneers in Policing* (Maidenhead: Patterson Smith), pp. 241–61.
Tonso, W. R. (1982), *Gun and Society* (Washington DC: University Press of America).
Torczyner, J. (1987), 'The Canadian welfare state: retrenchment and change', in R. R. Friedmann and N. G. M. Sherer (eds), *Modern Welfare States: A Comparative View of Trends and Prospects* (Brighton: Wheatsheaf), pp. 264–81.

Tsirlin, Y. (1988), 'The young turn to crime', *Moscow News*, June, p. 13.

Tsou, T. (1973), 'The values of the Chinese Revolution', in Oksenberg (ed.), op. cit., pp. 27–41.

Tsui, Y. K. (1979), 'Problems of a para-military police force in a changing society: a case study of the Royal Hong Kong Police Force', dissertation, Chinese University of Hong Kong.

Tulkens, H. (1979), *Some Developments in Penal Police and Practice in Holland* (Chichester: Barry Rose/NACRO).

US Department of Justice (1989), *Sourcebook of Criminal Justice Statistics – 1988* (Washington DC: US Government Printing Office).

Ushkalov, I. G. and Khorev, B. S. (1989), 'The USSR: territorial and administrative structure', in Bennet (ed.), op. cit., pp. 124–37.

Vass, A. A. and Menzies, K. (1989), 'The community service order as a public and private enterprise', *British Journal of Crimonology*, vol. 29, no. 3, pp. 255–72.

Vergara, F. (1983), 'Cuba: economic crises and US pressure', in Ayrton (ed.), op. cit., pp. 175–8.

Visser, B. R. and Wierda, H. (1987), 'The arousal of social awareness at neighbourhood level, as taking justice into one's own hands with social sauce: policing in a hostile environment', in Junger-Tas *et al.* (eds), op. cit., pp. 80–101.

Vogel, E. F. (1971), 'Preserving order in the cities', in Lewis (ed.), op. cit., pp. 75–93.

Volgyes, I. (ed.) (1978), *Social Deviance in Eastern Europe* (Boulder, Col.: Westview).

Walczak, S. (1976), 'Police and other agencies inside and outside the CJS in Poland', in Outrive and Rizkala (eds), op. cit., pp. 287–313.

Walden, K. (1982), *Visions of Order: The Canadian Mounties in Symbol and Myth* (Toronto: Butterworth).

Walklate, S. (1987), 'Public monitoring and police accountability', paper to British Criminology Conference, Sheffield.

Wall, D. (1987), 'Chief constables: a changing elite', in R. I. Mawby (ed.), *Policing Britain* (Plymouth: Plymouth Polytechnic), pp. 84–100.

Waller, I. and Okihiro, N. (1978), *Burglary: the Victim and the Public* (Toronto: University of Toronto Press).

Waller, M. and Szajkowski, B. (1986), 'The communist movement: from monolith to polymorph', in White and Nelson (eds), op. cit., pp. 9–26.

Ward, R. H. (1984a), 'Police and criminal justice in Hungary', *Police Studies*, vol. 6, pp. 31–4.

Ward, R. H. (1984b), 'The police of Hungary', *Law and Order*, April, pp. 39–41.

Ward, R. H. (1984c), 'Policing in the People's Republic of China', *Law and Order*, April, pp. 24–5, 65.

Ward, R. H. and Bracey, D. H. (1985), 'Police training and professionalism in the People's Republic of China', *Police Chief*, May, pp. 36–8.

Washnis, G. (1976), *Citizen Involvement in Crime Prevention* (Lexington, Mass.: Lexington).

Webster, J. A. (1970), 'Police task and time study', *Journal of Criminal Law, Crimonology and Police Science*, vol. 61, no. 1, pp. 94–100.

Weller, G. R. (1981), 'Politics and the police: the case of the Royal Canadian Mounted Police', paper to Annual Conference of Political Studies Association, Hull.

Westney, D. E. (1982), 'The emulation of Western organizations in Meiji Japan: the case of the Paris prefecture of police and the Keishi-cho', *Journal of Japanese Studies*, vol. 18, part 2, pp. 307–42.

White, L. T. (1977), 'Deviance, modernization, rations, and household registers in urban China', in Wilson *et al.* (eds), op. cit., pp. 151–72.

White, S. and Nelson, D. (eds) (1986), *Communist Politics* (London: Macmillan).

Whittingham, M. D. (1981), 'The evolution of the public police . . . a social history', *Canadian Police Chief*, July, pp. 27–9, and October, pp. 67–70.

Whyte, M. K. and Parish, W. L. (1984), *Urban Life in Contemporary China* (Chicago: University of Chicago Press).

Wiebrens, C. (1989), 'Police manpower re-allocation: the Dutch case', paper to British Criminology Conference, Bristol.

Willett, T. and Chitty, P. O. (1982), 'Auxiliary police in Canada – an overview', *Canadian Police College Journal*, vol. 6, no. 3, pp. 188–92.

Williams, A. (1979), *The Police of Paris 1718–1789* (Baton Rouge: Louisiana State University Press).

Wilson, J. Q. (1968), *Varieties of Police Behaviour: The Management of Law and Order in Eight Communities* (Cambridge, Mass.: Harvard University Press).

Wilson, J. Q. and Kelling, G. L. (1983), 'Broken windows', *Atlantic Monthly*, March, pp. 29–38.

Wilson, R. W. (1977), 'Perceptions of group structure and leadership position as an aspect of deviance and social control', in Wilson *et al.* (eds), op. cit., pp. 52–66.

Winant, T. T. (1972), 'The police of Tokyo', in Bopp (ed.), op. cit., pp. 304–11.

Womac, B. (1984), 'Modernization and democratic reform in China', *Journal of Asian Studies*, vol. 43, no. 3, pp. 417–39.

Xu, G. (1983), 'Combating criminal offenders by relying on the masses in the People's Republic of China', *Police Studies*, vol. 6, no. 1, pp. 3–5.

Yun, T. (1983), 'The police and the people', *Beijing Review*, 23 May, pp. 22–7.

Zeldes, I. (1981), *The Problems of Crime in the USSR* (Springfield, Illinois: Charles C. Thomas).

Zhu-cheng, C. (1983), 'Prevention of crimes in China', unpublished paper.

Index